Praise for *Aspect-Oriented Software Develo*

"A refreshingly new approach toward improving use-case modeling by fortifying it with aspect orientation."

—RAMNIVAS LADDAD
author of AspectJ in Action

"Since the 1980s, use cases have been a way to bring users into software design, but translating use cases into software has been an art, at best, because user goods often don't respect code boundaries. Now that aspect-oriented programming (AOP) can express crosscutting concerns directly in code, the man who developed use cases has proposed step-by-step methods for recognizing crosscutting concerns in use cases and writing the code in separate modules. If these methods are at all fruitful in your design and development practice, they will make a big difference in software quality for developers and users alike."

—WES ISBERG
AspectJ team member

"This book not only provides ideas and examples of what aspect-oriented software development is but how it can be utilized in a real development project."

—MICHAEL WARD
ThoughtWorks, Inc.

"No system has ever been designed from scratch perfectly; every system is composed of features layered in top of features that accumulate over time. Conventional design techniques do not handle this well, and over time the integrity of most systems degrades as a result. For the first time, here is a set of techniques that facilitates composition of behavior that not only allows systems to be defined in terms of layered functionality but composition is at the very heart of the approach. This book is an important advance in modern methodology and is certain to influence the direction of software engineering in the next decade, just as *Object-Oriented Software Engineering* influenced the last."

—KURT BITTNER
IBM Corporation

"Use cases are an excellent means to capture system requirements and drive a user-centric view of system development and testing. This book offers a comprehensive guide on explicit use-case-driven development from early requirements modeling to design and implementation. It provides a simple yet rich set of guidelines to realize use-case models using aspect-oriented design and programming. It is a valuable resource to researchers and practitioners alike."

—DR. AWAIS RASHID
Lancaster University, U.K., and author of
Aspect-Oriented Database Systems

"AOSD is important technology that will help developers produce better systems. Unfortunately, it has not been obvious how to integrate AOSD across a project's lifecycle. This book shatters that barrier, providing concrete examples on how to use AOSD from requirements analysis through testing."

—CHARLES B. HALEY
research fellow, The Open University, U.K.

Aspect-Oriented Software Development with Use Cases

The Addison-Wesley Object Technology Series

Grady Booch, Ivar Jacobson, and James Rumbaugh, Series Editors
For more information, check out the series web site at www.awprofessional.com/otseries.

Ahmed/Umrysh, *Developing Enterprise Java Applications with J2EE™ and UML*

Arlow/Neustadt, *Enterprise Patterns and MDA: Building Better Software with Archetype Patterns and UML*

Arlow/Neustadt, *UML and the Unified Process: Practical Object-Oriented Analysis and Design*

Armour/Miller, *Advanced Use Case Modeling: Software Systems*

Bellin/Simone, *The CRC Card Book*

Bergström/Råberg, *Adopting the Rational Unified Process: Success with the RUP*

Binder, *Testing Object-Oriented Systems: Models, Patterns, and Tools*

Bittner/Spence, *Use Case Modeling*

Booch, *Object Solutions: Managing the Object-Oriented Project*

Booch, *Object-Oriented Analysis and Design with Applications, 2E*

Booch/Bryan, *Software Engineering with ADA, 3E*

Booch/Rumbaugh/Jacobson, *The Unified Modeling Language User Guide*

Box/Brown/Ewald/Sells, *Effective COM: 50 Ways to Improve Your COM and MTS-based Applications*

Carlson, *Modeling XML Applications with UML: Practical e-Business Applications*

Collins, *Designing Object-Oriented User Interfaces*

Conallen, *Building Web Applications with UML, 2E*

D'Souza/Wills, *Objects, Components, and Frameworks with UML: The Catalysis(SM) Approach*

Douglass, *Doing Hard Time: Developing Real-Time Systems with UML, Objects, Frameworks, and Patterns*

Douglass, *Real-Time Design Patterns: Robust Scalable Architecture for Real-Time Systems*

Douglass, *Real Time UML, 3E: Advances in The UML for Real-Time Systems*

Eeles et al., *Building J2EE™ Applications with the Rational Unified Process*

Fontoura/Pree/Rumpe, *The UML Profile for Framework Architectures*

Fowler, *Analysis Patterns: Reusable Object Models*

Fowler et al., *Refactoring: Improving the Design of Existing Code*

Fowler, *UML Distilled, 3E: A Brief Guide to the Standard Object Modeling Language*

Gomaa, *Designing Concurrent, Distributed, and Real-Time Applications with UML*

Gomaa, *Designing Software Product Lines with UML*

Graham, *Object-Oriented Methods, 3E: Principles and Practice*

Heinckiens, *Building Scalable Database Applications: Object-Oriented Design, Architectures, and Implementations*

Hofmeister/Nord/Dilip, *Applied Software Architecture*

Jacobson/Booch/Rumbaugh, *The Unified Software Development Process*

Jordan, *C++ Object Databases: Programming with the ODMG Standard*

Kleppe/Warmer/Bast, *MDA Explained: The Model Driven Architecture™: Practice and Promise*

Kroll/Kruchten, *The Rational Unified Process Made Easy: A Practitioner's Guide to the RUP*

Kruchten, *The Rational Unified Process, 3E: An Introduction*

Lau, *The Art of Objects: Object-Oriented Design and Architecture*

Leffingwell/Widrig, *Managing Software Requirements, 2E: A Use Case Approach*

Manassis, *Practical Software Engineering: Analysis and Design for the .NET Platform*

Marshall, *Enterprise Modeling with UML: Designing Successful Software through Business Analysis*

McGregor/Sykes, *A Practical Guide to Testing Object-Oriented Software*

Mellor/Balcer, *Executable UML: A Foundation for Model-Driven Architecture*

Mellor et al., *MDA Distilled: Principles of Model-Driven Architecture*

Naiburg/Maksimchuk, *UML for Database Design*

Oestereich, *Developing Software with UML, 2E: Object-Oriented Analysis and Design in Practice*

Page-Jones, *Fundamentals of Object-Oriented Design in UML*

Pohl, *Object-Oriented Programming Using C++, 2E*

Pollice et al. *Software Development for Small Teams: A RUP-Centric Approach*

Quatrani, *Visual Modeling with Rational Rose 2002 and UML*

Rector/Sells, *ATL Internals*

Reed, *Developing Applications with Visual Basic and UML*

Rosenberg/Scott, *Applying Use Case Driven Object Modeling with UML: An Annotated e-Commerce Example*

Rosenberg/Scott, *Use Case Driven Object Modeling with UML: A Practical Approach*

Royce, *Software Project Management: A Unified Framework*

Rumbaugh/Jacobson/Booch, *The Unified Modeling Language Reference Manual*

Schneider/Winters, *Applying Use Cases, 2E: A Practical Guide*

Smith/Williams, *Performance Solutions: A Practical Guide to Creating Responsive, Scalable Software*

Stevens/Pooley, *Using UML, Updated Edition: Software Engineering with Objects and Components*

Unhelkar, *Process Quality Assurance for UML-Based Projects*

van Harmelen, *Object Modeling and User Interface Design: Designing Interactive Systems*

Wake, *Refactoring Workbook*

Warmer/Kleppe, *The Object Constraint Language, 2E: Getting Your Models Ready for MDA*

White, *Software Configuration Management Strategies and Rational ClearCase®: A Practical Introduction*

The Component Software Series

Clemens Szyperski, Series Editor
For more information, check out the series web site at www.awprofessional.com/csseries.

Allen, *Realizing eBusiness with Components*

Apperly et al., *Service- and Component-based Development: Using the Select Perspective™ and UML*

Atkinson et al., *Component-Based Product Line Engineering with UML*

Cheesman/Daniels, *UML Components: A Simple Process for Specifying Component-Based Software*

Szyperski, *Component Software, 2E: Beyond Object-Oriented Programming*

Whitehead, *Component-Based Development: Principles and Planning for Business Systems*

Aspect-Oriented Software Development with Use Cases

Ivar Jacobson

Pan-Wei Ng

✦✦ Addison-Wesley

Upper Saddle River, NJ · Boston · Indianapolis · San Francisco
New York · Toronto · Montreal · London · Munich · Paris · Madrid
Capetown · Sydney · Tokyo · Singapore · Mexico City

The publisher offers excellent discounts on this book when ordered in quantity for bulk purchases or special sales, which may include electronic versions and/or custom covers and content particular to your business, training goals, marketing focus, and branding interests. For more information, please contact:

U. S. Corporate and Government Sales
(800) 382-3419
corpsales@pearsontechgroup.com

For sales outside the U. S., please contact:

International Sales
international@pearsoned.com

Visit us on the Web: www.awprofessional.com

Library of Congress Cataloging-in-Publication Data

Jacobson, Ivar.
    Aspect-oriented software development with use cases / Ivar Jacobson, Pan-Wei Ng.
        p.   cm.
    Includes bibliographical references and index.
    ISBN 0-321-26888-1 (pbk. : alk. paper)
    1.   Computer software—Development.   2.   Object-oriented programming (Computer science)   I.   Ng, Pan-Wei, 1969-   II. Title.

QA76.76.D47J343   2004
005.1—dc22   2004023750

Pearson Education, Inc.
Rights and Contracts Department
One Lake Street
Upper Saddle River, NJ 07458

ISBN 0-321-26888-1
Text printed in the United States on recycled paper at Courier in Stoughton, Massachusetts.
First printing, December 2004

Contents

Preface

What Is Aspect-Oriented Programming?

That you have picked up this book tells us that you are a member of the software development community: a tester, a developer, a project leader, a project manager, an architect, an analyst, or a member involved in one of the many other aspects of developing. We also know that you are someone who wants to improve the way you develop software. You want your system to be more maintainable, more extensible, more reusable, and if you are a project leader, you want your team to be more productive. You know that these goals are not always easy to achieve.

Why is software development so difficult? One reason is that there are many things to watch out for. On the human side, you have to watch out for time, budget, resources, skills, and so forth. Frequently, as a team member, you have many tasks—some of them beyond what you are paid for. You report to two different people and each expects 100 percent from you, so you must give 200 percent to your work. As the developer, you must understand the application, the domain, and the idiosyncrasies of the platform. When you design the system, you need to deal with and balance many difficult concerns: how the system meets its intended functionality, how it achieves performance and reliability, how it deals with platform specifics, and so forth. You may find that your code—your classes, your operations, your procedures—must perform many functions, which may lead to spaghetti code, an indication of poor design. So, you need to improve design—improve modularity and provide better *separation of concerns*. Just as each team member must be clearly focused on his or her work, each component, each class, each operation must be focused on what is its specific purpose.

But there is a limit to what you can do with existing techniques. No matter how far you go, you find that many parts of your system have code fragments that have to do with logging, authorization, persistence, debugging, tracing, distribution, exception handling, and other such tasks. Sometimes, a sizeable portion of an operation or class has nothing to do with what it is supposed to do. Aspect-oriented programming (AOP) refers to such redundancy as *crosscutting concerns* because you find these code fragments in many operations and classes in your system—they *cut across* operations and classes. Crosscutting concerns are not limited to the technical concerns such as authorization and persistence. They include system and application functionality, and you find that a change in functionality often results in changes in many classes too.

AOP gives you the means to separate code that implements crosscutting concerns and modularize it into *aspects*. Aspect-orientation provides the mechanism to compose crosscutting behaviors into the desired operations and classes during compile time and even during execution. The source code for your operations and classes can be free of crosscutting concerns and therefore easier to understand and maintain.

What Is Aspect-Oriented Software Development?

In order to progress beyond AOP, you need a holistic approach to developing software systems with aspects from requirements, to analysis and design, to implementation and test. This is aspect-oriented software development (AOSD).

AOSD is about better modularity for the entire system, encompassing concerns of many different kinds—better modularity for functional requirements, nonfunctional requirements, platform specifics, and so on—and keeping them separate from each other. Keeping all concerns separate allows you to construct systems that have a more understandable structure and are easily configured and extended to meet the evolving needs of stakeholders.

AOSD is not just AOP. It encompasses a whole range of techniques to help you achieve better modularity. These techniques include object orientation, component-based development, design patterns, object-oriented frameworks such as J2EE and .NET, and more. AOSD does not compete with existing techniques but is built on top of them.

AOSD with Use Cases

How do you conduct AOSD? How do you identify aspects? When do you use classes as opposed to aspects? How do you specify aspects? You need a sound and systematic approach to help you conduct AOSD. The development community is crying out for this kind of systematic approach to software development.

In fact, there is such a systematic approach—and a mature one too. It is called the use-case-driven approach. It provides a sound method for developing applications by focusing on realizing stakeholder concerns and delivering value to the user.

It is well known that aspect orientation helps modularize crosscutting concerns during implementation, but there is a need to modularize crosscutting concerns much earlier, even during requirements. Use-cases are an excellent technique for this purpose. Use-cases are crosscutting concerns, since the realization of use cases touches several classes. In fact, you can model *most* crosscutting concerns with use-cases, and we demonstrate use-case modeling in the book.

The underlying concept in aspect orientation is similar to the concept of use-case-driven development. This means that you get a seamless transition from expressing requirements of stakeholder concerns with use-cases to implementing them with aspects.

Briefly, you conduct AOSD with use-cases as follows: You model crosscutting concerns with use-cases. You design use-cases in terms of overlays on top of classes—overlays called use-case slices and use-case modules. You use aspect technology to compose use-cases slices and use-case modules to form the complete model for the system.

We use a home-construction analogy to explain the approach further. Let's say you have a new house, but it is just an empty house with no fixtures—no lights, no phone lines, no wiring, no gas, and no Internet! Each missing fixture or service is a distinct concern, evidenced by the fact that you need to call different specialists to install each fixture or service. The fixtures and services are *crosscutting concerns*—they cut across different rooms (i.e., objects). They are analogous to use-cases. To determine how he or she will go about his or her job, each specialist must design a plan, often in terms of a diagram based on the floor plan. The floor plan shows where the rooms and the walls are. The electrician makes a photocopy of the floor plan and draws how she intends to install electric wiring; the plumber sketches out how he plans to run water pipes around the house; and so on. Each specialist can work separately, but all of them base their work on the same floor plan. The overall work to be done is the sum of all these diagrams.

If each specialist were to draw his or her diagram on a transparency, the transparencies could be merged by overlaying them on a projector. These overlays are analogous to what we call use-case slices and use-case modules. As long as the overlays are based on the same dimensions of the floor plan, you can get a perfect image on the screen showing *all* the work to be done. If there is a need to change the laying of Internet lines, you just rework the overlay that describes that plan and update the merged model. When you project it with the other overlays, you get the updated image of the house. You can easily stack more overlays on the picture or swap in and out overlays. You get a coherent image provided that the dimensions correspond to each other. This represents the architectural work involved.

Systems developed using use-case slices and use-case modules have a clear separation of crosscutting concerns. You can evolve them and extend them. It is easier to make each slice reusable. You can automatically generate certain slices because they do not interfere with other slices. You get better maintainability, better extensibility, and greater productivity with this approach.

The development community can gain even more from conducting AOSD with use-cases. We believe that the adoption of aspect orientation will accelerate significantly by basing it on the use-case-driven approach because this approach has already been widely accepted as a means to drive system development, testing, and delivery. Much literature on the use-case-driven approach is readily available for the development community. A good number of professionals, even companies, exist primarily to instruct and promote its use. Project teams both large and small have been successful in adopting the approach. Thus, it is attractive and even natural to base AOSD on the use-case-driven approach.

What This Book Is

This book systematically outlines how to conduct AOSD with use-cases. We cover requirements, analysis, design, implementation, and test. We demonstrate how to model crosscutting concerns and aspects with UML and how to establish a resilient architecture that is based on use-cases and aspects. We highlight key changes in practice and the paradigm shifts that you must note when applying AOSD. We give pointers on how you can quickly reap the benefits of AOSD in your projects.

We demonstrate how you conduct AOSD in a mixed environment of object-oriented frameworks such as J2EE, object-oriented design patterns, AOP, and so on, because we recognize that these are the challenges you face in practice. We show you how to map aspect and use-case analysis to different design and implementation technologies.

We spend a great deal of time in this book describing how to establish a firm architecture based on use-cases and aspects—an architecture that is resilient to changes.

Some of you may be familiar with earlier works by Ivar Jacobson, such as *Object-Oriented Software Engineering: A Use-Case Driven Approach* (Addison-Wesley, 1992) and *The Unified Software Development Process* (Addison-Wesley, 1999). This book should be read in conjunction with those books.

Some of you may have read books on aspect orientation and wondered about its implications for software development as a whole. This is the book for you. Newcomers to aspect orientation will learn its principles and application. If you are familiar with the use-case-driven approach, you should readily recognize the benefits and implications of aspect orientation. This book will help you to appreciate the larger context of aspects—not just AOP, but AOSD.

In this book, we use a single example of a Hotel Management System, which you become familiar with as we progress through the book. By building upon a single example, we keep our discussion of aspect orientation and use-cases focused and concrete.

What This Book Is Not

This book is not a programming book. We do not go into details about AOP languages or aspect-oriented frameworks that are currently available. For those details, refer to guide books and tutorials. This book is about aspect-oriented *software development* (not just programming). The emphasis is on a software development approach from requirements to code, applying a number of techniques in a balanced and iterative manner to help you succeed in building your software systems.

This book does not attempt to be an aspect-oriented design cookbook. We do not attempt to discuss all conceivable crosscutting concerns (synchronization, transaction management, caching, etc.). Nevertheless, we believe that the breadth of this book provides the principles and the basis for you to deal with many kinds of crosscutting concerns that you will encounter in practice.

What You Need Before Reading This Book

There are several prerequisites to getting the most out of this book. You must have at least some understanding of the Unified Modeling Language (UML). We include some explanation of UML in this book, but we largely expect you to know the basics. We expect you to know what classes are and that you can read use-case diagrams, class diagrams, sequence diagrams, and collaboration diagrams. Incidentally, the last two are called *interaction* diagrams and *communication* diagrams in UML 2.0.

If you have ever applied use-case-driven development in a project, then you will really benefit from this book—even if you do not have any background in aspect orientation. We had you in mind when we wrote this book and spent some time to ground you in the basics of AOP.

If you are knowledgeable about aspect orientation and have little idea about use-case-driven development, do not fret. We have you in mind, too. Part II is devoted to acquainting you with use cases and use-case realizations.

We show some code examples in AspectJ to give you a concrete picture of our proposed extension to the UML notation to support AOSD. AspectJ is a language extension of Java that supports AOP. Some understanding of Java is therefore helpful. However, we want to highlight that this is not an AOP book. This book does not intend to teach you the complete AspectJ syntax.

Since we are showing you how to apply AOSD in a mixed environment and how to deal with platform specifics, we need to use some platform to make our discussion concrete. For this purpose, we chose J2EE, so some knowledge of J2EE is useful. If you have ever heard about servlets and EJBs, you should have sufficient background. If you know the J2EE core patterns, better still.

So, welcome—and read this book.

How to Read This Book

We organized this book into five parts:

Part I, The Case for Use Cases and Aspects

Part I is basically an expansion of this preface. The goal is to help you understand what AOSD with use cases is all about. We highlight some basic cases of crosscutting—peers and extensions—and how aspects solve them. Through some simple code examples, we introduce AspectJ, which is currently the most popular AOP technology. We provide an overview of use-case-driven development as it is today—what use cases are, how use cases are realized, and how they are mapped to classes—and what we expect it to be like tomorrow—with aspects, use case slices and use case modules.

Part II, Modeling and Capturing Concerns with Use Cases

Whether you are familiar with use cases or not, you should read Part II. It gives you an overview of the use-case technique and clarifies common misconceptions about use cases. Part II also enhances the use-case modeling technique to provide a seamless transition from use-case modeling to aspect-oriented analysis and design. In particular, we show how point-cuts are modeled within use cases. Part II culminates by walking through a rich example of applying use-case modeling to different crosscutting concerns—both functional and nonfunctional. They are modeled with use cases of different kinds—application use cases and infrastructure use cases. Subsequent parts of the book demonstrate how to drive these different kinds of use cases all the way to implementation.

Part III, Keeping Concerns Separate with Use Case Modules

Part III goes deeper into the concept of use-case slices and use-case modules. Use-case slices help you keep the specifics of a use case separate in the design model. They are the overlays we mentioned to keep crosscutting concerns separate. We show you how to model use-case slices and aspects with UML and how our extensions to the UML notation map to AOP. We use this notation and the underlying concepts in Part IV, and the notation is summarized in Appendix B.

Part IV, Establishing an Architecture Based on Use Cases and Aspects

The most important determinant to the success of a project lies in its architecture. Part IV demonstrates how to get good architecture, step by step. Among other things, a good architecture keeps concerns of different kinds separate. It separates the use-case-specific from the use-case-generic, the application-specific from the application-generic; the plat-form-specific from the platform-independent; and so on. This separation not only makes your system more understandable and maintainable, it also makes your system extensible. It makes parts of your system reusable without causing those parts to be entangled. It also provides room for significant automation when implementing the system.

In Part IV, there are plenty of useful tips and guidelines to such an architecture. You might need to refer to Appendix B on the notations used in the book as you read Part IV.

Part V, Applying Use Cases and Aspects in a Project

You might be at the beginning, middle, or final stages of your project: No matter what stage you are at, you can apply the practices advocated in this book. In Part V, we demonstrate how to tailor our approach to different project scenarios. We also show you how to effectively manage a project that is based on use cases and aspects.

How This Book Came About

Research papers often have many authors, and you may wonder what each author contributed to the work. Here, we reminisce about how this book came about and explain our individual contributions to the concepts and pragmatics described in this book.

In the Beginning
By Ivar

The first time I heard the term aspect-oriented programming was back in 1997. I immediately saw it as an interesting technology, but at the time, I couldn't take a serious look at. I was working on the first version of UML, and on getting Rational Unified Process (RUP) right, and I was initiating an effort on active software processes—actually what is now Jaczone Way-Pointer. When I finally had time to take a good look at aspects, it was in September 2002. I downloaded a lot of papers and studied them for a couple of days. Then I contacted Harold Ossher at IBM Research and Karl Lieberherr at Northeastern University in Boston. They are two of the leaders in this space. The most well-known person on aspects is Gregor Kizcales. I tried to get his attention as well, but he was too busy at that time. However, he contributed to this book by reviewing it extensively, and we benefited significantly from his comments.

In November 2002, I visited the IBM folks and spent a day with them learning about their work. After the meeting, I was very impressed and excited about what they had done. I left their office and rushed to Newark airport; I had to run to the gate. This is normal. I was on my way to Stockholm. When I was seated in the plane, I ordered some champagne and began to relax and think a little. Suddenly, it struck me. Didn't I do something similar before? Didn't I write a paper on the same subject for OOPSLA '86—the very first OOPSLA conference?

When I got to Stockholm, I hunted for the paper. It was a paper that discussed a topic that I mentioned as future work in my Ph.D. thesis from 1985. However, the ideas in the paper had generated no interest, so I decided to leave the subject. I felt it was too early to push those ideas and just forgot about them. Besides, my work on component-based development with objects and use cases was so successful that there was no room for new inventions. However, now I wanted to find the paper. I went to the publisher's Web site and found it. I had to pay $95 to download it! My own paper!

The title of the paper is "Language Support for Changeable Large Real-Time Systems" [Jacobson 1986]. In that paper, I introduced several concepts—existion, which represents a base, and extension, which represents separate functionality that you want to add to the existion. Instead of modifying the existion to invoke an extension, we used a mechanism to allow the extension to add behavior into the existion. Thus, from the perspective of the existion, no modification was needed. This meant that you could add extension after extension without breaking the existion. The key idea is this: By keeping extensions separate from the base from the developer's perspective, the system is much easier to understand, maintain, and extend.

The basic idea sounded very much like what aspect-orientation research is trying to achieve. But I needed confirmation. Two hours after I downloaded the paper, I sent it to Karl Lieberherr. He responded, "Wow, Ivar, this is an early paper on aspect-orientation." He asked me if I had anything more. Since I throw away everything I don't work with, my first thought was that there was nothing more. However, I was excited, and my thoughts went back to the time before the paper. My memory asked me, "Didn't you file a patent for a similar work?"

The patent was filed in 1981, and I filed it as an employee of Ericsson. I called the Ericsson patent department and asked if they had saved the application. After a week, they produced a copy of the application—in Swedish. The application used typical patent language, so I had actually never understood it. It was written by a patent engineer. However, attached to the application was an internal Ericsson paper that described the whole idea in a couple of pages. It was quite a detailed paper with a practical example. This paper was also in Swedish. I had both documents translated into English by a professional translator, and you can find them on *www.ivarjacobson.com* (look for published papers and aspect-oriented software development).

The patent was about what we called a *sequence variator*. It works at the microprogram instruction level. The highlight of the design is this: A program has a list of instructions. To each instruction, I added a flag. If this flag is turned on, it means that there is an extension that needs to be executed at this point. The sequence variator fetches instructions from the extension and, thereafter, resumes at the next instruction. This branching is taken care of by the sequence variator. The developer of the original instructions does not need to code branch statements.

To make a long story short, Karl Lieberherr and Harold Ossher liked my early work. Karl wrote an email that compared my early work with modern aspect-orientation: extension aspect, extension point join point, and so on. I then wrote a couple of papers on aspects and use cases (see *www.jaczone.com/papers*) and as a result, I was invited to speak at an international conference on aspect orientation. I was very happy to be recognized for my early work. It spurred me to start a book on the technique, and I needed someone to work with me to make the approach practical.

I am often asked which is my favorite country. In addition to Sweden, where I grew up and have family, I have many favorites. Most countries have something that makes me feel happy and at home. Singapore is certainly one of them. In Singapore is Pan-Wei Ng. Pan-Wei was quite familiar with use-case-driven development, model-driven development, and similar methodologies. He had been helping me to review recent papers I'd written about use-case aspects, so I asked him to join me to write the book.

Pan-Wei immediately agreed, and we started work. That was sometime in December 2002. It took us almost two years to write this book. I leave it to Pan-Wei to tell you what happened thereafter and how we wrote the book together.

Working Together
By Pan-Wei

Writing the book has not been easy. This was originally intended to be a 150-page book, but it has grown much. Ivar's papers on use cases and aspects essentially set the framework for whole book, but they were not enough, and we needed to map Ivar's concepts (specifically use-case slices) into implementation and a set of guidelines for practitioners. This was my contribution to the book. Of course, Ivar had earlier works on use-case-driven development and related topics, and I had quite a lot of resources to draw from.

During the writing, Ivar made hundreds of comments, some of which changed the direction of the book dramatically. While I did most of the writing, Ivar supervised and had many strong opinions about the foundational concepts that shaped the book:

1. Modeling crosscutting concerns with use cases—peer and extension use cases
2. Use-case slices and use-case modularity
3. Model-driven development use case by use case
4. Use-case-driven development (as per OOSE and USDP)

We discussed many issues together, and my contributions include the following:

1. Mapping use-case slices to AOP—structural and behavioral context of operation extensions
2. Platform specifics as extensions to platform-independent elements and infrastructure as extensions to the application

My main contribution lies in making Ivar's ideas concrete through examples and discussing pros and cons of different approaches in the book. In doing so, I had to pull together existing practices in design patterns, J2EE patterns, layering, mock objects, and so on. Although these practices are mostly well described individually, finding a more adequate formulation to put them together was a challenge. This is why writing this book took longer than expected.

Many of these contributions would not have been possible without the foundations set by Ivar. But regardless of whether the contributions were made by Ivar or by me, we discussed and debated them heavily, often seeking the advice of others.

It was indeed lots of fun working on the book. It resulted in our becoming really good friends, and we plan to continue working together. This project inspired Ivar to form a company in Singapore and another in Korea. Life is exciting, and there is never a dull moment.

Acknowledgments

No book is purely the work of the authors. There are many people behind the scenes who in one way or another help shape the book. We are just the lucky ones with our names in the front of the book.

We thank Gregor Kiczales and his team for giving us AOP. It is indeed a wonderful and exciting technique that will shape the industry. Thanks to Harold Ossher with his IBM colleagues, and to Karl Lieberherr and team for giving us hyperslices and adaptive programming.

We thank Gregor Kiczales for his review and comments on the draft manuscript and his emphasis on modularity. We also thank other reviewers who in one way or another made this a better book: Omar Aldawud, Kurt Bittner, Ron Bodkin, Charles B. Haley, Wes Isberg, Ramnivas Laddad, Miguel Jorge Tavares Pessoa Monteiro, Roger Oberg, Awais Rashid, Therapon Skotiniotis, Dean Wampler, and Michael J. Ward. We are grateful for their detailed and precise comments.

Thanks to Gunnar Overgaard, who went to great depths on modeling, and to Magnus Christerson for his comments on dealing with platform specifics. Thanks to Stefan Bylund, too, for his input on use-case modeling and testing.

We thank Steve Ballard, Ivan Ng, and Kathleen Koh, who gave us useful tips on the earlier chapters of the book. Also thanks to D. J. de Villiers and Eric Lopes Cardozo for their helpful comments.

Special thanks to Andrei Stepanov for his extremely detailed reviews and for making this book much more approachable.

Thanks to Julie Nahil and Mary Sudul at Pearson Addison-Wesley Professional for their production supervision; and to Carol Lallier for copyediting, Carol Cramer for proofreading, and Barbara Palumbo for indexing.

Finally, we thank our families for their understanding and support as we took time away from them to write this book.

PART I

The Case for Use Cases and Aspects

In Part I, we build the case for use cases and aspects—why we need use cases, why we need aspects, and how the two complement each other. Conventional modularity approaches such as classes and components cannot keep crosscutting concerns separate. To solve this problem, you need two things: a separation technique to keep crosscutting concerns separate and a composition mechanism to compose these concerns to form the desired system.

Thanks to aspect technologies, you have a composition mechanism. You can compose parts of classes or components that realize different crosscutting concerns to form the complete classes or components. Through some simple code examples in AspectJ, an aspect-oriented language extension to Java, we demonstrate how such composition mechanisms work.

In addition to a composition mechanism, you need a separation technique to identify crosscutting concerns, to capture them, and structure them during requirements and preserve that separation all the way through analysis, design, and code. This is achieved with use cases. You express crosscutting concerns with use cases. **You can model and structure almost any crosscutting concerns with use cases—in fact we don't know any crosscutting concern that is functional in nature that can't be represented as use cases**. You analyze, design, implement, and test crosscutting concerns in basically the same way as you do use cases.

We also introduce the concepts of a *use-case slice* and a *use-case module*. A use-case slice contains the specifics of a use-case in a model. Use-case slices employ aspects to compose the different parts of a model together. A use-case module contains the specifics of a use case over all models of the system. We briefly demonstrate how use-case slices and use-case modules help you streamline software development. The rest of the book expands on the concepts of use-case slices and use-case modules, and explains how to develop a resilient architecture—one that keeps concerns of different kinds separate through use-case modules, use-case slices, and aspects.

Part I includes the following chapters:

Chapter 1, "Problem to Attack"

Chapter 2, "Attacking the Problem with Aspects"

Chapter 3, "Today with Use Cases"

Chapter 4, "Tomorrow with Use-Case Modules"

1

Problem to Attack

Component-based development is a widely used approach to build complex systems. Basically, you allocate requirements to components of some kind—classes, packages, services, and so forth. Although many requirements can be effectively localized to individual components, you find many requirements that cannot be localized to an individual component and that sometimes even impact many components. In aspect-speak, these requirements cut across components and are called *crosscutting concerns*. The inability to keep such concerns separate during design and implementation makes a system difficult to understand and maintain. It inhibits parallel development and makes a system difficult to extend and results in many of the problems that plague so many projects today. A successful solution to this problem involves two things: an engineering technique to separate such concerns from requirements all the way to code and a composition mechanism to merge the design and implementation for each concern to result in the desired system. With aspect orientation under the guidance of an appropriate methodology, you do have such a solution today.

1.1   The Use of Components Today

Software systems are important to businesses today. Most, if not all, businesses today cannot run without the help of software to conduct business operations. As we all know, software systems are complex and when we design such complex systems our limited minds cannot possibly consider everything and solve everything at once.

Our natural inclination is to break the problem into smaller parts and solve them one by one. This is why we have components. Each component plays its specific role and has specific responsibilities and purposes. We assemble components of various kinds to form the complete system. This is basically how we develop any kind of product: electronic devices, cars, and more.

In a generic sense, components are elements that conform to well-defined interfaces, and if you invoke them through their interfaces, they produce some well-defined responses. For example, a computer chip is a component. It has pins through which you can send electric signals. Upon receiving the signal, the chip performs some actions and possibly returns some response through some other pins. Your video projector is also a component. If you plug in a video cable from your laptop to the projector, you can make images appear on the wall.

A component encapsulates its contents. Its internals are all hidden from you. As a user of the component, you do not need to know how it really works on the inside. All you need to know is that you send the correct signals to it through its interfaces in some acceptable sequence and you get your desired response. This characteristic of components is very attractive because as long as the interfaces do not change, you can replace them with other components that conform to those same interfaces. This substitutability is extremely useful if you want to extend the system with some new capabilities—all you need to do is replace an existing component with a better one that conforms to the same interface. Even if you have to change an interface, you may delimit the changes to a few components. It allows you to gracefully grow a complex system.

1.1.1 Building a System with Components

The usual approach to building systems in terms of components is as follows: You begin by first understanding what the system is supposed to do: What are the stakeholder concerns? What are the requirements? Next, you explore and identify the parts (i.e., components) that will constitute the system. You then map the world of requirements to the world of components. This is an M-to-N mapping and, normally, M is much larger than N. For example, you might have 1,000 requirements and maybe 50 components. The common approach to mapping is as follows: You identify a set of candidate components and check that each requirement will be implemented with these components. In this process, you may learn more about the requirements and, provided that the requirements are not too critical, change them so that they are easier to implement. Alternately, you might modify components to improve the fit. Once the required set of components is found, they are connected to form the desired system.

Figure 1-1 shows the components for a Hotel Management System. We use this system as an example here and throughout the rest of the book. Briefly, this system provides the functionalities to Reserve Room, Check In, and Check Out to be used by both customers and hotel staff.

Figure 1-1 shows components of various kinds. The Customer Screen and Staff Screen components deal with presenting information to the users and accepting and validating input from them. The Reserve Room, Check In, and Check Out components encapsulate the business and control logic for the respective functionalities. The reservation and the room components maintain information in a data store. This separation of roles and responsibilities across components is essential to a system that is resilient—one that will not easily break when changes are introduced.

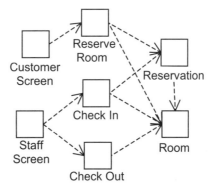

Figure 1-1   *Hotel Management System made up of interconnected components.*

1.1.2   Benefits of Components

Components are useful and important because they represent the static structure of a system such as that depicted in Figure 1-1. They are essential to understanding, designing, implementing, distributing, testing, and configuring the system. They are the most important asset for reuse in practice. Components contain things that change together. They keep concerns about a kind of object or an abstraction of a real-world phenomena separate.

For instance, a component (e.g., the Room and Reservation components in Figure 1-1) may encapsulate the manipulation of data structures capturing room and reservation information. If you change the data structure, you change the operations that touch these data. There are also components encapsulating the specifics of user interfaces. If you want to change the look and feel of the system, you simply change the screen components. Thus, you see that components make a system resilient to changes as you add new requirements to the system.

You can also meet customers' new demands by configuring the system using the components. New features or use-cases are usually provided by adding a new component and changing some already existing components.

In recent years, component frameworks such as J2EE and .Net have evolved and gained widespread popularity. Basically, all new software being developed is componentized.

1.2   Limitation of Components

To understand the limitations of components, we start with concerns. The goal of a system is to meet requirements or, more generally, concerns. A concern is anything that is of interest to a stakeholder, whether an end user, project sponsor, or developer. For example, a concern can be a functional requirement, a nonfunctional requirement, or a design constraint on the system. It can be more than a requirement of the system. It can even be a low-level concern such as caching or buffering.

Breaking down a problem into smaller parts is called *separation of concerns* in computer science. Ideally, we want to be able to cleanly separate the different concerns into modules of some kind and explore and develop each in isolation, one at a time. Thereafter, you compose these software modules to yield the complete system. Thus, the concept of separation of concerns and the concept of modularity are two sides of a coin—you separate concerns into modules, and each module solves or implements some distinct set of concerns.

Successful separation of concerns must start early. You begin software development by attempting to understand the stakeholder concerns. You explore and collect the requirements for the system according to stakeholder concerns. Although some concerns can be realized by distinct and separate components, in general, you find many concerns for which components are not adequate. These are known as *crosscutting concerns*—concerns that impact multiple components. There are different kinds of crosscutting concerns: *infrastructure* concerns are crosscutting concerns to meet nonfunctional requirements—for instance, logging, distribution, and transaction management. Some crosscutting concerns deal with functional requirements as well. You frequently find that the realization of functional requirements (which can be specified as use-cases) cut across multiple components. Thus, even use-cases are crosscutting concerns.

Sidebar 1-1   How Does Aspect Orientation Impact Object Orientation?

Aspect orientation is established precisely to overcome the limitation of object orientation. Conventional modularity such as classes and services suffer from their inability to keep crosscutting concerns separate. It does not matter whether or not you are implementing your system using object-oriented programming languages: they are all inadequate in dealing with crosscutting concerns.

As we write this book, we find that having to list all the conventional modules (components, classes, services, etc.) every time we talk about their limitations can be quite lengthy. So, for brevity, we simply use the term *components* as a representative of conventional modularity. So, when we say a "crosscutting concern can cut across classes," it applies to components as well.

1.2.1   Inability to Keep Peers Separate

We particularly want to highlight two kinds of crosscutting concerns. The first is what we call *peers*. These are concerns that are distinct from each other. No one peer is more important than another. If you consider the familiar ATM example, cash withdrawal, fund transfer, and cash deposit are all peers. In our hotel management example, Reserve Room, Check In Customer, and Check Out Customer are peers. These concerns do not need each other to exist. In fact, you can build separate systems for each one. However, when you start to implement peers in the same system, you find significant overlap between them. This is illustrated in Figure 1-2.

Figure 1-2 depicts concerns in different shades on the left-hand side. The right-hand side shows the components with multiple shades. Each shade represents the codes that implement the respective concerns. The limitation of components to keep peers separate is evident in Figure 1-2. It results in two effects, which in aspect-speak are known as *tangling* and *scattering*.

Tangling. You find that each component contains the implementation (i.e., code) to satisfy different concerns. For example, in Figure 1-2, you see that the Room component is involved in the realization of three different concerns. This means that as a developer/owner of a component, you need to understand a diverse set of concerns. The component, instead of single-mindedly fulfilling a particular concern, participates in many. This hinders understandability and makes the learning curve steeper for developers.

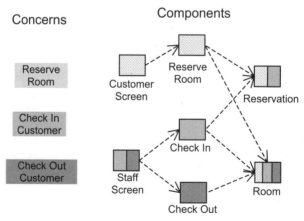

Figure 1-2   *Tangling and scattering when realizing peers.*

Do not confuse tangling with reuse. Reuse implies that the same code or behaviors are useable under different contexts. Definitely, some parts of the Room component will be reusable without changes. However, in many cases, as highlighted in Figure 1-2, each concern demands additional and distinct behaviors on the Room component not needed to realize other concerns. There is no reuse among them, and they result in tangling.

Scattering. You also find codes that realize a particular concern are spread across multiple components. For example, in Figure 1-2, you see that the realization of Check In Customer imposes additional behaviors on four components. So, if ever the requirements about that concern change, or if the design of that concern changes, you must update many components.

More importantly, scattering means that it is not easy to understand the internals of a system. For instance, it is not easy to uncover requirements by reading the source code of each component or a set of components. If the requirement for a particular concern changes, different classes need to be updated as well. Poor understandability leads to poor maintainability, and it is not easy to make enhancements, especially for large systems.

1.2.2   Inability to Keep Extensions Separate

The second kind of crosscutting concern is what we call *extensions*. Extensions are components that you define on top of a base. They represent additional service or features. For example, the Hotel Management System has a waiting list for room reservations. If there are no rooms, the system puts the customer on a waiting list. Thus, the provision of a waiting list is an extension of Reserve Room. Keeping extensions separate is a technique to make a complex problem understandable. You do not want to be entangled by too many issues, so you keep them separate as extensions.

Although it is natural to describe the base and extension separately, there is a problem when it comes to implementing the extension, as exemplified in Figure 1-3.

Figure 1-3 shows the Reserve Room component, which serves as the base. To incorporate the Waiting List extension, a corresponding component is added (shown in a darker shade). But in addition, you need to add some code fragments in the Reserve Room component at a particular location,

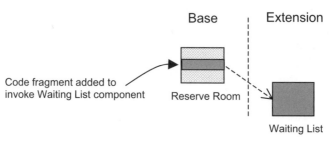

Figure 1-3   *Extensions inserted intrusively.*

which we call an extension point. The purpose of this code fragment is to connect or invoke the Waiting List component.

The problem is this: some code has been added to a place that didn't really need it before we added the new feature. It is there for the purpose of hooking the new component onto the existing component. This code fragment is affectionately known as *glue code*. In aspect-speak, such a change is known as *intrusive*.

No matter how good your design is, you still need glue code, and if you need to extend the system at another location, you must add the glue code there too. For example, if you need to support different payment methods for the Hotel Reservation System, you need additional glue code to open up an extension point in the system.

Adding all this glue code and making all these changes to existing code definitely makes the original classes harder to comprehend. But a greater problem exists: you cannot possibly identify all the extension points a priori. Thus, what is really needed is a way for you to designate extension points on demand at any time during the system's life cycle. Although this is a significant advantage, there is a limit to how far you can go. If a system is poorly designed, designating extension points is definitely not easy. In addition, after adding several enhancements, you have a better picture of the whole system and you might want to separate concerns differently. In this case, you might dispense some effort to refine the base.

Sidebar 1-2   The Difference Between Concerns and Requirements

---

You might be wondering what the difference between a concern and a requirement is. They are not the same. Developing a system involves specifying requirements, which are then refined into design and subsequently to implementation. So, requirements are only part of the software development life cycle. A concern represents something of importance to some stakeholder, and it encompasses everything: you must specify concerns, design them, and implement them. So, requirements are simply for specifying concerns.

In general, for each concern, you will have many requirement statements to clarify what the concern is. For example, the Reserve Room functionality is a concern. There will be many requirement statements because the system deals with the Reservation of kinds of Rooms, different Reservation schemes, and so on.

In addition to specifying the concern, you must design and implement it. When we talk about separating concerns, we mean separating at requirements time and keeping the separation during design and implementation.

1.3   Approaching a Solution

So, you find that even though components are excellent tools to structure a complex system in some hierarchical fashion, they are nevertheless insufficient. Components cannot keep crosscutting concerns separate all the way down to code. Adding a new concern (a set of requirements) to the system becomes very painful.

The search is on for a new kind of modularity, one that can keep crosscutting concerns separate throughout the life cycle of the module—from requirements to analysis, design, code, and test. To achieve this modularity, you must also have a corresponding way to integrate or compose the new modularity into a coherent whole to get executable code. The new modularity must also help you collect all work on a concern, not just the code, but requirements, analysis, design, implementation, and test for that concern.

To achieve this new modularity, you need two things: a concern separation technique and a concern composition technique.

Concern Separation Technique. In order to keep concerns separate, you must model and structure concerns. The use-case technique is quite helpful in modeling concerns during requirements and analysis. We discuss use-cases in greater detail in Chapter 3, "Today with Use-cases," and in further depth in Part 2 of the book. Separating peer use-cases is easy (that is how use-cases are normally defined). Separating extension use-cases requires new language constructs. On top of that, you also need techniques to preserve the separation during design and implementation.

Concern Composition Mechanism. At some point in time, you need to compose the concerns. This can happen during compile time, post-compilation time, or even during execution. Composing normal extensions is relatively easy, since all that is needed is some automated way to monitor the execution of the base and execute the extension when required.

Composing peer use-cases is much harder—you must deal with overlapping behavior, conflicts, and other problems. Thus, the early efforts have been to keep extensions separate. In the next section, we discuss some of these early efforts to highlight that crosscutting concerns is not a new problem. Keeping extensions separate is also not a technique that is invented only recently. But certainly, aspect orientation (which we discuss in Chapter 2, "Attacking the Problem with Aspects") provides an elegant solution and hence a renewed interest in the problem of dealing with crosscutting concerns. Another reason we highlight earlier works is to show that aspect thinking is very much in line with use-case thinking and, hence, use-case–driven development is a strong candidate for conducting aspect-oriented software development.

1.3.1   Early Support for Extensions

The idea of keeping extensions separate dates back a long way and appeared in a 1986 paper discussing "Language Support for Changeable Large Real-Time Systems" [Jacobson 1986]. Jacobson introduced several terms in that paper; see Figure 1-4. The original program, that is, the base, is termed an *existion*. The new functionalities to be added to the existion are termed *extensions*. Extensions are inserted at designated execution points in the existion. These execution points are known as *extension points*.

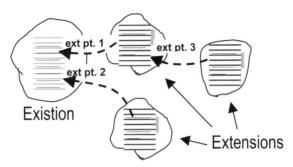

Figure 1-4   *Existions, extension points, and extensions.*

The key idea behind the approach is that you insert extensions into the existions during compilation or execution—not during coding. Thus, the source code of the existing system and even possibly its binaries remain clean and free of any extensions.

Structuring a system as shown in Figure 1-4 has several advantages. First, it makes extending an existing system a lot easier. When you want to introduce an extension, all you need to do is designate the extension point where the extension needs to be inserted. But this is no excuse for poor programming and design practices. Good development and programming practices make it easier for you to specify extension points.

Second, and even more fundamentally, structuring a system this way makes systems much more understandable. You structure the system from a base and then add more functionality in chunks that are not necessary to understanding the base. This allows our limited minds to focus on a particular concern at a time in isolation without the disturbance of other concerns. You can apply this approach to structure almost anything beyond codes. You can even apply it to requirement specifications and design.

How is support for extensions achieved? It can be achieved in several ways—during compilation time or runtime. One of the possible ways to do so during runtime is through a much earlier work by Jacobson. It is known as a sequence variator, and its operation is depicted in Figure 1-5 [Jacobson 1981].

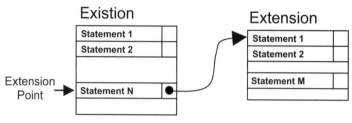

Figure 1-5   *Sequence variator.*

The sequence variator works at microprogram level. The program consists of a list of statements, and each statement has a bit flag to indicate whether an extension occurs at that point. In typical operation, the sequence variation takes a statement from memory and executes it, then takes and executes the next statement, then the next, and so on. If the extension bit flag is set, the sequence variator looks for an extension that references the current statement and proceeds to execute the statements in the extension. When all the statements in the extension have been executed, the sequence variator resumes with the statement at the existion and continues.

From the existion programmer's viewpoint, you only view the statements, not the extension bit flag. When an extension must be added later on, all that is needed is to code the extension statements and turn on the appropriate extension bit flags in the existion. The existion programmer does not have to worry about extensions that are added later. You can easily add extension after extension without breaking the modularity of the existion. There is no tangling or scattering.

Jacobson filed a patent for this approach in 1981, but the patent was not accepted. The idea was too close to a patented patching technique for which his proposal would have been an infringement, so Jacobson always had to apologize for this closeness before explaining the idea.

A common fear about adopting aspect orientation is that practitioners feel that it *is like patching*. Definitely, if used in an ad hoc manner, it indeed is like patching. But aspect orientation is not for patching. It is for you to achieve better separation of crosscutting concerns. It is for you to achieve better modularity. The goal of this book is to provide you with sound techniques and practical guidelines to achieve this.

1.3.2   Support for Extensions in UML

Even though the patent was not accepted, the concept of keeping extensions separate persists. It manifests as extension use-cases, which made it to the Unified Modeling Language. In fact, for those of you who have applied use-cases, you should be quite familiar with the use-case extension concept. We go into the details later, but what we want to say is that the idea of keeping extensions separate is not new. Briefly, use-case extensions permit us to describe additional behaviors that can be inserted into an existing use-case. For example, you have an existing use-case called Reserve Room, and you want to add some waiting list functionality, as exemplified earlier. With the use-case modeling technique, you simply add an extension use-case, which is modeled as the Handle Waiting List use-case in Figure 1-6. In use-case modeling terminology, the Reserve Room use-case would be a base use-case, and the Handle Waiting List would be an extension use-case.

The use-case technique provides the means to specify how behaviors described in the extension use-case are inserted at the extension points defined in the base use-case.

Nevertheless, the idea of keeping extensions separate remains a specification technique as opposed to an implementation technique. In *Object-Oriented Software Engineering* [Jacobson et al. 1992], there are techniques to keep extensions separate during analysis and during use-case modeling. However, there are no techniques to keep extensions separate during design, since there was no aspect-oriented programming language available when the book was written. In *Software Reuse* [Jacobson 1997], the authors generalize the concept of extension points into variation points, and many of these ideas have been carried over to the Reusable Asset Specification (RAS).

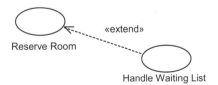

Figure 1-6   *Waiting list as an extension use-case.*

The first serious attempt to implement extensions was done in the early 1990s at Ericsson in the development of a new generation of switches. The people who adopted extensions took them into a new development environment called Delos, which supported extensions all the way down to code. Nevertheless, support for extensions in mainstream programming languages did not appear until the advent of aspect orientation technologies.

1.4   Keeping Concerns Separate

Being able to keep concerns separate is extremely important in software development. It helps you break down a complex problem into smaller parts and solve them individually. When it comes to large systems, it is the only way for you to build them. If you cannot keep concerns separate, the complexity of the system increases exponentially as you add enhancement after enhancement. By keeping concerns separate, on the other hand, the system is much easier to understand, maintain, and extend.

Existing modularity such as classes and components do help you keep concerns separate, at least to a certain extent. Each class keeps the specifics of a kind of object or real-world phenomenon separate; each component encapsulates the computation and data related for some functionality; and so on. However, when it comes to crosscutting concerns—concerns that cut across classes and components—you need another approach to modularity.

Moving ahead, in Chapter 2, we demonstrate how to maintain the separation of crosscutting concerns during implementation (i.e., code) using aspect orientation. In Chapter 3, we show how use-cases help us capture and model concerns. In Chapter 4, we show how, with use-cases and aspects, we can achieve separation of concerns from requirements to code, and we explain the steps necessary to get there.

2

Attacking the Problem with Aspects

We established in the previous chapter that existing techniques provide inadequate separation of crosscutting concerns. Aspect orientation solves this problem by providing a composition mechanism to compose additional behaviors from outside a class into the class itself. Composition can occur during compilation or runtime. But aspect orientation is more than just a composition mechanism. It is a way for you to separate the implementation of different concerns into separate modules. Through simple code examples in AspectJ—one of the most popular aspect technologies today—we demonstrate how aspects work and how aspect orientation helps you solve the problem of crosscutting and achieve better modularity.

2.1 Approaching a Solution with Aspects

Aspect orientation is a set of technologies aimed at providing better separation of crosscutting concerns. It is sometimes also known as advanced separation of concerns. Research in aspect orientation has been going on for a relatively long time, but it started gaining a lot of recognition from mainstream observers in 1997 when Gregor Kiczales from Xerox Parc presented his keynote presentation on aspect-oriented programming (AOP) at OOPSLA '97. AOP, and specifically, AspectJ, is the most popular aspect technology [Kiczales et al. 1997] [Kiczales et al. 2000]. AspectJ is an extension to the Java language with new constructs to separate and modularize concerns:

- **Intertype declarations** allow you to compose *new* features (attributes, operations, and relationships) into existing classes.
- **Advices** provide the means to extend *existing* operations at extension points designated by *pointcuts* in AOP.
- **Aspects** are a kind of building block used to organize intertype declarations and advices. Aspects can generalize other aspects.

AOP is not the only technique that deals with crosscutting concerns. A number of works from the research community, such as the following, address the issue:

- Composition filters (CF) originated from the TRESE group at the Department of Computer Science of the University of Twente, Netherlands [Aksit et al. 1998] [Bergmans et al. 2001].
- Multidimensional separation of concerns (MDSOC) originated from IBM Research [Tarr et al. 1999] [Ossher et al. 2000].
- Adaptive programming (AP) originated from Center of Software Sciences, Northeastern University (NEU), Boston, Massachusetts [Lieberherr et al. 1994].

Furthermore, AOP is not just AspectJ. Other AOP implementations include AspectWerkz and JBoss-AOP. You might wish to take a look at these evolving technologies. Although we show some code samples for AspectJ, AOP has also been implemented in languages like C, C++, and C#. The truth of the matter is that the idea of keeping concerns separate pervades throughout all software development and is not limited to object-oriented systems alone.

In Chapter 1, "Problem to Attack," we highlighted two specific kinds of crosscutting concerns that you need to keep separate—peers and extensions. Through some code samples in AspectJ, we show you how the above constructs help you keep such crosscutting concerns separate. Our intent is to show how you keep concerns separate, not to explain the details of AOP or AspectJ, so our examples are significantly simplified. As a developer, you might want to learn the specifics of AOP and AspectJ. The downloads along with additional code samples and a description of the AspectJ language extension to Java are available at the AspectJ Web site: *http://www.eclipse.org/aspectj*.

2.2 Keeping Peers Separate with Aspects

As a quick recap, peer concerns are distinct from each other, but their realizations overlap classes. Let's consider the example of a Hotel Management System, which we use throughout the book. In particular, we discuss three specific functionalities in this example system: room reservation, customer check-in, and customer check-out. Briefly, the functionalities are as follows:

- To reserve a room, you check the room availability, and if a room is available, you create a reservation.
- To check in a customer, you assign him to a room and consume his reservation. At the same time, you create an initial bill for the customer.
- To check out a customer, you collect the payment for the bill. Once the bill has been paid, the customer is removed from the room.

Figure 2-1 shows how these functionalities (represented horizontally) cut across classes in the system (shown as boxes). Each box lists the operations imposed on the respective classes.

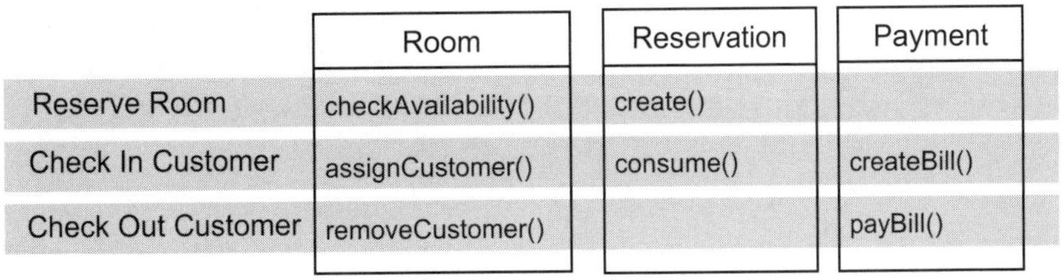

	Room	Reservation	Payment
Reserve Room	checkAvailability()	create()	
Check In Customer	assignCustomer()	consume()	createBill()
Check Out Customer	removeCustomer()		payBill()

Figure 2-1   *Classes composed from different concerns.*

Note that there are other operations not shown in Figure 2-1 that are common across the different functionalities. These operations are reusable, but our emphasis in Figure 2-1 is that the various functionalities impose different operations on the respective classes. As a developer, you need to collect all these responsibilities to implement each class. This is where crosscutting and, hence, tangling occurs. The Room class contains code needed by different peer functionalities. With AOP intertype declarations, you can indeed keep the specifics of each peer concern separate. Simplified Source Code to Check In Customer 0-1 shows the simplified listing that implements the Check In Customer functionality as an **aspect** using AspectJ.

Listing 2-1   Simplified Source Code to Check In Customer

```
1.  public aspect CheckInCustomer {
2.     ...
3.     public void Room.assignCustomer ()
4.     {
5.       // code to check in customer
6.     }
7.     public void Reservation.consume()
8.     {
9.       // code to consume reservation
10.    }
11.    public void Payment.createBill()
12.    {
13.      // code to generate an initial outstanding bill
14.    }
15.    ...
16. }
```

Line 1 in Listing 2-1 declares CheckInCustomer as an aspect, as indicated by the aspect keyword. It contains a series of intertype declarations. There are two segments of an intertype declaration we want to highlight. The first segment is the name of an existing class, and the second segment is the existing operation that you want to add into. So, for instance, in line 3, you see

```
Room.assignCustomer()
```

This adds the operation assignCustomer() into the Room class. Notice that although this operation is part of the Room class, it is defined outside the Room class itself. Thus, aspect orientation escapes from the restriction on a class property needing to be defined within the traditional class modularity. This allows us alternate ways of organizing code—one that keeps the realization of peer concerns separate.

2.3   Keeping Extensions Separate with Aspects

Let us now look at how AOP can help you keep extensions separate. Extensions are add-ons to some base behavior. In this case, we have a base reserve room functionality, which we want to extend. Figure 2-2 shows a state chart describing the steps within a `makeReservation` operation. A user wants to make a reservation for a room from a certain date to a certain date. If there are no rooms available, the system displays a message indicating there are no rooms. If rooms are available, the system creates a reservation.

Suppose that you want additional functionalities (i.e., extensions) specifically to ensure that only authorized users are permitted to make a room reservation, and if there are no Rooms available, you want to put the user on a waiting list. This can be achieved in two steps:

- Identify the extension points in the existing operation in which the behavior needs to be extended.
- Define the additional behavior that will be used to extend the behavior at these extension points.

The extension points where you need to add or modify are marked as ① and ② for the authorization check and waiting list functionality, respec-

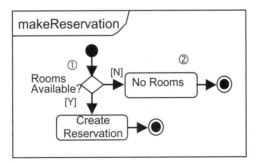

Figure 2-2   *makeReservation operation.*

tively. After composing the extension into the existing operation, you have the result in Figure 2-3. The shaded areas represent where updates have been made.

As shown in Figure 2-3, the additional behavior to check for authorization has been composed into the existing operation at marker ①. At marker ②, instead of displaying a message indicating there are no rooms, the customer is put in a queue.

As you can see in Figure 2-3, the original makeReservation operation is now entangled with code needed to fulfill requirements not directly related to making reservations. Worse, it makes the makeReservation operation less understandable for the developer. But Figure 2-3 does represent the final composed behavior you want. If you want to analyze the performance over all other runtime characteristics, you must analyze the composed result, but you normally do so with a perspective that treats functionality generically. We discuss this issue in Part 4 of the book.

We now illustrate how AspectJ can be applied to keep the waiting list and authorization extensions separate. Listing 2-2 shows the code fragment for the reserve room functionality implemented in a class named Reserve-RoomHandler.

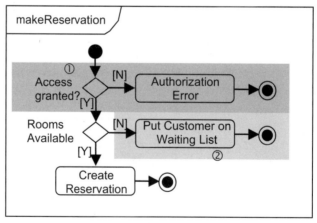

Figure 2-3   *makeReservation modified with authorization and waiting list.*

Listing 2-2 Simplified Source Code for ReserveRoomHandler

```
1.  class ReserveRoomHandler {
2.    ...
3.    public void makeReservation() throws NoRoomException
4.    {
5.      if(theRoom.getQuantityAvailable()<=0) {
6.         throw new NoRoomException () ;
7.      }
8.      createReservation() ;
9.    }
10.   ...
11. }
```

The `ReserveRoomHandler` class has an operation called `makeReservation()`, which as the name implies performs the reservation. It throws a `NoRoomException` if no rooms are available. The `makeReservation()` operation makes two calls:

- `getQuantityAvailable()`. This operation belongs to the `Room` class, and it returns the number of rooms available. If none are available, the `makeReservation()` operation throws a `NoRoomException`.
- `CreateReservation()`. This operation creates a reservation record in the data store if rooms are indeed available.

We look at how aspects in AOP help us keep the waiting list and the authorization extensions separate.

Handle Waiting List. Listing 2-3 shows the waiting list extension implemented as an aspect in AspectJ. The name of this aspect is `HandleWaitingList` (see line 1). It illustrates how aspects extend existing operations through *pointcuts* and *advices*. A pointcut identifies an execution point in the base, and an advice describes the additional behaviors that will run when execution reaches that point.

Listing 2-3 Simplified Source Code to Handle Waiting List

```
1.  aspect HandleWaitingList {
2.    ...
3.    pointcut makingReservation() :
4.        execution(void ReserveRoomHandler.makeReservation()) ;
5.    ...
6.    after throwing (NoRoomException e) : makingReservation() {
```

```
7.      // code to add customer to waiting list ;
8.    }
9.  }
```

Lines 3 and 4 show a pointcut named `makingReservation` that refers to the execution of the `makeReservation` operation. Lines 6, 7, and 8 show an advice that occurs when the operation referenced by this pointcut throws a `NoRoomException` (i.e., when `makeReservation()` throws a `NoRoomException`).

The body of the advice adds the customer to the waiting list. For simplicity, we use comments in line 7 to denote this action.

Thus, AspectJ allows you to extend existing operations with additional behaviors. In this way, the original operation (i.e., `makeReservation()`) is not entangled with the extension. Thus, the extension is kept separate from the developer's perspective. But that is not all: AspectJ allows us to extend multiple operations at once, as you shall see.

Check Authorization. Listing 2-4 implements the authorization extension. It applies not only to room reservation, but to any transactions that are performed on the system. You need to intercept all these transactions. Instead of specifying one pointcut for each transaction, AOP lets us use a limited form of pattern matching to specify multiple execution points at once. These execution points are collectively called `performingTransaction`, and we name the pointcut accordingly in lines 2, 3, and 4.

Notice the `||` and `*` in the pointcut expression: `||` refers to a logical `or` operator, and `*` is a wildcard to match names of packages, classes, operations, and so on. With the logical operators, we can combine multiple expressions to form a more complex pointcut. This is quite convenient to implement behaviors that impact a large number of operations. In lines 2, 3, and 4, the `performingTransaction` pointcut identifies all operations in the `ReserveRoomHandler` and `CheckInHandler` classes using the wildcard character `*`.

Listing 2-4   Simplified Source Code to Handle Authorization

```
1.  aspect HandleAuthorization {
2.    pointcut performingTransaction ():
3.            call(void ReserveRoomHandler.*(..))
4.            || call(void CheckInHandler.*(..));
5.    void around () : performingTransaction() {
6.        if(isAuthorized()) {
7.            proceed() ;
8.        }
9.    }
10. }
```

Now, we want calls to ReserveRoom and CheckIn operations to be bypassed if the caller has no authorization. In AspectJ, this is achieved with an around advice, as depicted in lines 5 through 9. This advice is inserted at the performingTransaction pointcut. By default, the advice causes the execution of the existing operations in the Reserve-RoomHandler or CheckInHandler to be bypassed (i.e., to go "around" them). The if condition in line 6 checks if there is sufficient authorization. If so, the advice invokes the existing operation using a proceed keyword (line 7); that is, you proceed with the existing operation.

The ReserveRoomHandler class in Listing 2-2 is totally free from any dealings with the waiting list or authorization extensions. This makes the ReserveRoomHandler class much easier to understand. In addition, all behaviors about the waiting list or authorization extensions are localized in their respective aspects: HandleWaitingList and HandleAuthorization. Thus, with aspects, you can indeed separate extensions from the base.

Note that Listing 2-2 has been simplified to make our discussion easier. In reality, you must pass the user object as a parameter into the around advice, and the isAuthorized() operation uses that parameter to perform the authorization check. Moreover, if the user has no authorization, you normally throw an exception as well. But all you need to know now is that the aspect-orientation technique provides an elegant means to keep extensions separate.

Our goal in this book is to identify, describe, and exemplify principles on how to apply aspect orientation effectively. We want to be as independent as possible of specific aspect-oriented implementations, and our proposed notation in Part III of can be mapped to the various existing implementations that we know of. Having a way to model aspects, we can proceed to discuss further principles on how to separate crosscutting concerns in Part IV of the book.

In this chapter, we limited our discussion to the programming part of aspect-orientation: AOP. Note that AOP is only part AOSD (aspect-oriented software development). AOP is about the programming part, whereas AOSD ranges from the requirements of some stakeholder concern (be they crosscutting or otherwise) to design, implementation, and test.

Sidebar 2-1   Is AOP Another Code Generation and Merging Technique?

It is important to note that AOP is not about code generation and merging. According to Gregor Kiczales, the originators of AOP worked very hard with AspectJ for the semantics to be declaration of behavior, not composition of code fragments. This is what makes the AOP a powerful behavioral composition mechanism. Composition of code fragments is an implementation technique and a preliminary way of understanding a new programming paradigm. Consider the following: does defining a subclass imply (1) composing code fragments into an operation table? or (2) the behavior of a class of objects based on the behavior of another class? Surely, the semantics of subclasses are more important than the technique to perform the composition. Similarly, you should not treat advices as code fragments. Rather, advices are declarations of behavior applicable in circumstances. They are modular extensions to existing operations, which is why, in this book, we call them operation extensions.

Although AOP provides means to use wildcards and such, an important property of AOP (specifically AspectJ) is that the language is weaker than regular expressions. That weakness helps to limit people to writing code that is more reasonable than they might if they had true regular expressions. In this book, we highlight additional ways to make your pointcuts more understandable.

2.4   Need for Methodological Guidance

The composition mechanism in AOP gives you the ability to define behavior from outside a class. This is something relatively new to most of you. But a word of caution: we do not want you to be trigger-happy and poke advices into existing operations or add intertype declarations to existing classes in an uncontrolled manner. If you do so, you will end up with a patchwork system that is impossible to extend.

AOP provides a powerful composition mechanism for a reason: so you can achieve better separation of concerns and better modularity. Thus, you have to think about design and about when you should code behaviors into classes or aspects. To apply aspect orientation effectively, therefore, you need to know how to systematically identify aspects and classes. More accurately, the question should be how you identify concerns from which aspects and classes are derived.

In addition, keeping concerns separate does not mean that concerns are independent. For example, it is clear that waiting list functionality has dependencies on the room reservation functionality. This means that if the requirements for the latter changes, the former may also be impacted. You must be able to model concerns and their relationships. In this way you get a better understanding of stakeholder concerns and consequently can separate them better. The use-case technique provides such a method for you to model concerns and relationships, and the use-case–driven approach will help you drive the concerns all the way down to implementation.

3

Today with Use Cases

As we established in earlier chapters, to get a truly extensible system, we must keep concerns separate all the way to code and must modularize the implementation accordingly. We also showed how this can be achieved with AOP. However, there still remains a challenge—that of finding concerns and expressing them clearly. Fortunately, we already have a well-proven technique to find and express them. It is the use-case technique. Use cases help us explore the various ways in which the system is used. They provide a means to validate stakeholder concerns early in the project. They are also excellent tools to drive the definition of the system architecture and the development and delivery of the system. However, until now, use cases have lived with a gap—we have been unable to keep use cases separate during their realization. If we can bridge this gap with aspect orientation, not only can we preserve the modularity of concerns, we also can harvest all the knowledge we have regarding use cases and apply it to aspect-oriented software development (AOSD).

3.1   Use Cases in Brief

What makes use cases more attractive than traditional ways of capturing requirements such as through feature specifications? A feature specification attempts to reply to the question, What is the system supposed to do? The use-case strategy forces us to add three words to the end of that question: "for each user?" (Actually, we mean for each user type). Each use case is the system's behavior when interacting with a user. It considers the variations that the system must handle to meet that user's needs effectively. Since use cases explore requirements from the user's perspective, they are natural candidates as techniques to model and organize user and stakeholder concerns.

The concept of use cases and use-case-driven development was first introduced by Jacobson [Jacobson 1987] and since then has grown in popularity—project teams both large and small have applied it successfully. In fact, it is fast becoming the de facto standard means to elicit the needs of stakeholders and capture requirements. Along with its popularity comes a huge amount of knowledge and experience about how to apply the technique effectively.

So, what is a use case? Intuitively, a use case is a sequence of actions performed by the system to yield an observable result of value to a particular user. Formally, a use case is a class-like construct that describes a related set of usages of the system by a particular actor (user) type. In UML, actors are represented as stick figures, and use cases are represented by ellipses. Lines indicate which actors are involved in which use cases. We use the Hotel Management System (HMS) as an example. The two primary actors for the system are the customer who can reserve rooms and the hotel counter staff who can check in and check out customers (see Figure 3-1).

Each use case describes the necessary actions to perform the tasks, including the variations. For example, the Reserve Room use case collates stakeholder concerns about reserving rooms—how to deal with different types of rooms, different customer types, different reservation schemes, and so on. Success in applying use cases comes not just by being able to draw stick figures, ellipses, and arrows to present the requirements of a

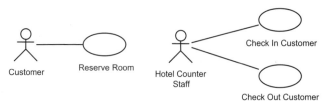

Figure 3-1   *Use cases for Hotel Management System.*

system. Success is attributed more to being able to systematically explore and validate the users' concerns in terms of how the desired system is used under different scenarios and highlighting how variations are handled. This promotes a better understanding between user representatives and the development team.

The *use-case model* contains actors, use cases, and relationships between them. It is a kind of requirements model. As mentioned, the goal of use-case modeling is to separate user *concerns*. In addition, use cases help us to model the dependencies between concerns through several defined use-case relationships: *include, generalization,* and *extend.*

The *include* relationship allows you to factor out common behaviors between use cases. So, instead of describing such behaviors repeatedly, you only need to include them. The *generalization* relationship between use cases is similar in meaning to classes. It connotes an "is-a-kind-of" semantics between two use cases and is used when the sequence of actions of one concrete use case (the child) is similar to, but refines those of, the other abstract use case (the parent). For example, Reserve Facility is an abstract use case that describes how to reserve any kind of facility in generic terms, and the Reserve Room use case depicted in Figure 3-1 is a concrete use case that deals with the specifics of Room Reservation.

The *extend* relationship allows us to add behavior to a base use case at a set of extension points without changing the base use case. The added behavior is specified in the extending use case, which is inserted into the base use case. An *extension point* unambiguously references a point in a base use-case description. At this point (and possibly using *before* and *after* qualifiers), the *extension use-case flow* as specified in the extending use case is inserted when the use case is interpreted. You probably notice that there is some resemblance between use-case extensions and aspects discussed in Chapter 2. This is important because the resemblance implies a seamless transition as we move from use cases to implementation (with aspects), as you shall see in Chapter 4, "Tomorrow with Use-Case Modules."

3.2   Use-Case-Driven Development

Use cases are not just a requirements technique. They are a software engineering technique used to drive the whole software development life cycle. All software development should be driven toward meeting user concerns. You should capture users' concerns, design the system to fit those concerns, and test the system against those concerns. As we mentioned earlier, use cases express stakeholder concerns and provide early validation of what needs to be built. Use cases are therefore a useful means to drive the development of a system. You build a system incrementally, use case by use case.

Use-case-driven development assumes that software development is *model-driven*. In its simplest form, this follows a sequence of models: use-case model to design model to implementation model. With each iteration of the software life cycle, the team performs the following activities:

1.   Find the use cases and specify each one.
2.   Design each use case.
3.   Design and implement each class.
4.   Test each use case.

Usually, each of the four activities represents a job to be taken on by one of the team members. Apart from designing and implementing each component, all the rest of the activities above are use-case-based. During these activities, we develop the following key elements: use cases, use-case realizations, and components.

There is of course more work to be done within an iteration, such as architectural analysis and design, but we deal with that in a later part of the book.

The use-case model describes the system from an external perspective— the internal building blocks are not represented in this perspective. The internals of the system are introduced in the *design model*. Each use case in the use-case model is realized by one *use-case realization* in the design model. A use-case realization is a UML *collaboration* describing (using, for instance, interaction diagrams) which classes participate, how they interact, and what responsibilities they take on to realize a use case. Figure 3-2 shows how three peer use cases in the Hotel Management System get

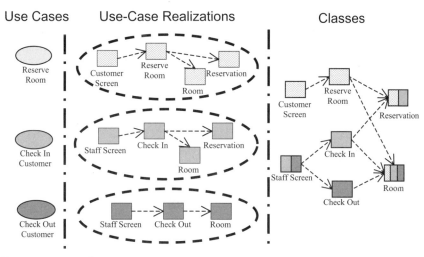

Figure 3-2   *From use cases to classes.*

mapped into their respective realizations and subsequently to classes. These use cases are considered peers because they are separate from one another, but their realizations make use of similar classes.

Each use case is designed, and the result is a use-case realization. From each use-case realization, you identify what responsibilities are imposed on each class. You then collate the responsibilities for each class and design, implement, and test that class.

Based on the use-case realizations, many of today's tools can generate a specification for each class by collecting all the responsibilities assigned to the class over all use cases. This is quite straightforward, since the responsibilities come directly from the use-case realizations.

The job for the class owner is to collect the responsibilities of each class from all relevant use-case realizations. The class owner also needs to reconcile the different needs of the use cases. For example, the realization of two use cases might result in the same operation in the same class but with slightly different behaviors. In addition, the class owner has to consider details such as concurrency (e.g., deadlock). The class owner tests the implementation of each class against the collated responsibilities, and finally, the entire use-case realization is tested.

3.3   Roles and Benefits of Use Cases

The role of use cases is important, and the benefits are many. Use cases are important tools to capture stakeholder concerns effectively. In fact, the majority of all concerns are extremely well mapped to use cases. When describing use cases, you walk through the desired behavior of the system step by step: what the actor does and what the system does in response. This helps you describe the context in which stakeholders' concerns and requirements apply. That is why we dare say that well-expressed concerns are well-expressed use cases.

In addition, use cases are advantageous in driving the development of a system.

- Since use cases are the behavior of the system from the user's perspective, they serve very well as preliminary test cases and provide early validation of acceptance criteria.
- Use cases thread through classes and drive how classes work together.
- Use cases help in planning: high-priority and critical use cases can be determined early and implemented first.

Use cases are useful for building systems in general and are not limited just to object-oriented systems. The use-case technique has been extended to incorporate business modeling, user experience modeling, systems engineering (including hardware systems), and more.

Many books have been written about use cases, and with the wealth of literature and experience behind us, it is no wonder that it is fast becoming a de facto standard in capturing requirements and driving software development.

3.4   Gaps in the Use-Case Technique

You have seen that use cases are good for capturing concerns and driving software development. But there is a problem, which is evident in Figure 3-2. Even though peer use cases are separate during requirements, their separation is not preserved during implementation. The realization of a use case touches many classes (scattering), and a class contains pieces of several use-case realizations (tangling). As a serious consequence, the realization of each use case gets dissolved in a sea of classes.

Recall that in use-case modeling, there are include, generalization, and extend relationships to relate different use cases. For the include relationship, we have the technique for a use-case realization to make use of another use-case realization. For the generalization relationship, we have the technique for a use-case realization to inherit from an abstract use-case realization. However, we have a problem when it comes to the extend relationship. We had previously no mainstream programming language supporting the implementation of extensions as we now get with AOP. The effect is that it is not possible to separate extension use cases from base use cases in design and implementation. The only way to implement extension use cases is to write some code in the base to invoke the extension. This runs counter to the idea of keeping extensions separate.

The major problem today is that traditional languages don't support separation of crosscutting concerns, so the impacts of the different use cases on the class can't be kept separate. As a consequence, you cannot keep peer and extension use cases separate during implementation.

3.5   Bridging the Gaps with Aspects

The two gaps we highlighted in the previous section by no means invalidate the usefulness of use-case-driven development. In fact, any development approach that does not have a means to maintain the modularity of concerns all the way down suffers from the same consequence, and all current approaches do.

From our discussion in the previous chapter, you know that aspects can help keep concerns separate during implementation, and they can certainly be used to bridge the gaps in use-case-driven development, as you see in Chapter 4.

But use cases are not the only one to benefit from aspects. Aspects benefit from use cases as well. The popularity of the use-case technique implies that a wealth of knowledge already exists on use cases regarding the modeling of concerns and regarding driving software development. It will be a tremendous advantage if this knowledge can be harvested and applied to aspect orientation. This is important because aspect orientation has been missing methodological guidance until now.

Sidebar 3-1   What Are Early Aspects?

There have been some discussions in the aspect-orientation community on what is termed *early aspects* [Rashid et al. 2002]. Proponents of early aspects highlight that current efforts in identifying crosscutting concerns usually occur at the programming level. They consider early aspects as crosscutting concerns that are usually found at early stages (and hence the name) of the software development life cycle, that is, during requirements. We do not treat early aspects as something special. They are just part of AOSD. You need to identify, specify, design, and test every crosscutting concern. It does not matter when they are identified. The same technique of specifying, analyzing, designing, and testing them still applies. In this book, we do so with use cases.

4

Tomorrow with Use-Case Modules

Use cases provide the means to model and separate crosscutting concerns effectively, but you must preserve the separation of concerns through design and implementation. This means that you have to collate the specifics of a use case during design in some modularity unit, which we call a *use-case slice*. Each use-case slice collates parts of classes, operations, and so forth, that are specific to a use case in a model. The task of composing these parts is left to some composition mechanism (provided by aspect technology). The developer no longer needs to perform this step, and from this perspective, he or she no longer faces tangling from other concerns. This makes his or her code much cleaner and easier to understand. We extend this concept even further—a use-case module that collates the specifics of a use case from all models and artifacts in a project into a single unit. This is advantageous because it is now much easier to manage system configurations, and parallel development is now simplified tremendously.

4.1   Building Systems in Overlays with Use-Case Slices

When you realize a use case, you identify the required classes and features (attributes, operations, and relationships) of these classes. Some of these classes and their features are specific to this use-case realization, while others are needed by other use-case realizations. In this section, we introduce the concept of a use-case slice. Each use-case slice keeps the specifics of a use-case realization in one model (e.g., the design model). Those generic and reusable parts are kept in non-use-case-specific slices. All these slices are then superimposed to form the entire design model.

Recall our home construction analogy in the preface. This analogy helps us understand what a use-case slice is. When an electrician wants to wire the house, he first describes his intent by drawing lines on a floor plan. The floor plan gives the locations and dimensions of walls, doorways, and so on. From this information, the electrician knows how much work needs to be done. If another specialist wishes to lay phone lines, she takes a floor plan and draws out where the phone lines will be laid. You can get each specialist to draw what he or she intends to do on an overlay (a transparency used on overhead projectors). You can easily sum up the work done by stacking up these overlays and projecting them on the screen. Of course, each overlay must be based on the same floor plan and the same scale.

So, use-case slices are analogous to overlays, and composition is simply stacking them on top of each other. The floor plan is analogous to what we call the *element structure*. A model (e.g., a design model) comprises a hierarchy of elements. You find packages containing classes, classes containing operations, and so on. This hierarchical organization is the *element structure*.

An element's qualified name within the element structure is the path from the top-most element to the element itself. This means that you can uniquely identify a particular element in the model by looking at its fully qualified name. This qualified name is extremely important during composition because it is used by the composition mechanism to determine if elements on two separate use-case slices refer to the same element in the element structure.

Use-case slices are separate from the element structure. They are overlaid on top of the element structure and define its contents; that is, they define behaviors that extend the element structure. Use-case slices have dependencies among themselves that describe which use-case slice (or overlay) should be placed first, which should be next, and so on. This leads to another structure, which we call the use-case structure. It is a hierarchy of use-case slices. Thus, a model comprises two structures:

- The element structure, which identifies elements.
- The use-case structure, which defines the content within these elements.

This composition is illustrated in Figure 4-1. On the left, you see the element structure organized hierarchically in terms of layers, packages, and classes. On the right, you see the use-case structure. For simplicity, we show only one use-case slice, which is stereotyped as «use-case slice». The use-case slice contains element extensions that will be composed (such as through an aspect weaver) into the model with reference to the element structure.

As can be seen in the figure, the element structure is just a means to identify where elements in the model reside. You treat the elements (i.e., classes) like empty boxes. Their contents (i.e., behavior) will be filled by use-case slices during composition.

Up until now, the use-case structure could not be kept separate from the element structure. A developer would have to collate all responsibilities on each class from different use cases and develop the class. This leads to tangling and scattering. But now, by keeping the use-case structure separate from the element structure, the separation of use cases can be preserved.

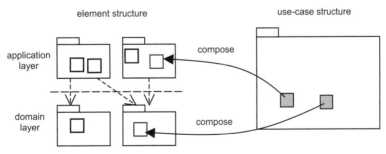

Figure 4-1   *Element structure space and use-case slices.*

Sidebar 4-1   How Are Use-Case Slices and Hyperslices Related?

The term use-case slice is very much in line with the concept of hyperslices in a particular branch of aspect-orientation research known as multidimensional separation of concerns (MDSOC) [Tarr et al. 1999], [Tarr et al. 2000]. Whereas aspects allow you to add features into existing classes, hyperslices allow you to add new classes as well. In essence, when two hyperslices are merged, elements that coincide at the same namespace are merged. This is similar to the «merge» dependency in UML. However, AOP has rich and expressive power for you to define how you can add extensions into existing classes and in multiple extension points at once through the use of wildcards and regular expressions in pointcuts. In this book, we discuss how use-case slices are modeled and implemented through AOP and particularly as a programming language extension like AspectJ [Laddad 2003]. Note that use-case slices are still applicable even if you use MDSOC or, in general, any aspect technology.

Although there are similarities between use-case slices and hyperslices, they have different roots and motivations. Hyperslices have their roots in subject-oriented programming. [Harrison et al. 1993]. Use-case slices are motivated by the need to keep peers and extensions separate. Their origins are discussed in Section 1.3.1, "Early Support for Extensions."

4.2   Keeping Peer Use Cases Separate

We earlier highlighted two specific cases that we have been unable to keep separate—peers and extensions. We demonstrate how this is solved through use-case slices.

Let us begin with the realizations of peer use cases. Peer use cases are those that have no relationships between them. They are distinct and separate use cases, but their realizations overlap and they impose responsibilities on the same classes. The three use cases Reserve Room, Check In Customer, and Check Out Customer depicted in Figure 4-2 are peers. Their realizations impose a set of responsibilities on the classes listed in Figure 4-2.

After identifying classes, you must identify the features (i.e., attributes, operations, and relationships) of each class needed to realize the use cases. You do not sum up the features for each class from the various use-

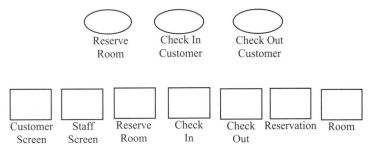

Figure 4-2   *Use cases and classes in the Hotel Management System.*

case realizations, since doing so would end the separation of use cases and result in tangling within classes.

Instead, you collate the features of each class that are specific to a use-case slice. Thus, each use-case slice may not have complete classes. Instead, they have parts of classes, which we call *class extensions*. In essence, a class extension contains only the features of a class needed to realize a specific use case. The result is depicted in Figure 4-2. It shows three use-case slices containing extensions of classes identified in Figure 4-2.

In Figure 4-3, the horizontal axis shows the element structure that identi- fies the classes in the system. The vertical axis shows the use-case struc- ture. It identifies the use cases being realized, each with a different shade. Each horizontal row depicts a use-case slice containing the extensions of classes needed to realize the use case for that row. Thus, we have the ReserveRoom use-case slice, the CheckInCustomer use-case slice, and the CheckOutCustomer use-case slice.

Each use-case slice contains partial class definitions (i.e., class extensions) specific to the use-case realization. If you want complete class definitions, all you need to do is merge all the use-case slices. In essence, the merging operation takes elements of the same name and merges them together. For example, the ReserveRoom use-case slice has a class extension named Room, and so do the CheckInCustomer and CheckOutCustomer use-case slices. Since the class extensions have the same name, they will be merged. The result is depicted in the bottom row of Figure 4-3. The resulting Room class is a composition of all the class extensions from the respective aspects as depicted by the different shades.

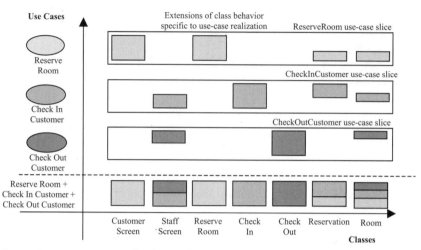

Figure 4-3   *Composing peer use-case realizations with use-case slices.*

In UML today, the merge operation is modeled using the stereotyped «merge» dependency between packages. This merge operation can be implemented in AOP using intertype declarations. You can now keep the realizations and implementation of peer use cases separate from one another.

4.3   Keeping Extension Use Cases Separate

We now show how the realizations of extension use cases are kept separate. Let's quickly recap extension use cases using our waiting list example in Chapter 2. Recall that we wanted to add a waiting list functionality (the extension) on top of the existing reserve Room functionality (the base). This is modeled through the extend relationship between two use cases, as depicted in Figure 4-4. The Handle Waiting List extension use case extends the Reserve Room base use case. The extension use case has a sequence of actions that must be inserted into the base use case at the extension point defined within the base use case. This sequence of actions is known as an extension use-case flow. It puts a customer on the waiting list. It is a separate concern from Reserve Room, but it is needed to provide the Handle Waiting List functionality and is, therefore, specified within the Handle Waiting List use case.

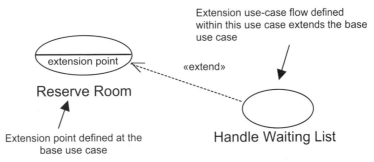

Figure 4-4   *Extension use case.*

Extension Points in UML. In UML today, extension points are just a means to give a label or a name to a point in the execution sequence of a use case. The extension use case references the extension point to indicate when the extension use-case flow will be inserted. AOP uses the concept of pointcuts to identify execution points during implementation.

Join Points and Pointcuts in AOP. The corresponding concept of extension points in AOP is known as join points. A join point is a point in the execution flow of a program with well-defined semantics (the execution of an operation, a call to an operation, the throwing of an exception, etc.). Pointcuts in AOP are a larger concept than extension points, as they are currently defined in UML today. In addition, pointcuts in AOP have the capacity to refer to multiple extension points (i.e., join points) that may be defined in multiple classes at once. This is advantageous especially for infrastructure mechanisms (authorization, logging, etc.) that cut across many classes. We show how pointcuts are modeled in use-case slices in Part III of this book.

An *extension use-case flow* is realized by an *advice* in AOP. An *advice* is the behavior to be executed at extension points designated by pointcuts. The equivalent of an AOP advice in use-case slices is what we term an *operation extension*. An operation extension is a modular extension to an existing operation to perform a behavior different from the operation's main responsibility.

We can describe how we keep the realization of extension use cases separate as we did with peer use cases earlier. Figure 4-5 shows the composition of the realization of the Reserve Room and Handle Waiting List use cases. The horizontal and vertical axes represent the element structure and the use-case structure, respectively.

Each horizontal row in Figure 4-5 shows a use case and the class extensions (shown shaded) needed by its corresponding realization. Compared to the earlier example in Figure 4-3, we have an additional `WaitingList` class in the element structure. This class is required by the `HandleWaitingList` use-case realization but not by the `ReserveRoom` use-case realization. Hence, it does not appear in the `ReserveRoom` use-case slice.

In addition, the `HandleWaitingList` use-case slice has two operation extensions. These operation extensions (indicated by the arrows in Figure 4-5) are defined within the `CustomerScreen` and `ReserveRoom` class extensions, respectively. If you want the complete class definitions (with the complete operation behaviors), you need to merge the two use-case slices. The result is depicted in the bottom row of Figure 4-5. The merging works at a finer level of resolution compared to that discussed earlier regarding peer use-case realizations. This is because with peer use-case realizations, you merge complete operations by their names. With extension use-case realizations, however, you need to specify what the existing operation is doing when the operation extension must be inserted. This fine-grain merging or weaving is supported through pointcuts. Thus, with the advice and pointcut mechanism, you can keep the realization of extension use cases separate from the base.

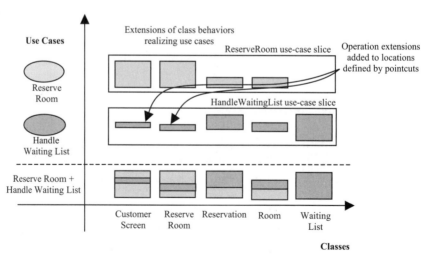

Figure 4-5   *Composing extension and base use-case realizations.*

We kept the above discussion simple by indicating that you compose peer use-case slices with intertype declarations and extension use-case slices with advices. In general, composition of both peer and extension use-case slices require both intertype declarations and advices.

4.4   Developing with Use-Case Modules

Now that you can modularize extensions of classes needed by a use case in design using use-case slices, you can take a step further. You can modularize all elements and artifacts specific to a use case into a single module—we call this a use-case module. When we say *all*, we mean over *all* lifecycle models. Thus, a use-case module contains the use-case specification for the use case, the analysis of the use case, the design and implementation of the use case, the test associated with the use case, and all configuration and parameters needed by the use case. Just as you can compose extensions of classes and operations from multiple use cases to form the desired executable, you can likewise compose the extensions of other kinds of model elements and artifacts (analysis elements, design elements, implementation elements, etc.).

Parallel Development with Use-Case Modules. The ability to work with use-case modules independently greatly and positively impacts the way you conduct software development. Work on each use-case module can proceed separately and in parallel as separate projects. Of course, there is some architecture work to coordinate the names of elements, pointcuts, and so on.

Stakeholders and project managers benefit because the project team can attend to business concerns of the system early in the project. The project manager can postpone the selection of platform specifics (such as security, persistency, and distribution) and deal with them in a later iteration. In short, we now have more options to organize which part of the system we want to develop first. You can *almost* choose to deal with any concern in any iteration. We say *almost* because there will be some dependency between concerns, but being able to effectively separate concerns better than before allows greater freedom to choose which concerns to deal with first.

Develop Incrementally with Use-Case Modules. In addition, since most interesting concerns are modeled as use cases, the use-case model helps you identify relationships between concerns and decide how to plan iterations. You normally start with a set of core use cases that do not depend on anything else and gradually grow the system to incorporate use cases on top of this core.

If you apply use-case modularity to the Hotel Management System, you might, for instance, start to build the use-case module for the Reserve Room use case (see Figure 4-6). In the next iteration, you can develop the use-case modules for Check In and Authorization separately and compose them onto the Reserve Room use-case module. The composition action is indicated by the «compose» relationship in Figure 4-6, which essentially means that you overlay a module onto another module. At a later stage, you might choose to develop and compose the use-case module for the Check Out use case. Or you might want to choose a different use case. If a use-case module needs to be modified, you simply replace it with a new one. The choice is really flexible, and all this is possible thanks to new modularity that is enabled by aspect orientation.

Architecture Unifies Use-Case Modules. It is evident that keeping use cases separate all the way down gives tremendous benefit to the project team. Since everything about a use case is contained within a use-case module, systems developed this way are much easier to understand, maintain, and extend. But this does not mean that use-case modules can be developed totally independent of each other. There must be some

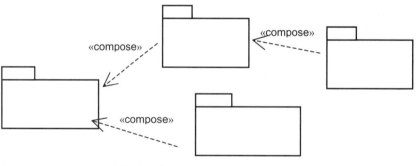

Figure 4-6   *Composing use-case modules iteratively.*

architecture work involved. The architecture is not just about separation. It is also about composition. You need to analyze and evaluate runtime characteristics of the composed system as well. After all, the response time is the sum of all responses from all the use-case slices through which the execution path flows.

PART II

Modeling and Capturing Concerns with Use Cases

We have established that the goal aspect-oriented programming is to keep concerns separate. In order to do so, you must correctly identify and structure concerns early in the life cycle of the project rather than as an afterthought during design and implementation. In other words, separation of concerns must start during requirements. This does not mean capturing every detailed requirement for each concern at the beginning of the project. Instead, you systematically organize stakeholder concerns to scope the system. The detailing and refinement of the requirements for each concern can be prioritized and allocated across the project life cycle in an iterative manner.

The use-case technique provides the means to systematically model stakeholder concerns by walking through meaningful interactions between end users and the system. In doing so, you get a better idea about stakeholder concerns and a better idea of whether concerns overlap or cut across each other. The use-case technique further provides means to structure concerns through use-case relationships such as include, extend, and generalization.

Part II provides an overview of what use-case modeling is about. In this part of the book, we propose some enhancements to the use-case modeling technique, which you will find useful whether you are familiar with the technique or not. In particular, we provide better visualization of the complexity of each use case and show how to model pointcuts in use cases. Use-case extension pointcuts help clarify the relationship between extension use cases and the use case being extended. They also facilitate identifying pointcuts during analysis and design.

We demonstrate how to apply the technique to the Hotel Management System example. In particular, we show how to model functional requirements with application use cases and nonfunctional requirements with infrastructure use cases (which deal with nonfunctional requirements). This common approach to modeling most crosscutting concerns with a single technique—use cases—simplifies the approach to building the system.

Part II includes the following chapters:

Chapter 5, "Modeling Concerns with Use Cases"

Chapter 6, "Structuring Use Cases"

Chapter 7, "Capturing Concerns with Use Cases"

5

Modeling Concerns with Use Cases

Software development starts with understanding and capturing stakeholder concerns. The use-case technique models stakeholder concerns by walking through the interactions between users and the system. This provides early validation of stakeholder concerns and acceptance criteria, and leads naturally to the identification of test cases. In addition, the way you specify use cases follows very much the idea of building a system incrementally—you build the core functionalities before adding more advanced capabilities on top. Likewise, when describing use-case flow of events, you begin with the most basic of scenarios with basic flows and then describe how more complex variations are handled in separate, alternate flows. This early separation of concerns improves the overall comprehensibility of the system.

5.1   Use-Case Modeling

We established in Part I that it is important to keep concerns separate. This is the only way to make complex systems comprehensible. Keeping concerns separate should begin right from the start during requirements.

In addition, they should be modeled in a way that facilitates early validation and incremental development of the system. The use-case technique does precisely that.

Use cases are a means to specify required usages of a system. They are used to capture the requirements of a system—that is, what a system is supposed to do. When modeling the use cases of a system, you represent the users and any other external systems that may interact with the system as actors. Actors always represent entities that are outside the boundaries of the system.

The required behavior of the system is specified by one or more use cases, which are defined according to the needs of actors. Each use case specifies a unit of useful functionality that the system provides to its actors.

A use-case model contains all the use cases of a system. It is the sum of all the possible uses of a system. You depict the different use cases for a system on a use-case diagram, where a stick figure represents an actor and an ellipse represents a use case. Lines between actor use-case pairs indicate that the actor can interact with the associated use case. For our Hotel Management System, the use-case diagram is depicted in Figure 5-1. A use-case diagram specifies who can do what with the system. For example, a customer can reserve a room. Hotel counter staff can check in or check out the customer.

For larger systems, you may partition the use-case model into various use-case packages. Each package can contain a set of use cases for a group of actors, such as for a department in a company. Alternately, you might wish to package use cases according to entities that the use cases manipulate. For example, you may have use cases to manipulate inventory entities, sales entities, and so on. A third way is according to functional areas. For

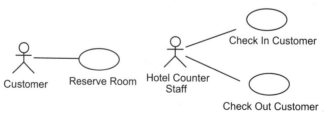

Figure 5-1   *Use-case diagram.*

example, sales can be one functional area of a system, customer relationship can be another functional area, and so on. Each use-case package should have a use-case diagram to provide an overview of the use cases contained within it.

5.2   Use-Case Instances and Flows of Events

Just as drawing classes in a class diagram does not give you code, drawing a use-case ellipse is only a small part of the use-case technique. When applying the use-case technique, you find that a significant portion of time is spent on specifying the behavior for each use case, or more specifically, the behavior of each use-case instance.

Both actors and use cases are classifiers or class-like elements in UML. Both have attributes and operations. Both are instantiable and generalizable. When you describe the behavior of the system through use cases, you follow through the execution of a use-case instance. A use-case instance is created when an actor instance initiates a use case. For example, for the Reserve Room use case, the use-case instance is created when a customer indicates that she wants to reserve a room (see Figure 5-2).

Once a use case is instantiated, a dialog between the use-case instance and its actor instances can occur as specified by the use-case specification. This continues until it is terminated as specified by the use-case specification. Just as a class instance follows through a particular path defined by its class source code, a use-case instance follows one path through the use case.

Tracing through the different execution paths of a use case is an important part of understanding what the user wants, what she wants to do with the

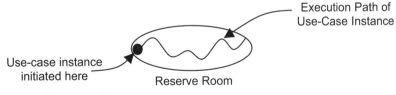

Figure 5-2   *Execution of a use-case instance.*

system, and how she wants the system to respond as she interacts with it. This provides early validation of what the system needs to do.

This execution of a use case results in a use-case scenario. A use-case scenario is made up of one or more use-case flow of events. A use-case flow can be either a complete path or a segment of a path through the use case. The smaller segments allow us to focus attention on specific areas of the system behaviors and are especially useful when considering how variations are handled.

5.3   Describing Use Cases

When describing a use case, you start with the simplest or the most typical scenario and trace through the sequence of events in it. We call this the basic flow. A use case has one or more basic flows depending on the number of ways the use case can be instantiated.

After describing the basic flow, you gradually describe how different variations are handled on top of the basic flows; that is, you describe them in separate use-case flows, which we call alternate flows. By keeping the descriptions separate, you prevent the basic flow from being entangled by all the variations that the use case needs to handle.

As you describe the use-case flows in a use case, you may find that some of the interaction sequences are repetitive, and you might want to factor and describe them separately. We call such use-case flows subflows.

The behavior of a use case can be specified in a number of ways depending on who the intended reader is. Today, the textual form is the most frequently used approach to specify the behavior of a use case. This form is most easily understandable by end-user representatives. Listing 5-1 provides an example of a use-case specification for the Reserve Room use case.

Listing 5-1   Use-Case Specification: Reserve Room

Brief Description
This use case describes how the customer reserves a room.

Basic Flows
B1. Reserve Room
The use case begins when a customer wants to reserve a room.
1. The customer selects to reserve a room.
2. The system displays the types of rooms the hotel has and their rates.
3. The customer <u>Check Room Cost</u>.
4. The customer makes the reservation for the chosen room.
5. The system deducts from the database the number of rooms of the specified type available for reservation.
6. The system creates a new reservation with the given details.
7. The system displays the reservation confirmation number and check-in instructions.
8. The use case terminates.

Alternate Flows
A1. Duplicate Submission
If in step 5 of the basic flow there is an identical reservation in the system (same name, e-mail, and start and end dates), the system displays the existing reservation and asks the customer if he wants to proceed with the new reservation.
1. If the customer wants to continue, the system proceeds with the reservation, and the use case resumes.
2. If the customer indicates that the new reservation is a duplicate, the use case terminates.
A2. . . .

. . .

Subflows
S1. Check Room Cost
1. The customer selects his desired room type and indicates his period of stay.
2. The system computes the cost for the specified period.

Preconditions
The customer has logged in to the system.

Postconditions
Upon successful reservation, a new reservation record is created, and the number of rooms available for the specified dates is decreased. If reservation is unsuccessful, there is no change in the database.

Special Requirements
The system must handle five concurrent reservations. Each reservation should not take more than 20 seconds.

Listing 5-1 follows a typical use-case specification template. It has a brief description and a number of flows, which we discuss shortly. The use case also has preconditions and postconditions. They respectively indicate the circumstances in which the use case can be instantiated and the system state when the use-case instance terminates. There is also a section that describes special requirements for the use case. In this case, there are some performance requirements.

The textual specification of a use case may not adequately describe what the user representative wants. Thus, it is not uncommon that the use-case specification is supplemented with additional tables and diagrams, such as user interface descriptions and flow charts.

Let's look at the flows in Listing 5-1 more closely. It shows one basic flow and one alternate flow for the Reserve Room use case. The basic flow describes the steps leading to a successful reservation of a room for a specified time period. Step 3 refers to the subflow Check Room Cost. We use an underline in Listing 5-1 to denote a reference. This subflow is defined later in S1 to describe the steps to choose rooms for reservation. By using subflows, you keep the basic flow less cluttered. In addition, multiple flows can reference or "use" the subflow. Thus, instead of specifying the interaction multiple times, you need to specify it only once.

Listing 5-1 shows an alternate flow, A1, that handles the case of duplicate submission of reservations. Note that the basic flow has no checks for duplicate submission or any reference to the alternate flow. All such details are in the alternate flow. Using this approach, you can keep concerns about duplicate submissions totally separate from the basic flow and localize them to the alternate flow A1. But you must somehow indicate where the behavior for handling duplicate submissions is inserted into the basic flow. This is achieved with the phrase that says, "If in step 5 of the basic flow. . . .". Note that in general a use case specification will contain a number of alternate flows. We indicate this in Listing 5-1 through A2, … It is important that you explore these alternatives and describe how the system should use them appropriately.

Aspect orientation applies a similar mechanism and thus provides a seamless transition when we attempt to realize a use case. We discuss more of that in Chapter 6, "Structuring Use Cases."

Multiple Basic Flows. In the example above, there is only one basic flow named Reserve Room that allows a customer to book a room online. In general, there are multiple entry points. For example, a customer might make a phone call or send a fax to a hotel staff who will then make the actual reservation. It is possible to use an alternate flow to describe such variations. However, since the way the use case is initiated is different for each situation, it is not easy to identify where the alternate flow will be inserted if we choose to use alternative flows. Hence, having multiple basic flows becomes an effective option. These basic flows usually reference the same subflows. For example, the Check Room Cost subflow will be used repeatedly.

Referencing Subflows. In our example, we use the underline to denote how a flow references a subflow. In practice, you might use the hyperlink capabilities available in most word processors today. Some practitioners use a keyword to indicate the referencing of a subflow. A more technical keyword you can use is an "include," which we explain later in this chapter when we discuss how to structure use cases.

Sidebar 5-1   Are Use Cases the Use-Case Specifications?

You have to take note that use case and use-case specifications are two different things. Even though they exist together in pairs, they are nonetheless two separate things—a use case lives in a use-case model, but a use case specification is an artifact that is outside the use-case model but associated with the use case. This is the same with classes—a design class in the design model is not the same thing as the source code for that design class even though they are closely associated.

A use-case specification describes not only what the use case does, but also what actor instances do as well. In other words, use-case specifications describe the dialogue between actor instances and use-case instances.

5.4   Visualizing Use-Case Flows

The complexity of a use case is very much dependent on how many variations or scenarios it must handle. The use cases identified in Figure 5-1 may apply to a simple hotel or even to small a bed and breakfast accommodation. A sophisticated hotel chain might have the same set of use cases, but each use case will have to handle a much larger number of variations.

The ellipse notation on its own does not give any indication of the complexity of a use case. For example, Figure 5-3 illustrates the Reserve Room use case. It has no indication of how complex the Reserve Room use case is or the multitude of variations or scenarios the use case needs to handle.

Although the ellipse is the most well-known notation for use cases, there are also other ways to display it. A use case is actually just a special case of classifiers or a stereotype of classifiers. A classifier in UML is a class-like thing—it can be instantiated, and it is generalizable. You can denote a use case using the standard rectangle notation for classifiers with an ellipse icon in the upper right-hand corner of the rectangle with optional separate list compartments for its contents, as exemplified in Figure 5-4. Figure 5-4 illustrates the Reserve Room with its flows in a compartment. This notation gives us an overall perspective of the responsibilities of a use case.

As illustrated by the earlier Reserve Room example, each use-case flow can be a basic flow, an alternate flow, or a subflow. In Figure 5-4, we distinguish between different kinds of flows using tags denoted as strings within brackets: {}. While UML allows us to define tag values to give more information about particular elements in our model, the tags {basic}, {alt}, and {sub} are not defined in UML. However, we believe that they should be added, since they reflect the standard practice in writing use cases.

Use cases, like classes, are generalizable elements, and their flows can be either concrete or abstract. A flow is concrete when the steps that consti-

Reserve Room

Figure 5-3   *Reserve Room use case using ellipse notation.*

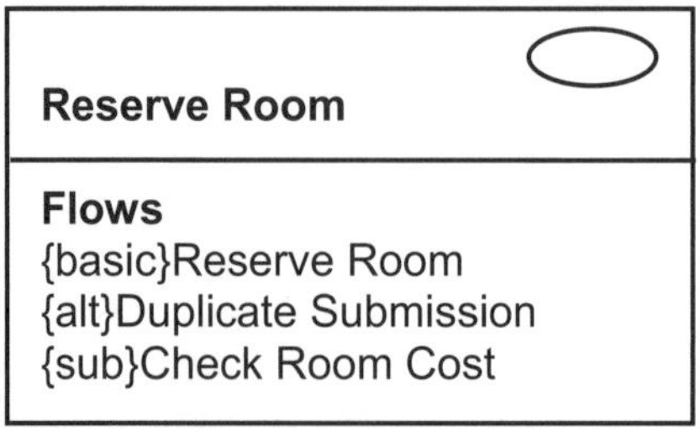

Reserve Room ⬭
Flows {basic}Reserve Room {alt}Duplicate Submission {sub}Check Room Cost

Figure 5-4   *Flows as compartments.*

---

tute the flow are defined—that is, you have all the text that describes flow. A flow is abstract when you have given the flow a name, but the flow itself is unspecified. The actual specification is defined as a child use case.

Sidebar 5-2 When to Use Rectangular Notation for Use Cases

Whether use cases are depicted as ellipses or with the standard classifier notation depends on what you want to emphasize. If you want to show the use cases in a system as an overview, the ellipse notation is better. This is because at this level of abstraction, you do not need to present the flows.

If you want to explore the details of one or a few use cases, such as during a requirements workshop, the ellipse notation may not provide sufficient visualization power. In this case, the standard classifier (i.e., rectangular) notation is more appropriate. You can quickly list out the important flows of events and start to discuss them.

The rectangular notation is also useful when you want to highlight the important flows of a use case. This occurs, for example, when you want to indicate which parts of a use case will be implemented in a particular iteration or when you want to highlight the architecturally significant parts of a use case.

Sidebar 5-3 Why You Must Avoid Functional Decomposition

We frequently encounter situations in which practitioners simply create one use case per use-case flow, leading to what we call functional decomposition— the breaking up of use cases such that the smaller use cases provide no real value to stakeholders. For example, if you have 200 use cases, you are likely to have fallen into the functional decomposition trap. To get out of this trap, think about what value the actor is trying to derive and the full sequence of behaviors that lead to that value. Another way to get out of functional decomposition is to have real people play the role of actors and observe what they do to complete their job responsibilities.

One possible reason for practitioners to fall into functional decomposition is that the ellipse notation gives the illusion that a use case is simple when in fact it is not, and it contains many flows and variations. In the absence of the rectangle notation listing the use-case flows, practitioners resort to creating a use case for each flow. With the ability to visually represent the complexity of a use case through the flow compartment, they are less likely to fall into this trap.

5.5   Summary and Highlights

Each use case is a unit of useful functionality that the system provides to its actors. A use-case specification contains a number of flows that describe how variations are handled. You can easily verify that you have captured stakeholder concerns by walking through the flows with the stakeholders.

The use-case technique is a widely adopted technique to model the requirements of a system. Use cases are a huge topic, and while we do not explore them in depth, many books have been written to demonstrate how to apply the technique effectively. If you want to learn more about use cases, we recommend the following books as references:

1. Ivar Jacobson, Magnus Christerson, Patrik Jonsson & Gunnar Övergaard, *Object-Oriented Software Engineering: A Use-Case Driven Approach*, Addison-Wesley, Boston, 1992.
2. Kurt Bittner & Ian Spence, *Use-Case Modeling*, Addison-Wesley, Boston, 2002.
3. Gunnar Övergaard and Karen Palmkvist, *Use-Cases: Patterns and Blue Prints*, Addison-Wesley, Boston, 2004.

There have not been many changes to the use-case technique or the representation of use cases since their introduction. In this chapter, we introduced a small enhancement—to represent use-case flows as a compartment within the use-case classifier. This helps us visualize the responsibilities of the use case and prevents practitioners from falling into the functional decomposition trap. More importantly, it is the starting point for us to model pointcuts in use cases, which we discuss in Chapter 6.

6

Structuring
Use Cases

As you attempt to model the concerns about a system, you will find that they are not independent from one another. In fact, you frequently find relationships between them and must understand what these relationships are to effectively structure and separate the concerns. The use-case technique provides the means for you to model the relationships between concerns through relationships between use cases, such as use-case extend, use-case include, and use-case generalization. We pay particular attention to use-case extensions because they translate to advices in AOP during implementation. Here, we propose the modeling of pointcuts in extension use cases. This early identification of pointcuts during use-case modeling facilitates the identification of pointcuts during analysis, design, and implementation.

6.1   Use-Case Relationships

As you specify use cases for a system, you might sometimes find common behavior across use cases, which you might want to factor out. Other times, you might want to add behaviors to an existing use case, but you do not want to entangle the existing use case. So, what you must do is to specify use-case flows in a different use case from the one executing the flow. What you need then is some way for a use case to refer to another use case. For this reason and several others, as you shall see, you need to model relationships between use cases.

In UML, there are three kinds of relationships between use cases: extend, include, and generalization. These three relationships are illustrated in Figure 6-1.

Figure 6-1 shows the three use cases from Chapter 5, "Modeling Concerns with Use Cases": Reserve Room, Check In Customer, and Check Out Customer, which are represented in white. Three additional shaded use cases are related to the original ones through the use-case relationships. The Handle Waiting List use case extends the Reserve Room use case. This means that it adds new capabilities on top of the existing use case. The Check Room Details use case factors out common behaviors to be included by other use cases. The Reserve Facility use case generalizes the Reserve Room use case and serves as a template for other use cases that deal with reservations. In the rest of this chapter, we discuss each of these relationships, when to use them, and how to model them.

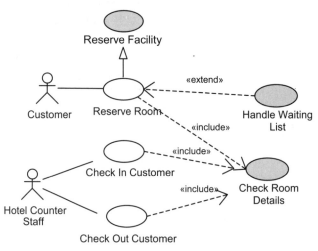

Figure 6-1   *Use-case relationships.*

6.2   Use-Case Extend Relationship

Extension use cases allow you to add new behaviors into existing use cases (which we call the base, or extended, use case). The use-case technique is formulated such that the new behavior is described totally separate from the base use case. Thus, the base use case is not entangled with the details of the new behavior. This bears a close resemblance to AOP, in which aspects are kept separate from the classes they extend. If you have in the past applied extension use cases, then you have in effect applied aspect orientation all along during requirements (i.e., during use-case modeling). This resemblance is important because it provides a natural transition as you proceed from use-case modeling to design and implementation with aspects.

An extension use case contains one or more extension flows. Extension flows are like alternate flows except that they add to the behaviors of a different use case. Figure 6-2 provides an example of an extension use case. The Handle Waiting List use case is an extension use case that extends the Reserve Room base use case. It introduces a waiting list capability and is used when there are no rooms available during reservation.

Listing 6-1 shows the Reserve Room and the Handle Waiting List use-case specifications side by side. The Reserve Room basic flow on the left is the same basic flow described earlier in Listing 5-1.

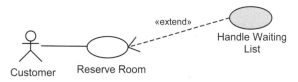

Figure 6-2   *Extension use cases.*

Listing 6-1 Reserve Room Use Case and Handle Waiting List Use Case

Use Case: Reserve Room

Basic Flow

The use case begins when a customer wants to reserve a room(s).

1. The customer selects to reserve a room.
2. The system displays the types of rooms the hotel has and their rates.
3. The customer Check Room Cost.
4. The customer makes the reservation for the chosen rooms.
5. The system deducts from the database the number of rooms of the specified type available for reservation.
6. The system creates a new reservation with the given details.
7. The system displays the reservation confirmation number and check-in instructions.
8. The use case terminates.

Alternate Flows

. . .

Extension Points

E1. Update Room Availability
The Update Room Availability extension point occurs at step 5 of the Basic Flow

Use Case: Handle Waiting List

Basic Flow

. . .

Extension Flows
EF1. Queue for Room
This extension flow occurs at the extension point Update Room Availability in the Reserve Room use case when there are no Rooms of the selected type available.

1. The system creates a pending reservation with a unique identifier for the selected Room type.
2. The system puts the pending reservation into a waiting list
3. The system displays the unique identifier of the pending reservation to the customer.
4. The base use case terminates.

Extension Points. At the bottom of Listing 6-1 is a section called Extension Points, a standard compartment of a use case in UML. An extension point identifies a specific execution point in the execution path of a use-case instance where additional behaviors can be inserted. In practice, they are named steps in a use-case specification. In our example, the step of interest is when the use-case instance attempts to Update Room Availability, which occurs at step 5 of the basic flow.

In AOP, the points in the execution flow are known as *join points*. They correspond to extension points in use cases. You do not need to explicitly identify join points in classes, since they are described with a programming language with a formal syntax. The expressiveness of AOP allows you to refer to any possible join point using a combination of pointcut primitives (call, execution, set, cflow, etc.). The semantics of these pointcut primitives identifies join points.

Since use cases are meant for stakeholders, who are usually not as technically inclined as developers, we should not make use cases too formal. That is why use cases are described textually and informally. Consequently, use-case specifications are not as precise as using a programming language to describe them. This means that the use of pointcut primitives, which have formal semantics, is not suitable during use-case modeling. To overcome the informality in use cases, you name a step in the use-case flow that you want to extend. This is achieved with extension points. Note that it is not necessary to name every step, nor should you attempt to do so.

Extension Pointcuts. The right-hand side of Listing 6-1 shows the specification of the Handle Waiting List use case. The Handle Waiting List use case has basic flows that permit an actor to view the contents of the waiting list and so on, but that is not the focus of our discussion at the moment. So we leave the basic flow with "…" in Listing 6-1. Let's bring our attention to the extension flows. In our example, we have one extension flow named Queue for Room. It describes the additional behavior that occurs when a reservation is submitted. The text in italics is very important because it specifies where the extension flow will be inserted into the base use-case instance.

There is currently no construct in UML for the text in italics. In AOP terminology, it corresponds to a pointcut. A pointcut is an expression that indicates where operation extensions are to be inserted into an existing operation. The concept behind pointcuts and the text in italics are the same except that we are dealing with use cases as opposed to classes. We call the text in italics *extension pointcuts*.

Please do not get confused between *extension points* and *extension pointcuts*. They are different things and occur on different ends of the extension relationship. Extension points are defined in the base use case (see left side of Listing 6-1), whereas extension pointcuts are defined in the extension use case (see right side of Listing 6-1).

The author of the extension use case should not make a reference to the actual step in the base use case, as he has no control of how the base use case will be written or updated. Thus, the author of the base use case is responsible to name the extension points, which are then referenced by the extension pointcuts. In Part 3, we show how use-case pointcuts are mapped to pointcuts during design.

As suggested by UML, the current approach to visually model extension pointcuts is to use a note, as shown in Figure 6-3, but we find this approach inadequate. It is not uncommon to have extension use cases that may be applied to multiple base use cases. Using a note implies that you have a note per extension point-extension flow pair. You may encounter situations in which there are multiple extension flows in one extension use case that are applicable to different extension points in another use case. Thus, you end up with many notes for a single extend dependency between use cases. In both cases, using notes makes the use-case diagram extremely cluttered.

In addition, some segments of the extension pointcut descriptions may be reusable across flow and extension flow pairs. The UML note does not provide a way for you to systematically reuse such segments.

We apply the approach taken by AOP and define a new compartment to house all extension pointcuts. An extension pointcut is an expression that specifies where the base use case is extended. Figure 6-4 illustrates how the extension use case looks if you use this approach.

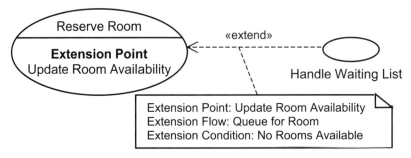

Figure 6-3   *Handle Waiting List extends reserve room.*

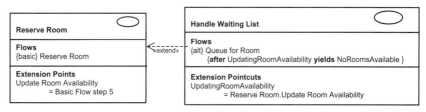

Figure 6-4 *Extension pointcut as a compartment.*

Figure 6-4 depicts both use cases using the standard rectangle classifier notation. The Reserve Room use case has a basic flow, tagged {basic}.

Extension Flow Declaration. The extension use case has an extension flow Queue for Room. Since an extension flow is, in reality, an alternate flow defined in a different use case, we tag the Queue for Room flow as an alternate flow {alt}. The extension flow has a suffix to indicate when this extension flow will execute. In the case of Figure 6-4, the suffix indicates that the Reserve Room basic flow will be extended **after** the extension point referenced by pointcut UpdatingRoomAvailability **yields** NoRoomAvailable. The extension condition (e.g., **yields** NoRoomAvailable) is not always necessary. Sometimes, you might want an extension flow to always execute. For example, you might want to monitor use-case behaviors all the time.

In general, you can insert *before* or *after* the extension point referenced by an extension pointcut. When the extension flow completes, the existing flow resumes. Sometimes, you need to bypass the existing flow if some conditions are not met. For example, if a customer is blacklisted, he cannot make a reservation. AOP permits us to bypass execution of a join point using an around keyword, and you can likewise in your models use this keyword with the same semantics.

Extension Pointcut. The extension pointcut UpdatingRoomAvailability is defined in the extension pointcuts compartment. In this case, it is an expression with two segments connected by a dot.

1. The first segment points to the existing use case, Reserve Room.
2. The second segment points to the extension point, Update Room Availability.

Listing 6-2 also shows how you specify the extension flow and extension pointcut within the use-case specification.

Listing 6-2   Use-Case Specification: Handle Waiting List

Use Case: Handle Waiting List

Basic Flows

. . .

Extension Flows
EF1.Queue For Room
This extension flow occurs after UpdatingRoomAvailability yields No Rooms Available.
1. The system creates a pending reservation with a unique identifier for the selected Room type.
2. The system puts the pending reservation into a waiting list.
3. The system displays the unique identifier of the pending reservation to the customer.
4. The base use case terminates.

Extension Pointcuts
extension pointcut `UpdatingRoomAvailability = Reserve Room.Update Room Availability`

In Listing 6-2, we did not describe the basic flow. If you were to write the full specification for this use case, you would indeed have one. For example, you might have a basic flow that is initiated periodically to notify customers the subsequent availability of a room.

In general, extension use cases may or may not have basic flows. Unlike the Handle Waiting List use case, some will be pure extensions. They do not have basic flows, and they can never be instantiated directly. We discuss more about pure extensions in Section 6.5.

Let us look at what happens when you execute the Reserve Room use-case instance. This is depicted in Listing 6-5. An actor instance triggers the base use case (Reserve Room) and a use-case instance it created. This Reserve Room use-case instance goes through the steps in the basic flow until step 5. The use-case execution environment knows that there is an extension flow and executes this extension flow (Queue for Room). The first step of the extension flow checks if there are rooms available. In this case, none is available, and the rest of the extension flow is executed. In the last step of the extension, the base use-case instance is terminated.

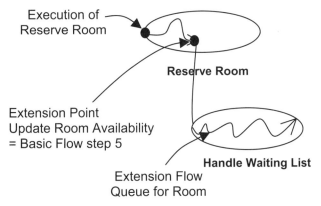

Figure 6-5   *Execution of use-case extensions.*

Sidebar 6-1   Guidelines on Applying Extension Points and Extension Pointcuts

Extension points are defined in the base use case, and the extension pointcuts are defined in the extension use case. This is analogous to join points being part of classes and pointcuts being part of aspects in AOP. However, in normal programming, you do not need to name join points within existing classes. But with use cases, you do—simply because of the deliberate lack of formality in use-case modeling. Putting extension points in the base use case reflects the current practice in use-case modeling and what is currently defined in the UML specification.

Does having extension points in the base use case mean modifying the original use case or being aware that the extension use case exists? In a way, yes, because you add an extension point to the base. However, you do not change the flow. You add the extension point in a separate compartment of the use case. If the use-case flow changes, the name of the extension point still remains. Hence, the extension use case will not be impacted.

You can also define extension points in several ways

Extension point occurring at a single step. The extension point occurs at a specific point in a use-case flow—for example at step 5 of the basic flow.

Extension point occurring over multiple steps. The extension point occurs over a sequence of points—for example, over steps 1 through 4 of the basic flow.

Sidebar 6-1   Guidelines on Applying Extension Points and Extension Pointcuts *(continued)*

Extension point occurring for steps with behavioral properties. The extension point occurs when some behavioral properties are true—for example, *whenever the actor submits a request to the system*. The submission of a request is, therefore, a behavioral property. In this case, the extension point can occur at any step of a use case and, hence, it is not practical to name each step. That is why we identify the steps according to their behavioral properties. This approach is useful when you want to describe when infrastructure concerns (such as logging or authorization) extend existing use cases.

Having the extension use-case flow to refer to the extension pointcut, which refers to the extension point in the base use case, which in turn refers to a step within a flow in the base use case, may seem quite indirect. At this point, we have defined what extension points and extension pointcuts are. How to apply them when expressing your use cases depends on pragmatics. You can do the following:

Direct Reference. Have an extension pointcut refer to a step in the extended use case step directly.

Indirect Reference. Have an extension pointcut refer to an extension point which then refers to a step in the extended use case.

Indirect reference is useful if two or more extending use cases extend an existing use case at the same extension point all the time.

What we have discussed here are merely guidelines on using extension points and extension pointcuts. We believe that as experience in the software development community grows, this set of guidelines will grow. For the time being, note that use-case specifications do not need to use an exact and precise language. As long as you can effectively communicate the behavior of the use case between stakeholders and developers, you are on the right track.

6.3   Use-Case Include Relationship

You often find certain steps that are similar across different use cases. You can factor these common flows of events into what is termed an *inclusion use case*. Other use cases can then reference the flows within this inclusion use case. This referencing from an including use case to an inclusion use case is modeled with an include relationship. Figure 6-6 provides an example of the use-case-include relationship. The Check Room Details, shown shaded, is an inclusion use case. This use case is included by the Reserve Room and Check In Customer use cases to allow actors to check availability of rooms, find rooms that are available for specified periods, and so on.

Figure 6-7 depicts the relationship between the Reserve Room and Check Room Details use cases in greater detail than by explicitly listing the use case flows. We have relocated the use case flow Check Room Cost from the Reserve Room use case (see Listing 5-1).

The tag {basic} indicates that a flow can be triggered by an actor, whereas the tag {sub} indicates that a flow can be referenced or included only by another flow. The execution of a Reserve Room use case instance is illustrated in Figure 6-8.

The execution path begins at the Reserve Room use case, continues through an included flow within the Check Room Details use case, and resumes at the Reserve Room use case. In this example, the included flow is used to Check Room Availability.

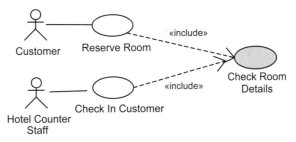

Figure 6-6   *Use-case inclusions.*

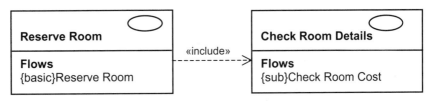

Figure 6-7   *Reserve Room includes Check Room Details.*

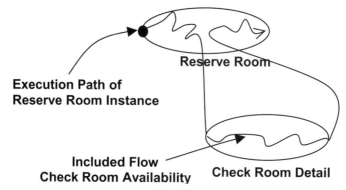

**Execution Path of
Reserve Room Instance**

**Included Flow
Check Room Availability**   **Check Room Detail**

Figure 6-8   *Execution of use case inclusion.*

Note that the referencing from an including use case flow to an included use case flow is not the same as a function call. As we mentioned in Chapter 5, use-case flows are not functions. When you do an include, you take the included flow and expand it in the including flow. You can think of include conceptually like macro expansions such as #include and inline in C++ and JSP, and like include in Web modeling. The included files are not invoked but are inserted and expanded at the same level as the including use case at the point when the inclusion is made.

Also note that no use-case instances are instantiated when an include occurs. The same goes for all kinds of use-case relationships. Remember, use-case instances do not communicate. The various use-case relationships discussed in this chapter are just different means for you to reuse flow descriptions.

Inclusions and Extensions. Inclusions and extensions are opposites. With extensions, an extension flow inserts itself into the existing use-case flow, whereas with inclusions, it is the responsibility of the existing use-case flow to insert the inclusion flow.

The question is then which one to use. Since an inclusion is essential to follow the flow of a use case, one way to determine whether a flow is an inclusion flow is to remove it. For example, if we remove Check Room Cost completely from the Reserve Room use case, the Reserve Room makes no sense because checking Room Cost is an integral part of making a Reservation. You do not make a Reservation without knowing the cost. Thus, Check Room Cost is in an inclusion use case, not an extension use case.

By contrast, if we were to remove the waiting list completely, making a reservation would still be useful to the actor by itself. So, we find that the waiting list is quite a separate capability of the system and, hence, we have a separate extension use case for it.

6.4   Use-Case Generalization

Use-case generalization is another technique to structure the use-case model. It takes the same meaning as class generalization and connotes an "is-a-kind-of" relationship between use cases. You apply use-case generalization when a group of use cases have similar sequences or when similar set of constraints are imposed on them. Rather than specifying the sequences and constraints repeatedly in individual use cases, you generalize them and describe them in parent use cases. Child use cases then inherit these properties. The parent use case is usually abstract, which means it has some flows that have been identified but are deliberately left unspecified. These flows are considered abstract because at the parent level, terms are still generic and details are not yet described. The actual specifications of these abstract flows are postponed to child use cases because the child use cases include the details. In UML-speak, we say that the child use cases make the flows concrete—by providing the specifications for these flows.

In the Hotel Management System example, there are different kinds of facilities in addition to just Rooms. Customers can make reservations for restaurants, video equipment, and other hotel services. You can generalize Reservations with a Reserve Facility use case. Figure 6-9 shows our use-case model with the Reserve Facility use case added.

Figure 6-9 depicts an additional Reserve Restaurant use case. For every generalized use case in your use-case model, you should have at least two child use cases. Otherwise, there is no point in generalizing. It is only when you have several concrete use cases that generalizations can be meaningful. You need to go through all of them at once to sift out the common sequences and push them to a generalized use case.

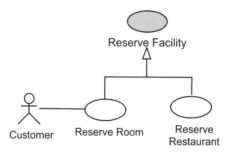

Figure 6-9   *Use-case generalization.*

Listing 6-3 shows the specifications of the Reserve Facility and Reserve Room use cases side by side.

Listing 6-3   Reserve Facility Use Case Generalizes Reserve Room Use Case

Use Case: Reserve Facility	**Use Case: Reserve Room**
Basic Flow	**Basic Flow**
The use case begins when a customer wants to reserve a facility (s).	. . .
1. The system displays the facilities available.	**Subflow**
2. The customer <u>Choose Facility</u>.	**S1.Choose Facility**
3. The system displays the total costs for the facilities chosen.	1. The customer selects to Reserve Room.
4. The system deducts from the database the number of facilities available.	2. The customer selects his desired room type and indicates his period of stay.
5. The system creates a new reservation for the chosen facilities.	3. The system computes the cost for the specified period.
6. The system displays the reservation confirmation number.	
7. The use case terminates.	
Alternate Flows	
. . .	
Subflows	
{abstract} Choose Facility	

The left-hand side of Listing 6-3 shows the specification of the Reserve Facility use case. In our example, the steps to reserve a facility are all the same. Thus, the basic flow Reserve Facility is concrete. In step 2, it includes a subflow to Choose Facility. This subflow is intentionally left unspecified (i.e., abstract) because it is specific to the child use case. On the right-hand side of 3, we have a concrete case for Reserve Room.

Figure 6-10 shows the generalization relationship between Reserve Facility and Reserve Room. The Reserve Facility use case is an abstract use case because it has an abstract flow. Note that an abstract use case can have concrete flows, but it must have at least one abstract flow.

In UML, the way to represent an abstract element is to use italics. However, when attempting to draw diagrams on paper, and especially if you conduct use-case modeling by hand on a whiteboard (as opposed to using a modeling tool), italics are not easily recognizable. To circumvent this problem, we use an {abstract} tag in Figure 6-10.

The execution of a child use-case instance is illustrated in Figure 6-11. Instantiation occurs at the child use case (Reserve Room in our example) and follows a basic flow. The execution path of a child use-case instance follows through a number of flows. If a flow is defined in the child, it is executed; otherwise, the flow defined in the parent is executed. In our example in Figure 6-11, the Reserve Room use-case instance follows the basic flow of the Reserve Facility use case. This is because the Reserve Room use case does not define it, but inherits it from the parent. When the use-case instance reaches the point to choose a facility, we find that the parent use case has left it abstract. Thus, the Choose Facility flow of the Reserve Room use case is executed.

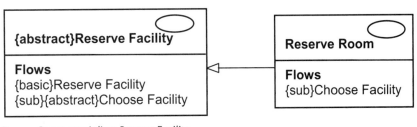

Figure 6-10 *Reserve Room specializes Reserve Facility.*

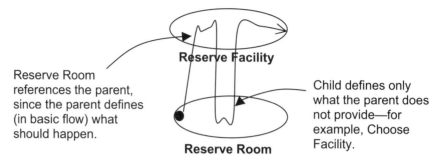

Reserve Room references the parent, since the parent defines (in basic flow) what should happen.

Reserve Facility

Child defines only what the parent does not provide—for example, Choose Facility.

Reserve Room

Figure 6-11   *Execution of use-case generalization.*

Generalization and Extensions. Generalization and extensions should not be confused with each other. If you are a developer, you may be familiar with the *extends* keyword in Java. Extends in our discussion refers to generalization, not extension.

With generalization, we want to factor out the common behavior into a parent use case and put the specific behavior in a child use case. It is the child use case that is instantiated and executed. With extension, there is no requirement for common behavior: the extension flow merely hooks on to some location in the existing use-case flow to add new behavior.

In addition, with generalization, parent and child use cases have between them an is-a-kind-of relationship. For example, Reserve Room is a kind of Reserve Facility. With extensions, this is not true. For example, Handle Waiting List is not a kind of Reserve Room, nor vice versa.

Generalizations and Inclusions. Generalizations and inclusions are both used to factor out the common behavior of use cases, so at times they can be confused with one another. They are different ways of achieving reuse of common behaviors. Generalizations always require an is-a-kind-of semantics between the parent and the base so that inheritance is meaningful, but this is not necessary with inclusions.

With inclusions, we reuse common behavior by merely delegating the description of a flow to another use case. When the execution of a use case reaches a step that needs common behavior, the use case must make an explicit reference to the included use case and the flow therein.

6.5   Utility Use Cases

In addition to generalization, inclusion, and extension use cases, we also have another kind of use case called a utility use case. Utility use cases, by nature, do not provide functionalities that are of direct usefulness to actors and stakeholders, so they are never instantiated on their own. There are either pure inclusions or pure extensions. For example, a utility use case might have functions such as open file, close file, and rename files. These functions need to be used in a larger context before they are useful. Therefore, utility use cases can never be instantiated. They always execute in the context of another use-case instance.

Recall that the purpose of basic flows is to specify the behavior that emerges when a use case is instantiated. Therefore, a use case without a basic flow cannot be instantiated. Since utility use cases are never instantiated, they do not need any basic flow. This is a distinguishing characteristic between utility and non-utility use cases.

Utility use cases are analogous to utility classes in UML. They are merely a container of related flows very much like utility classes, which are containers for related methods.

There are two kinds of utility use cases: utility inclusions and utility extensions. Utility inclusion use cases have subflows that are included by other use cases, whereas utility extension use cases have alternate flows that hook onto other use cases. Neither has basic flows.

Examples of utility inclusions are file operations and basic create, read, update, and delete operations on different kinds of information stored within the system. Such operations are always performed as part of a larger goal of the system, such as to reserve a room.

Utility extensions usually appear as add-on features that do not require further processing. Context-sensitive help is one such example, and so are features that help remember information about a customer so that default values can be entered automatically for her. Such utility extension use cases work simply by hooking on to existing use cases. With aspect orientation, it is very easy to hook such utility extensions onto existing use cases and, therefore, we can make them highly reusable.

Sidebar 6-2   Does Structuring Use Cases Lead to Functional Decomposition?

Structuring use cases with include or extend or generalization, as we have discussed in this book, should not be done when you first identify use cases. It is only when you have a good understanding about the identified use cases that you structure them. So, you structure the use-case model later, and only when it leads to a better understanding of the system.

We mentioned in Chapter 5, Sidebar 5-3, that you should avoid functional decomposition, or breaking down the system into many small use cases to the extent that it becomes difficult for the reader to understand what the system is for and the value it brings to the stakeholder. Some practitioners are concerned that introducing use-case relationships may lead to functional decomposition, and their worries are valid because of possible abuse of these relationships.

While we agree that functional decomposition must be avoided at all cost, having use cases include, extend, and generalize does not necessarily lead to functional decomposition. In fact, if done correctly, you get better use-case models. That is why we have them in the first place. If an inexperienced practitioner falls into the trap of functional decomposition, he will do so regardless of whether or not he uses include/extend. The analogy is as follows: if a person has no driving experience, he will likely crash into something regardless of whether he drives a small car or a big car, or whether it has a manual transmission or an automatic transmission.

Consider use-case include. When the concept of use cases was first introduced, the originators did not introduce the include, not because they did not know it could be valuable, but because people would misuse it. At that time, Objectory (the origin of the Unified Process) and the tool that supported it had text objects in place of include.

Today, use cases are understood by more people, but the risk of misuse is still substantial. However, today, use-case include is part of the UML specification, and many practitioners are familiar with it. Still, we need to caution about its appropriate use.

The same applies to use-case extends and generalization. Although there is potential for abuse, there is greater value to achieve a more understandable and, hence, better use-case model.

6.6   Summary and Highlights

The whole idea of use-case modeling and structuring use cases is to clarify stakeholders' concerns and to make the requirements of the system more understandable. The use-case-extend relationship is one possible technique you can use. In this chapter, we propose the explicit representation of pointcuts in extension use cases. The extension pointcuts help to identify pointcuts during analysis, design, and implementation. This provides a seamless transition as you move ahead in subsequent development activities.

In addition to use-case extend, you can apply use-case include and generalization as well. You can also apply use-case packages to group-related use cases. But structuring use cases occurs not just at the use-case model but also within the use-case specification itself through basic, alternate, and subflows. In fact, the bulk of the time spent in use-case modeling is with the use-case specifications. You normally make several iterations before you can finally evolve a good structure for your use-case model.

7

Capturing Concerns with Use Cases

Understanding stakeholders' real concerns is critical to successful software development. Concerns come from various sources and can be about different aspects of the system. Use cases provide a single technique to describe what the system must do to address these concerns. We distinguish between two major categories of use cases: application and infrastructure use cases. Application use cases describe how users interact with the system to perform the desired functionality. Infrastructure use cases describe what the system does to add qualities such as usability, reliability, performance, and supportability to each step of an application use case.

7.1 Understanding Stakeholder Concerns

If you want to build the correct system, you have to get the requirements correct. This does not necessarily mean thick and huge volumes of documents. You must understand the motivation behind the stated requirements—the stakeholders' concerns. And that is paramount. If you ever feel that stakeholders keep on changing their requirements, ask yourself these questions: do you have a good feel for the stakeholders' concerns, and do you share their vision of the desired system? Even if your answer is yes, you must continually validate your understanding with them.

In addition, you have to understand stakeholder priorities. Not all concerns are created equal. Some are more important than others. The priority determines which requirements have to be developed before others and how their development will be spread across the project schedule. If things do not turn out well, you know which requirements can be dropped out, and your stakeholders can still get an acceptable, albeit incomplete, functionality.

7.1.1   Understanding the Problem Domain

The whole idea of requirements is about nailing down the problem that the system is intended to solve. You must be able to elicit and explore the root problem with the stakeholders. You must understand the business domain; you must walk through the business scenarios with the stakeholders; you must identify key desirable features of the system with them. You frequently do these activities in parallel, and the goal is to draw out the stakeholders' real needs.

It is an important stakeholder concern that the system correctly and accurately captures the problem domain. This can be effectively achieved through classes. When being introduced into a new problem domain, you need to quickly grasp its essential concepts that distinguish this new problem domain from another. Classes are excellent tools for you to describe such concepts. For example, if you are ever required to build a hotel management system, you need to understand what constitutes such concepts as Room, Promotion, Reservation, Customer, and Bill. Even if you have built such a system for Hotel Chain ABC, the terms used by Hotel Chain XYZ might be different. It is extremely important that you clarify these concepts. You can capture them in a glossary. You can most certainly depict them visually as classes through a class diagram such as that shown in Figure 7-1, which further shows the relationships between these classes.

Finding these classes constitutes what is known as domain modeling, or business object modeling [Jacobson et al. 1994]. You go through the essential business scenarios that your system will be supporting to identify what information the system needs to keep track of or manipulate. Such

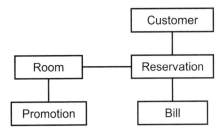

Figure 7-1   *Domain classes for the Hotel Management System.*

information will be modeled as domain classes. It is usually sufficient to identify the essential attributes and relationships between these classes. At this point, you are merely capturing the essential concepts and their relationships. You should not go into too much detail as if you were doing data modeling in database design. You will do that later.

7.1.2   Eliciting System Features

Stakeholders and project sponsors normally justify the need for a new system or an enhancement by emphasizing the benefits and payoffs of specific features. Features are high-level statements of desired system capability, which can either be in terms of functionality (i.e., what the system can do) or some other quality attribute (performance, security, etc.). There are many ways to come up with the features for a system. You can conduct some brainstorming with the stakeholders; you can look at the problems they are facing; you can walk through the business process with them; and so on. But whichever method you use, you end up with a list of key features for the system. As an example, Listing 7–1 itemizes the key features of the Hotel Management System.

Listing 7-1 Key Features of Hotel Management System

1. A customer can make a reservation for a hotel room.
2. Counter staffs can check in and check out customers.
3. Hotel management can define standard room rates and promotional offers when room rates are reduced for limited periods.
4. Members can accumulate loyalty points and use them for any payment.
5. There will be a waiting list in case the rooms are fully reserved.
6. Different types of customer (individual, corporate, members) must be handled.
7. The room reservation can be over different channels, such as through agents, Internet, or via phone.

8. The system has to be Web-enabled.

9. The system will store all records in a relational database.

10. For audit purposes, all transactions in the system have to be logged.

11. Only authorized personnel can perform their functions.

12. To promote ease of use, the system will track the users' preferences and use them as default.

13. All retrieval of records should take no longer than 2 seconds.

Listing 7–1 gives us, in concise terms, an overview of the system's requirements. However, it definitely does not constitute all the requirements for the system. Listing 7–1 is still a long way from that. From the perspective of the developer, the features are still open to many interpretations, and different acceptance criteria can be proposed for each one. Additional work is necessary to clarify what each feature means. One way to find out more about these features is to refine them one by one, resulting in a long requirement list. But if you do this, you end up with loose bits of information.

A more effective approach is to walk through the use of the system and uncover how the features are put into effect. This is a better approach because it puts the features in the context of the system operation. This is what use-case modeling is all about. The remainder of this chapter describes how to map these features to use cases. We also describe how to explore and uncover requirements surrounding these features and how to capture them through use cases. Through use cases, you clarify stakeholders' concerns about the system's functionality and quality.

7.1.3   Dealing with Functional and Nonfunctional Requirements

Most analysts distinguish between two kinds of requirements: functional requirements (FRs) and nonfunctional requirements (NFRs). Typically, functional requirements refer to what users can do with the system, whereas nonfunctional requirements usually refer to qualities of the system. Features 1 through 7 in Listing 7–1 are usually considered functional requirements; whereas features 8 through 13 are considered nonfunctional, or at least cross-functional: that is, they apply to all the functions in features 1 through 7.

Today, most practitioners model functional requirements with use cases, but they tend to leave nonfunctional requirements out of use-case modeling. However, use cases are applicable to nonfunctional requirements too. So long as a requirement requires some observable response to be programmed into the system, you can apply use cases. Always ask yourself, is there something the system must do to meet a particular requirement? If the answer is yes, then use cases can be applied because use cases help you capture desired system behaviors. Also ask if there is a way to test the system for conformance to the requirement. As long as you can define a test, you can indeed define a use case for it. After all, a use case is a set of test cases. Basically, each scenario in the use case is a preliminary test case. To complete the test case, you need to add test data. Making use cases/test cases upfront has been popularized through test-first-design techniques.

Nonfunctional requirements usually need the support of some underlying infrastructure mechanisms. For example, feature 12 needs some infrastructure mechanism to track user inputs. Feature 13 requires an infrastructure mechanism to utilize some form of caching to meet the 2-second response time requirement. So, these nonfunctional requirements do impose some behaviors on the infrastructure. You can most certainly model these infrastructure mechanisms with use cases. To distinguish such use cases from others, we call them *infrastructure use cases*. We call the others *application use cases*. Infrastructure use cases deal with infrastructure concerns, and application use cases deal with application concerns.

Most of you are familiar with writing application use cases. Here, we recommend that you specify the use cases for infrastructure mechanisms as well. The advantages for doing so are many. It helps the development team understand how the infrastructure mechanism will be used. Too frequently, we find that infrastructure mechanisms are poorly described. There might be a bunch of diagrams that attempt to describe the realization of the infrastructure mechanism, but they generally describe only the basic use of it. How exceptions and variations are handled is usually either not considered or poorly described. This leads to obscure defects in the system. You apply the same technique as you do with application use cases to explore the different scenarios that each infrastructure mechanism has to handle. There will be basic and alternate flows and so on in infrastructure use-case specifications just as in typical use-case specifications. We discuss how to model such infrastructure use cases later in this chapter.

7.2   Capturing Application Use Cases

Let us look at how you can distinguish application use cases from functional requirements. Features 1 to 5 are functional features and describe what users can do with the system; they lead to the identification of use cases for our system. But since features are rarely complete, we often supplement the identification of use cases by first identifying who the actors for the system are and what they are using the system for. Each use of the system is described through use cases.

A first attempt at identifying use cases that address features 1 to 5 is depicted in Figure 7–2.

Most, if not all, businesses exist for two groups of people: customers who need some products and services, and business owners who believe they can earn some money from the customers. The rest of the folks in the business are workers; they are there to do their jobs and get paid. In our Hotel Management System, the actors that have been explicitly identified are:

- Customers (and members)
- Hotel counter staff
- Hotel management

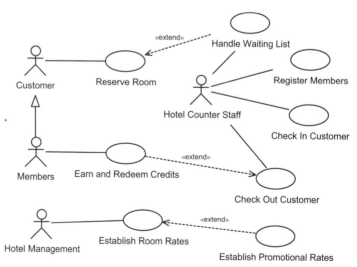

Figure 7-2   *Application use cases for Hotel Management System.*

The goal of customers is to reserve rooms and stay there happily for a period of time. In our system, our stakeholders (the business owners) want the customer to reserve rooms over the Internet and thus broaden the hotel's sales channel. Counter staff help customers check in and out of their rooms. Of course, counter staff must collect payment from the customers when they check out. The hotel management specifies the room rates and specials, but a frequent scenario is defining promotional offers when rooms are offered at a discount. As an attempt to capture more customers, the hotel offers a loyalty program whereby members can earn and redeem credits. Credits are earned when the member makes payment on a 10 to 1 ratio—that is, for every 10 dollars spent, the member earns one credit, which is equivalent to 1 dollar. Credits can be used to make subsequent payments. To participate in this program, the customer has to register through the counter staff. The stakeholder indicates the need for a waiting list as well.

The use cases Reserve Room, Check In Customer, Check Out Customer, and Establish Room Rates are core use cases.

The use case Earn and Redeem Credits is an extension of the check-out use case to permit payment by loyalty credits earned by previous payments. A prerequisite for using loyalty credits is that the customer be registered as a member. This is provided by the Register Members use case.

The Establish Promotional Rates use case is an extension of the Establish Room Rates use case. The key difference between promotional rates is that they are time-limited, whereas room rates remain fairly constant.

The use cases and their relationships in Figure 7–2 are by no means complete. They represent an initial understanding of the system's requirements. As you proceed through the project, the use-case model gets updated.

7.2.1 Identifying Use-Case Variability

Once you have identified the use cases for the system, you have in effect separated the different concerns for a system from the actor or user perspective. Now you can explore the concerns of each use case in greater detail. For each use case, there are many flows of events, each describing how a particular variation is handled through that use case. It is important to have a systematic way to explore variations. Otherwise, you risk missing key requirements of a system. To avoid this risk, you have to identify variables for your system or for each use case. Some of these variables may be critical concerns to your stakeholders. In our example Hotel Management System, they are so important that they appear in the key feature list in Listing 7–1. Features 6 and 7 identify two variables, Customer Types and Reservation Channels. Each variable may take on different values. You may have values for the Customer Types variables such as individual customer, corporate customer, registered customers, and customers from an affiliate hotel. You may have values for different Reservation Channels such as through an agent, a telephone (i.e., an interactive voice response unit), or the Internet. Customer Types and Reservations Channels are not the only variables: as yet another example, you can have a variable for reservation schemes with values such as a single period reservation, reservation over multiple time periods, recurring reservations, and so on.

Identifying variables and their values is important because they help you to understand the complexity of the system you are developing. They identify the universe of your requirements gathering effort—that is, your project scope. Forgetting to deal with a variable or a variable value has negative consequences on the completeness of requirements. Thus, it is important to identify them early in the project.

The domain model shown in Figure 7–1 is quite useful in identifying the variables. The domain class itself and the attributes of the domain class and associations between domain classes are all candidates of use-case variability.

7.2.2   Handling Use-Case Variability

Use-case variables will likely affect multiple use cases. For example, most of the use cases identified earlier in Figure 7–2 will be affected by the Customer Type variable; thus, you might have scenarios describing how corporate customers reserve room, check in, check out, and use their loyalty credits, and those customers may be given higher priorities on the waiting list. In other words, the variables crosscut use cases, and you might consider them "aspects of use cases" (see Sidebar 7–1).

The handling of each variable value tends to be use-case-specific. Hence, while the variables may cut across use cases, it is better to leave them within the use cases and describe how to handle them as alternate flows. In fact, use-case variables help you organize your alternate flows. You can have one section per use-case variable, and within each of these sections, describe how each variable value is handled. This organization is shown in Listing 7–2.

Listing 7-2 Organizing Alternate Flows with Use-Case Variables

Basic Flow
The use case begins when an individual customer wishes to make a reservation for a single period over the Internet.
1. . . .
2. . . .
3. . . .
Alternate Flows
   Customer Types
      Corporate Customer
   Reservation Periods
      Multiple Periods
   Reservation Channels
      Agent Reservation
      Phone Reservation

There are two ways to describe the basic flow, either generically and independent of each use-case variable or using a default value. Listing 7–2, shows the use of default values in the basic flow. It assumes that the customer is an individual customer, the reservation is for a single time period, and the reservation is made over the Internet. The variations to this default case are handled in the alternate flows, which are organized according to the use-case variables.

When describing the handling of each variable, you walk through the basic flow and identify steps or points that are affected by that variable. You consolidate these points (which we call variability points) as sort of an introduction for that variable. So, each variable becomes a subsection within the alternate flows. Within this subsection, you describe how each variation is handled as an alternate flow. Organizing use-case specifications in this way makes reading use-case specifications a lot easier. This is much better than merely producing a long list of alternate flows. It facilitates reviewing the use case for completeness. It also facilitates the subsequent transition to analysis and design.

When helping the stakeholders to describe how they intend the variations to be handled, you can use a diagram similar to Figure 7–3. The figure presents the variables on each axis, and the markings on each axis represent a particular value.

Using Figure 7–3, you can ask whether the use-case variables are independent of each other. For example, how different reservation channels are handled is independent of the other two variables in the figure. Customer types and reservation periods may have some relationships. For example, only a corporate customer can make reservations over recurring periods, or there may be different pricing between customer types and reservation periods. When there is interplay between use-case variables, you need to supplement your use-case specifications with tables and matrices to summarize how they are handled.

It is not always possible to describe precisely how the variables are handled through use cases. In such cases, you might want to postpone this to analysis or even just list them as test cases.

If the handling of each variable is generic across use cases, you may want to factor them into a generalized use case. In this way, you avoid being repetitive in your use-case specifications.

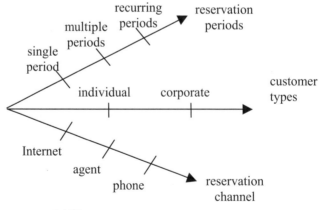

Figure 7-3   *Handling use-case variability.*

Sometimes, how variations are dealt with is dependent on the customer site (e.g., for Hotel Chain ABC or Hotel Chain XYZ). In this case, you may wish to describe them in a separate extension use case containing a number of extension flows that describe the desired behaviors to meet the needs of that customer site.

Identifying these variables is extremely important if you want to build an extensible system because the system will likely be extended on the basis of these variables. For the Hotel Management System example, you might wish to introduce a new customer type, a new reservation scheme, a new reservation channel, and so forth. We discuss how you can design your system to be extensible in Part 4 of the book, specifically in Chapter 13, "Separating Functional Requirements with Application Extension Use Cases."

Sidebar 7-1   How Do You Identify Aspects?

Whenever a new construct is introduced, you need a way to identify it. When object orientation was first introduced, practitioners asked, "How do we identify classes?" When use cases were introduced, practitioners asked, "How do we identify use cases?" With the introduction of aspect orientation, you expect a similar question: "How do we identify aspects?" In fact, it is a frequently asked question.

Aspects refer to crosscutting concerns. Use cases are crosscutting concerns in that their realizations cut across many classes. As you can see, each use case is subject to variables, which results in multiple alternate flows. These variables are crosscutting and are modeled as alternate flows or even extension use cases, as we see in the next section. Moreover, as you will see later, nonfunctional requirements (which are generally accepted to be crosscutting concerns) are also modeled with use cases, specifically with infrastructure use cases. To put this across explicitly: *when you identify use cases, you are indeed identifying aspects.*

7.2.3   Dealing with Extension Use Cases

Our use-case model survey in Figure 7–2 shows several extension use cases. Some of these extension use cases are what we call *concrete use cases*—they can be instantiated separately from the use cases that they extend. Examples are the Handle Waiting List and the Earn and Redeem Credits use cases. We discussed the Handle Waiting List use case in Chapter 6, "Structuring Use Cases." In this chapter, we discuss the Earn and Redeem Credits use case. Figure 7–4 provides a visual representation of this use case. With this use case, a customer can view the credit she has accumulated. She can also purchase reward items with the credits. These are achieved through the basic flows listed in Figure 7–4.

A customer's credits can be accumulated only when she makes payment for hotel facilities. This is achieved through the extension flow Earn Credits. The customer can also use credits to pay for the hotel facilities she uses. This is achieved through the extension flow Make Payment with Credits. Recall that extension flows are alternate flows that execute in the context of separate use case—the base use case. The base use case is identified through an extension pointcut. The Earn and Redeem Credits use case has an extension pointcut named `MakingPayment`. It is used in both extension flows and it is defined to refer to the extension point Collect Payment in the Check Out Customer use case.

As you can see, an extension use case itself can be modeled relatively independently from the use case it extends. Its basic flows are separate from the Check Out Customer use case. The extension flows can be described by referencing to `MakingPayment` pointcut as an indirect reference to some extension point in another use cases.

The details of the extend relationship between the base and extension use cases needs coordination between the authors of the respective use cases. The interface between the extension and the base use case is expressed in terms of extension pointcuts and extension points. So, there is some coordination between the authors of both use cases to define them (i.e., extension pointcuts and extension points). There are basically two methods of coordination. In the first method, the author of the extension use case lists

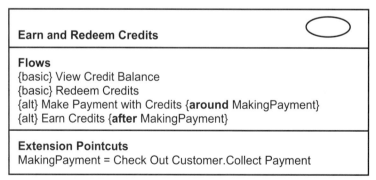

Figure 7-4   *Outlining an extension use case.*

the pointcuts he or she needs. The author of the base provides a suitable extension point. This is exemplified by the Earn and Redeem Credits use case. You want to provide this loyalty credit capability, and you determine where in which use case additional behaviors are required. In the second method, the author of the base provides a list of extension points. This is useful when you want to handle variations in the base use case, as discussed in the previous section. You can also combine both methods. Once you have clarified the interface between the base and extension use case, both authors can work on them separately.

The indirect reference from the extension pointcut to the actual execution point (the use-case step) in the base use case prevents changes in the base use case to propagate to the extension use case. If at any time the base use case gets modified, it is up to the base author to ensure that the extension point still points to a correct point in the base use case.

7.3   Capturing Infrastructure Use Cases

Let us now look at how you deal with nonfunctional requirements. Some nonfunctional requirements, such as authorization and transaction management, can be refined and kept separate as infrastructure use cases. As you will see shortly, these can be modeled as extensions to application use cases.

There are also other kinds of nonfunctional requirements that deal with system wide qualities such as performance and reliability. These system wide concerns are described simply as declarative statements during requirements. There are usually several key infrastructure use cases that are used to achieve these qualities, and you need to consider the sum of these infrastructure use cases to determine whether these qualities are met.

We again use the feature list for our Hotel Management System in Listing 7–1 for discussion. Features 8 to 13 are the nonfunctional requirements. To reiterate, these features are:

8. The system has to be Web-enabled.
9. The system will store all records in a relational database.
10. For audit purposes, all transactions in the system have to be logged.
11. Only authorized personnel can perform their functions.

12. To promote ease of use, the system will track the users' preferences and use them as default.
13. All retrieval of records should take no longer than 2 seconds.

These features affect all use cases identified earlier. If you take a closer look at the features listed above, you find that they affect each step of an application use case. For feature 8, every step in an application use case produces a Web page. For feature 9, each step in an application use case has access to the database. For feature 10, the action at each step is recorded. For feature 11, each step must ensure that the actor instance has sufficient privileges. For feature 12, each step attempts to profile the actor inputs. Finally, for feature 13, each step of an application use case should take no longer than 2 seconds.

As you can see, the features listed above are qualities of the system that are required for each step of an application use case. We call each step of a use case a use-case transaction. It is an actor request-system response pair—the actor does something, the system responds in return. Since the features require additional processing within the basic use-case transaction, you can model them as extensions to this basic transaction.

7.3.1   The Perform Transaction Use Case

You can model the basic transaction through a ⟨Perform Transaction⟩ use case, as shown in Figure 7–5. This use case is a pattern—a template bounded to each step of an application use case. We use the angle brackets, ⟨ ⟩, to indicate that both the Actor and the ⟨Perform Transaction⟩ use cases are parameterized elements.

⟨Actor⟩   ⟨Perform Transaction⟩

Figure 7-5   *<Perform Transaction> use case.*

The ⟨Perform Transaction⟩ use case collates the infrastructure requirements for the system. This is exemplified in Listing 7–3.

Listing 7-3   Use-Case Specification: ⟨Perform Transaction⟩

Basic Flow
The use case begins when an actor instance performs a transaction to view the values of an entity instance.
1. The system prompts the actor instance to identify the desired entity instance.
2. The actor instance enters the values and submits his request.
3. The system retrieves the entity instance from its data store and displays its values.
4. The use case terminates.

Alternate Flows
A1. Access Control
If in step 3 of the basic flow the request requires authorization, the system checks the actor instance's access rights.
1. If the actor instance does not have access rights, the request is rejected. The use case terminates.
2. Otherwise, the use case proceeds.
A2. User Preference
In step 1 of the basic flow, if prior preference is defined, the system retrieves the preference and uses those values as defaults for the actor instance's request. The use case resumes.
In step 2 of the basic flow, if the user indicates that the submitted values will be used as defaults, the system stores the values as the user's preference.
A3. Logging
In step 2 of the basic flow, the request has to be logged; the system stores the submitted request into the log database.

Special Requirements
All retrieval of records should take no longer than 2 seconds.

The basic flow in Listing 7–3 usually looks simple. The complexity of the ⟨Perform Transaction⟩ use case lies in the variations it needs to handle, as exemplified by the alternate flows.

We show only three alternate flows in Listing 7–3. In reality, there can be quite a large number of alternate flows, and an experienced architect will want to explore them and track their implementation. The ⟨Perform Transaction⟩ use case provides a convenient place to document these variations and the context in which they occur. If the ⟨Perform Transaction⟩ use case needs to deal with too many variations, you can factor out the different concerns into separate extension use cases, as we demonstrate in the next section.

The ⟨Perform Transaction⟩ use case is a convenient place to model the behavior required to meet nonfunctional requirements of the system. There are nonfunctional requirements that describe the system-level qualities such as that the response time should not exceed 2 seconds (see feature 13). For the time being, you model and express them using declarative statements in the special requirements section of the ⟨Perform Transaction⟩ use case. This is shown in the Special Requirements section of Listing 7–3.

The ⟨Perform Transaction⟩ use case is crucial to the architect. It is from this use case that she describes how infrastructure mechanisms are introduced. Expect that there will be different kinds of transactions, some involving the retrieval and displaying of an entity instance, some involving displaying a list of entity instances, and so on. In order for you to systematically extend them, you need to consider the different kinds of transactions that may occur. The use-case-specification technique itself offers a convenient way to describe the different kinds of transactions you have to handle. During analysis, design, and implementation, the realization of the ⟨Perform Transaction⟩ use case becomes a pattern that is applied to the realization of each application use-case step. Thus, the ⟨Perform Transaction⟩ use case also helps achieve consistency during analysis, design, and implementation.

7.3.2   Structuring Infrastructure Use Cases

As you explore more variants of the basic flow in the ⟨Perform Transaction⟩ use case, it will start to grow. For complex systems with many infrastructure considerations, a single ⟨Perform Transaction⟩ use case will be too large and difficult to manage. You can factor out different alternate flows from the ⟨Perform Transaction⟩ use case into extension flows in separate extension use cases when they represent a separate, nonfunctional concern. This is depicted in Figure 7–6. These extension use cases—Handle Authorization, Audit Transaction, and Track Preferences—are infrastructure use cases.

Accordingly, you need to identify extension points in the ⟨Perform Transaction⟩ use case and define pointcuts for each infrastructure use case in

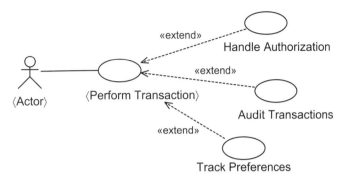

Figure 7-6   *Structuring infrastructure use cases.*

Figure 7–6. Treating infrastructure use cases as extensions of the ⟨Perform Transaction⟩ use case offers many advantages. It helps you visualize the context of infrastructure mechanisms. It serves as a base from which you identify extension points systematically.

From an application standpoint, the ⟨Perform Transaction⟩ use case serves as a template for realizing each individual use-case transaction. It greatly improves the consistency in naming conventions, structuring, and so on. This makes specifying extension points and extension pointcuts a lot easier.

Sidebar 7-2   What Is the Relationship between the <Perform Transaction> Use Case and Application Use Cases?

You might be wondering what relationship exists between an application use case and the ⟨Perform Transaction⟩ use case. Is it a generalization? It is not. You cannot say that the Reserve Room use case is a ⟨Perform Transaction⟩ use case. The Reserve Room use case has a number of steps, or transactions, whereas the ⟨Perform Transaction⟩ use case essentially refers to only one step, or transaction. Thus, they are of different granularity, and is-a-kind-of semantics do not exist between an application use case and the ⟨Perform Transaction⟩ use case.

As mentioned, the ⟨Perform Transaction⟩ use case is a template or a pattern. This means that the relationship between an application use case (e.g., Reserve Room) and the ⟨Perform Transaction⟩ use case is a "bind" relationship. In fact, each application use case binds the ⟨Perform Transaction⟩ use case many times—as many times as there are steps within the application use case.

7.3.3 Describing Infrastructure Use Cases

Now that you have identified the infrastructure use cases, you can describe them individually. Like application use cases, infrastructure use cases frequently have basic flows. The basic flows can be for several purposes:

- They can be used to set the conditions for the extension flows. For example, to check authorization, an extension flow must be able to determine which actor is submitting a request.
- They can be used to view the information collected by the extension flows. For example, in the Audit Transaction use case, you can view and analyze the logs collected from other use cases.

As an example, Figure 7–7 depicts the Handle Authorization use case. It has basic flows for the actors to define access permissions. This information is used to check if the actor is authorized to perform any transaction that arises through any application use cases.

The Check Authorization extension flow executes in the context of some base use-case flows. If the actor has no authorization to perform that request, this extension flow displays some message or notification of possible violations to interested parties.

In Figure 7–7, there is an extension pointcut, `PerformingTransaction-Request`, which is mapped to the Perform Request extension point in the ⟨Perform Transaction⟩ use case. This means that you need to identify the extension point in the base ⟨Perform Transaction⟩ use case. This can be mapped to step 3 of the basic flow in Listing 7–3. However, you need not

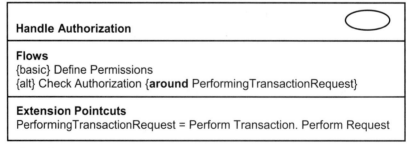

Figure 7-7   *Handle Authorization use case.*

always define extension points exactly during use-case modeling. The textual description used in use-case specifications is imprecise, and often it is more fruitful to define them during analysis and design. During use-case modeling, you just need to know the existence of the pointcut and roughly where it points to.

Not all infrastructure use cases are as visible to the users as Handling Authorization, Tracking Preference, and Auditing Transactions, as we described earlier. A number of infrastructure use cases work in the background. For example, to meet the 2-second response, you may have an infrastructure mechanism to describe how you Provide Cache Access of frequently accessed data, as depicted in Figure 7–8.

This use case has an extension flow that looks up a local cache to see if the requested data is available in the cache. If it is available, it returns the data in the cache. Otherwise, it reads from a back-end data store, updates the cache, and returns the data to the requestor.

In Figure 7–8, there is an extension pointcut, `AccessingData`, which corresponds to Access Frequently Used Data in the ⟨Perform Transaction⟩ use case. The question is then, What are the frequently used data? This answer will not be found in the ⟨Perform Transaction⟩ use case. Instead, it will be found in application use cases such as Reserve Room and Check In Customer that use the ⟨Perform Transaction⟩ as a template. In these application use cases, you can have a special requirements section that lists the frequently accessed data. For example, room rates can be a frequently accessed data.

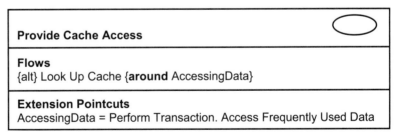

Figure 7-8   *Provide Cached Access use case.*

> ### Sidebar 7-3   Do You Have Infrastructure Use Cases for all Nonfunctional Requirements?
>
> Let's use performance as an example. Note that you do not simply add an infrastructure use case for caching whenever you find a performance requirement. Normally, you conduct some benchmark tests first. If the tests show that you cannot meet the performance requirement, then you add a caching capability or any other capability that will improve performance into the system.
>
> The fact that we treat infrastructure use cases as modular extensions of application use cases is beneficial. You can extend the application use cases with infrastructure use cases (via the ⟨Perform Transaction⟩ use case) only as needed.

You may be wondering why stakeholders may be interested in such low-level infrastructure use cases. There can be several possible reasons. First, the local cache might be on the end user's machine and may have security implications. The cache may contain valuable information that needs protection and cannot be stored in a local cache. This means that cached access is not a viable option. In addition, the end user's machine may impose size limitations on the cache. The stakeholder may also be interested in how frequently the cache gets refreshed so that the end user may have access to up-to-date data.

The level of detail you need to get into for these infrastructure use cases is very much dependent on what the stakeholder is concerned with. But please do not assume that they are not interested in such infrastructure details at all. Today's IT departments are usually concerned about such things. They will be more than happy to tell you their infrastructure concerns. Nevertheless, the description of the infrastructure use cases must be refined during analysis when more details are available.

7.3.4   Dealing with Systemwide Concerns

As you have seen, infrastructure use cases are excellent tools for expressing concerns about underlying infrastructure support. Infrastructure use cases help you keep infrastructure services separate. However, not all nonfunctional requirements can be kept separate this way. You will encounter requirements on the overall system characteristics. An example is feature 13. It requires that each step of an application use case should take no longer than 2 seconds. Although you indeed have an infrastructure use case, Provide Cache Access, to help improve response time, it is not enough. To ascertain whether each use-case step indeed takes 2 seconds or less, you must consider a combination of use cases. Recall that infrastructure use cases extend application use cases at each application use-case step. You need to sum up the time taken by each infrastructure use case to determine the total time taken. The use-case diagram in 7–6 tells you which infrastructure use cases you need to sum up. You add up the time spent in Handling Authorization, Auditing Transactions, and Tracking Preferences. If there are potential bottlenecks, you use the Provide Cache Access to improve the response time.

The summing up of response times can be performed by inspection. But to be certain about whether the response time can be met, you need to run some tests. Yes, you need to execute the system. With iterative development, you get an executable early in the project and you can verify the quality of your system. Once you have the test results, you can determine what additional infrastructure use cases you need.

7.4 Summary and Highlights

To reiterate, understanding stakeholder concerns is extremely important to building the correct system. Many failures in software development are attributed to poor understanding of requirements. In these situations, you normally find stakeholders and developers walking along different paths and speaking with different assumptions and terms of reference. Both seem to be unable to get their ideas across. For a project to be successful, there needs to be a common vision of what the system must do. With use cases, you can get that common understanding.

There are various types of requirements. Some are functional, some are nonfunctional. But so long as they impose behaviors on the system, use cases will be applicable. You have application use cases to deal with application concerns and infrastructure use cases to deal with infrastructure concerns. Thus, with use cases, you have a common way of modeling crosscutting concerns.

We have stressed the importance of exploring the variations your system needs to handle and a means to describe them. This applies to all kinds of use cases. It is important that you identify such variables and their values early in the project. Otherwise, you miss key requirements and get a rude shock about the perceived scope of the requirements. How these variables are handled can be described with use cases, or they can be postponed to analysis when you refine the use cases.

This chapter introduced the ⟨Perform Transaction⟩ use case. It describes a pattern for how each step of an application use case is conducted. It provides the context for you to generically describe where infrastructure use cases extend application use cases. As you will see in the subsequent chapters, this ⟨Perform Transaction⟩ use case is crucial to describe concerns regarding the distribution of the system into different processing nodes, concerns regarding the execution platform, and in fact a wide range of concerns about the architecture in general. Thus, as an architect, you need to pay special attention to this use case.

PART III

Keeping Concerns Separate with Use-Case Modules

Now that you have correctly modeled stakeholder concerns with use cases, the next step is to preserve that separation during design and implementation. Separation is maintained through a new modularity unit called a *use-case slice*. A use-case slice contains classes and extensions to existing classes (organized within aspects) that are specific to each use-case realization in the design model. Thus, the design model comprises an element structure (a hierarchical organization of elements in terms of layers, packages, subsystems, etc.) and a set of use-case slices that overlay behaviors onto these elements. In the past, developers have implemented directly on the element structure. The result is that concerns were entangled in these elements. With use-case slices, developers can now implement each use case separately and let the development environment compose the use-case slices to form the complete set of elements in the design model.

In Part III, we demonstrate with examples how to preserve the separation of both peer and extension use cases through use-case slices. In essence, you start with the realization of a use case with a set of classes, and then you determine which parts of these classes are specific to the use case and which parts are common among use cases. You collate the specific parts as class extensions within use-case slices. Use-case slices employ aspects to compose class extensions into their respective classes in the element structure. Thus, you must determine the structural context of the extension (i.e., to which class or operation the extensions will be added) and the behavioral context (i.e., when during execution of the operation the operation extensions will be executed). Our modeling construct for use-case slices highlights such context information explicitly and thereby helps you visualize how their use-case slices will be composed. It also provides a systematic means to identify intertype declarations, pointcuts, and advices during implementation.

Software development is the process of building models—each describing the system from a particular perspective—from the use-case model to the analysis model, to the design model, and finally to the implementation model. Whereas use-case slices keep together the specifics of a use case in *a* model, *use-case modules* keep the specifics of a use case together over *all* models for the entire system. Thus, use-case modules comprise slices for the various models in the system.

Part III includes the following chapters:

Chapter 8, "Keeping Peer Use Cases Separate with Use-Case Slices"

Chapter 9, "Keeping Extensions Separate with Pointcuts"

Chapter 10, "Building Systems with Use-Case Modules"

8

Keeping Peer Use-Case Realizations Separate with Aspects

With use cases, you can keep concerns separate during requirements time, but that is not enough. You also need to preserve that separation during design and implementation. In this chapter, we look at a particular kind of use case called a peer use case. Peer use cases have no relationship with one another, but their realizations involve the participation of some shared classes. You may find that some classes and some parts of classes are shared and reusable across use cases, while others are specific to each use-case realization. A use-case slice modularizes the specifics of a use case in a model. It utilizes aspects as a composition mechanism to extend use-case-specific features (attributes, relationships, and operations) onto these shared classes.

8.1   Realizing Peer Use Cases

From a use-case modeling perspective, peer use cases have no relationships (i.e., inclusion, extension, or generalization) between them. When attempting to realize peer use cases, you find that they impact the same classes, which is why they are called peers. The Reserve Room and Check In Customer use cases, as shown in Figure 8–1, are examples of peer use cases for the Hotel Management System. These two use cases affect the Room class, as we shall see in a minute.

The fact that there are no relationships between peer use cases means that it is possible to get different persons to detail peer use cases separately and in parallel. Some coordination definitely is required, since their authors have to use the same vocabulary. When you start to realize peer use cases, you want to work on them separately and in parallel.

8.1.1   Collaborations

The realizations of use cases are modeled using collaborations. Use cases describe a system from the external perspective—how actors interact with the system. Use cases do not describe a system's internals—how classes within the system collaborate to realize the use case. The internals are modeled by collaborations. A collaboration defines a set of class instances that cooperate to achieve a given task. The task can be the realization of a use case or the realization of an infrastructure mechanism,

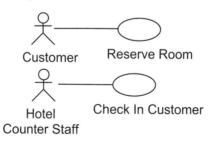

Figure 8-1   *Peer use cases.*

and so on. Thus, use cases and collaborations are two sides of a coin—the use case describes the system from the external perspective and the collaboration describes the system from an internal perspective. Figure 8–2 depicts the relationship between the Reserve Room use case and its realization modeled as a collaboration. UML denotes a collaboration as a dashed ellipse icon containing the name of the collaboration, and the dashed arrow with a triangle arrowhead in Figure 8–2 denotes the realization relationship in UML.

A collaboration identifies different roles classes play to realize a use case. The collaboration demands a number of features (i.e., attributes, operations, and relationships) on classes that play these roles. For example, the Reserve Room use-case realization (see Figure 8–3) requires a class to play the role of the resource being reserved. This role is fulfilled by the Room class. Assuming that the Room class at this moment has no such features, you have to extend (i.e., add onto) the Room class with the two required operations updateAvailability() and retrieve().

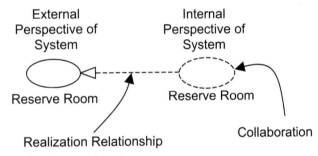

Figure 8-2   *A use case is realized by a collaboration.*

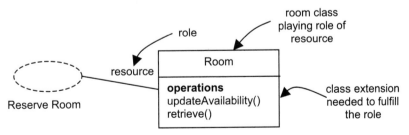

Figure 8-3   *Collaboration identifies class extensions.*

A *class extension* is a modular extension to an existing class to play the role identified by a collaboration (use-case realization). Sometimes, you do not need to add complete operations into the existing class. Instead, you might need only to extend an existing operation with some behaviors to play the role identified by the collaboration. This modular extension to an existing operation is known as an *operation extension*.

8.1.2   Realizing a Use Case

When you realize a use case, you identify classes that participate in the realization and the required roles thereafter expressed as features of these classes. You do this by walking through the use-case specifications, and at each step of a use-case flow, determining the classes you need. In the case of the Reserve Room use-case realization, we have identified two classes: the ReserveRoomHandler class and the Room class. Regarding the Reserve Room collaboration, the classes ReserveRoomHandler and Room play two different roles.

1. The ReserveRoomHandler class plays the role of a controller. It coordinates other classes in the realization of the Reserve Room use case. In particular, it has a makeReservation() operation to coordinate the actions to make a reservation.
2. The Room class plays the role of a resource that can be reserved. It is responsible for retrieving and updating information about the room's availability.

In reality, more classes are involved (e.g., a Reservation class), but for simplicity, we restrict our discussion to just these two classes. We deal with more complex examples in the next part of the book. In addition, the classes ReserveRoomHandler and Room may play other roles in other collaborations (i.e., use-case realizations).

You identify the features required for each class by walking through each step of a use-case description and determining how a particular class instance invokes another class instance. This can be represented using interaction diagrams such as that depicted in Figure 8–4. An interaction diagram depicts the chronological ordering from one class instance to another class instance.

Figure 8–4 shows the sequence of actions that occur when some client invokes the `makeReservation()` operation on a `ReserveRoomHandler` instance. The `ReserveRoomHandler` instance retrieves details of rooms and updates their availability accordingly. This is achieved by calling two operations on a `Room` instance: `retrieve()` and `updateAvailability()`.

Once you have identified the required features of each class, you present them in a collaboration, as shown in Figure 8–5. The roles played by the `ReserveRoomHandler` and `Room` classes are denoted by labels on the ends of the solid lines (known as associations in UML) joining the collaboration and the class extensions in Figure 8–5.

In Figure 8–5, each class extension identifies only a subset of a class's features. Consider the `Room` class extension. It identifies only the operations `updateAvailability()` and `retrieve()`. The complete `Room` class will have other operations. The final `Room` class is a composition of all `Room` class extensions over all use-case realizations.

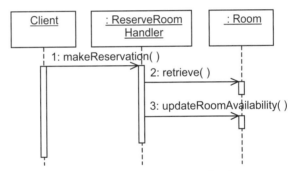

Figure 8-4   *An interaction diagram for the Reserve Room use-case realization.*

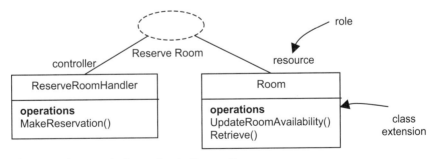

Figure 8-5   *Class extensions required to realize the Reserve Room use case.*

Figure 8–5 shows only operations in class extensions. In general, a collaboration identifies other kinds of features in a class extension, such as attributes and relationships. You identify these similarly to the way you identify operations. So, it suffices for us to limit our discussion to operations throughout this chapter. We want to keep the discussion simple.

8.1.3   Overlap between Peer Use-Case Realizations

To illustrate how the realization of peer use cases overlaps, we need the help of another use-case realization—the realization of the Check In Customer use case. It involves a new `CheckInHandler` class, which plays the role of a controller and the same `Room` class we had earlier. The interaction between these classes when a client invokes the `checkIn()` operation on a `CheckInHandler` instance is illustrated in Figure 8–6.

When a client invokes the `checkIn()` operation on a `CheckInHandler` instance, the latter retrieves details of rooms and assigns a lodger to the room. This is achieved by invoking two operations on a `Room` instance: `retrieve()` and `assignLodger()`.

The roles played by the classes and the operations required by the Check In Customer use-case realization are summarized in Figure 8–7.

Consider the realization of the two use cases above—Reserve Room and Check In Customer. You find that the roles in the Check In Customer collaboration and those in the Reserve Room collaboration are the same. This, however, does not constitute overlap, since these roles belong to different collaborations. This is analogous to two classes having some attributes with the same name. It is legal, and it does not constitute an overlap.

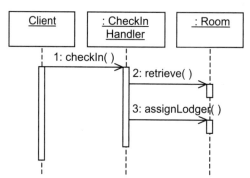

Figure 8-6   *An interaction diagram for another use-case realization: Check In Customer.*

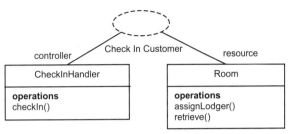

Figure 8-7   *Classes extensions required to realize the Check In Customer use case.*

The two use-case realizations require classes that are specific to them, such as `ReserveRoomHandler` and `CheckInHandler`. They require classes that are shared—the `Room` class—which constitutes overlap (i.e., overlapping classes). In addition, the `retrieve()` operation needed in the `Room` class extension is used in both collaborations—this also constitutes overlap (i.e., overlapping operations).

In the absence of aspect orientation, a developer today would collate the extensions for each class before implementing the class itself. Some of these classes would be existing classes, and he or she would add the new features into them. Some of these would be new classes that have not been previously identified, and the developer would need to create them in the correct package in the design model. This, as we all know, leads to scattering of the use-case realization and tangling of classes. You need to keep the specifics of a use-case realization separate, which we demonstrate in the next section.

8.2   Keeping Use-Case Specifics Separate

To preserve the modularity of use cases during their realization in a model, a new modularity unit is needed to contain the elements (and extensions of elements) that are specific to the use-case realization. We call this modularity unit a *use-case slice* because its contents are for a specific *use case* and it cuts, or *slices*, across a model (the design model in this case.)

A use-case slice contains the following:

1.   A collaboration that describes the realization of the use case.

2. Classes specific to the use-case realization.
3. Extensions of existing classes specific to the use-case realization.

For each use case, there will be a use-case slice in the design model. Thus, for the Reserve Room use case, there is a corresponding Reserve Room use-case slice. The Reserve Room use-case slice contains the following:

1. **Collaboration.** The collaboration contains a set of diagrams (interaction diagrams, class diagrams, etc.) that describe how the Reserve Room is realized.
2. **Specific Classes.** The `ReserveRoomHandler` class is specific to this use-case realization and is not needed in the Check In Customer use-case realization.
3. **Specific Extensions.** The `Room` class is needed by several use-case realizations. However, the `updateAvailability()` is specific to the Reserve Room use-case realization. This is defined within a class extension in the use-case slice.

The `retrieve()` operation is required by different use-case realizations and is defined in some other lower use-case slice (such as that for included use case or a generalized use case) or a non-use-case-specific slice. We discuss them in subsequent sections.

Figure 8–8 depicts the Reserve Room use-case slice. It is a special kind of package and is stereotyped as «use case slice». You normally name a use-case slice with the same name as its corresponding use case. The collaboration it contains is named the same way.

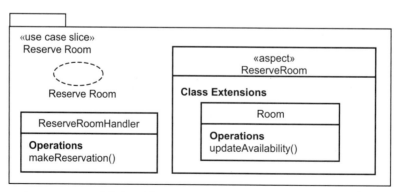

Figure 8-8   *Preserving use-case modularity with use-case slices and aspects.*

The Reserve Room use-case slice contains a class `ReserveRoomHandler` and a `Room` class extension. You need a mechanism to compose the `Room` class fragment into the existing `Room` class. This is achieved using aspects in AOP. We model aspects as an element stereotyped «aspect». It represents our proposed UML construct for modeling aspects. Aspects have a class extensions compartment to overlay class extensions onto existing classes. With AOP, this is achieved using intertype declarations and advices.

Each use-case slice keeps the specifics of a use-case realization in a model—in this case, the design model. Different use-case slices are then superimposed to form the design model. This concept is best explained through an overhead projector metaphor. Use-case slices are like slides (or transparencies) or overlays, and the design model is like the screen. We can put slides on top of each other and project the result on the screen. We can work on the slides independently, but some coordination is required so that we can project their contents coherently. For example, we can project the anatomy of the human body with one slide to show the bones, one slide to show the arteries and veins, and yet another slide to show the internal organs. We can draw each slide independently, but their positions must correspond across the respective slides.

With software design, the namespace in the design model ensures that use-case slices can be composed properly. In the remainder of this section, we discuss in detail how use-case slices are composed into the design model.

8.2.1   Composing Use-Case-Specific Classes

Let us look at how the classes specific to a use-case realization are composed into the design model by considering the `ReserveRoomHandler` class. Suppose you have organized your design model into layers and packages and you have an application layer, which contains a customer application package within it, and you want to add the `ReserveRoom-Handler` class into it.

You can add this class directly into the designated package in the design model, but that will result in a problem. If you want to remove the use-case slice, you would have to remove all classes that the use-case slice has added as well.

Instead, you want to keep the `ReserveRoomHandler` class within the Reserve Room use-case slice, as depicted in Figure 8–9. The left-hand side of Figure 8–9 depicts the design element structure. A structure is basically a containment hierarchy of elements of some kind—in this case, of the design element structure. It comprises layers and packages, and classes. The right-hand side depicts a use-case slice containing the specifics of the use-case realization.

We now discuss how to overlay the `ReserveRoomHandler` class in the Reserve Room use-case slice onto the design element structure (see Figure 8–9). First, you need to identify the class uniquely in the design element structure. This is achieved by giving a fully qualified name in the design element structure. Do note that at this moment, the `ReserveRoomHan-dler` in the design element structure is empty—you only have its name (see ①). A composition mechanism (such as a compiler) would then compose the `ReserveRoomHandler` in the use-case slice (indicated by ②) into the design element structure.

Today, composing use-case-specific classes such as the one in Figure 8–9 is achievable in all compilers. Identifying a fully qualified name is achieved by specifying the namespace of the class in the design model. Namespaces are available in most conventional languages like C++, Java, and C#. In Java, this is achieved with the **package** keyword, as shown in Listing 8–1.

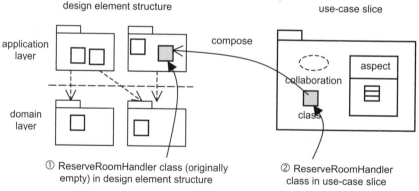

Figure 8-9   *Overlaying classes within use-case slice onto design element structure.*

Listing 8-1   Class Specific to Use-Case Realization: ReserveRoomHandler.java

```
1.  package app.customer ;
2.  public class ReserveRoomHandler {
3.    public void makeReservation() {
4.      // code
5.    }
6.  }
```

In line 1, we define the namespace for `ReserveRoomHandler` as residing in the customer package within the app (application) layer. After defining the namespace, we can start to define the `ReserveRoomHandler` class, as shown in line 2. Thereafter, we add the `makeReservation()` operation in lines 3, 4, and 5. Thus, we can keep classes specific to a use-case realization separate in a use-case slice.

When you are working with source code, you are dealing with the implementation model. The implementation use-case structure represents your source files (i.e., `*.java`). The implementation element structure represents the binary files (i.e., `*.class`). Note that AspectJ can perform what is known as byte code—it can insert behavior into binaries even without source code.

8.2.2   Composing Use-Case-Specific Class Extensions

Let us now look at how to compose class extensions onto existing classes in the design element structure. This capability was not available in conventional languages until the advent of AOP. AOP provides you with inter-type declarations to add features on top of existing classes. This is depicted in Figure 8–10 by the arrow labeled compose. The features to be overlaid onto an existing class are collated within a class extension.

In our example, the `Room` class is an existing class within the design element structure. It has been previously overlaid onto the design element structure, and now we want to overlay additional class extensions. Let's assume that the `Room` class resides in the room package in a domain layer. Having identified the `Room` class, we can now overlay the `Room` class extension specific to the Reserve Room use-case slice onto the Room class in the design element structure.

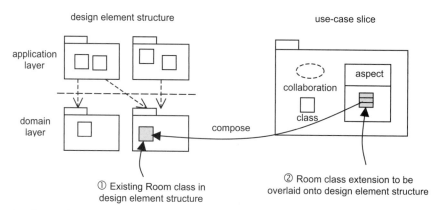

Figure 8-10   *Overlaying class extensions within use-case slices onto the design element structure.*

This is achieved in AOP using aspects with intertype declarations. We call this aspect `ReserveRoom`, since it is used in the realization of the Reserve Room use case—we simply remove the space within string "Reserve Room." Compilers today don't like spaces. Listing 8–2 shows how you can add an operation to the existing `Room` class.

Listing 8-2   Reserve Room Aspect in AspectJ: ReserveRoom.java

```
1.  package app.customer ;
2.  import domain.room.Room;
3.  public aspect ReserveRoom {
4.  public void Room.updateAvailability() {
5.  // code
6.  }
7.  }
```

Like the `ReserveRoomHandler` class, the `ReserveRoom` aspect resides in the application-layer customer package (see line 1 of Listing 8–2). This is the namespace for the aspect, not the class you are extending. Line 2 identifies the existing `Room` class that you want to extend. In lines 4, 5, and 6, we extend the `Room` class in the design element structure with a new operation, `updateAvailability()`.

In this case, the aspect contains an intertype declaration for only one class. However, in general, you will compose multiple operations onto multiple classes. It will be natural for you to organize these intertype declarations that add features to the same class together, which is not required by AOP or AspectJ, in particular, but we find it a good practice to do so. That is why we have class extensions—they are modular extensions onto existing classes.

In addition, it is important to have a means to visualize and understand the overall effects aspects have on each individual class. Hence, it is extremely useful to explicitly model all advices and intertype declarations on each existing class. Moreover, this is how you work with collaborations today—you identify roles and then the attributes, operations, and so on, for that role. So, you see that class extensions are derived naturally when you identify roles in a collaboration. Thus, there is indeed methodological support for using class extensions.

Our proposed UML aspect contains class extensions, as depicted in Figure 8–11. This figure shows the `ReserveRoom` aspect containing a class extension called `Room`. The class extension is named this way so that you know which class its features must be composed into. In this case, the class extension has an `updateAvailability()`operation. During compilation, this will be composed into the existing `Room` class.

8.2.3   Collaborations in Use-Case Slices

Recall that a use-case slice also has a collaboration describing the realization of the use case. The collaboration only describes a view of the model's internal structure (comprising classes, subsystems, components, etc.) to show which of these elements are needed to realize the use case. The collaboration is not part of the internal structure itself. Consequently, you do not need an implementation construct for a collaboration.

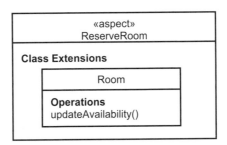

Figure 8-11   *Proposed UML aspect construct containing class extensions.*

Sidebar 8–1   How to Implement Use-Case Slices with Eclipse

For those who are familiar with Eclipse Integrated Development Environment (IDE), we show how to keep the use-case structure and the element structure separate. Note that this is but one example of applying the concept of use-case slices. In this case, we apply compile-time composition of use-case slices.

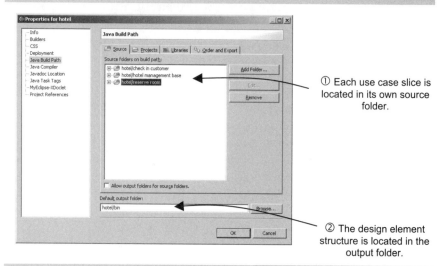

① Each use case slice is located in its own source folder.

② The design element structure is located in the output folder.

Each use-case slice or non-use-case-specific slice has its own source folder (① in the figure above). This is where developers spend their time writing Java codes for each slice. The design element structure is located in the output folder (② in the figure above). Basically, the AspectJ compiler compiles each use-case slice and composes the result into the design element structure.

8.3   Dealing with Overlap

As mentioned, a use-case slice contains elements that are specific to a particular use case. What about those elements that are required by more than one peer use-case slice? For example, the `retrieve()` operation in the `Room` class is used in both Reserve Room and Check In Customer use-case slices. You cannot put shared elements in any of the peer use-case slices because that will mean a dependency from one peer use-case slice to another, which violates the very idea of peers—there should not be relationships between them.

Recall that in use-case modeling, you can factor out common behaviors with use-case include and generalization. You can apply a similar technique with use-case slices and define corresponding semantics for include and generalization relationships between use-case slices. Another way is to put these common classes and features into what we call a non-use-case-specific slice.

8.3.1   Included Use-Case Slice

An included use-case slice is used to factor out commonalities across use-case realizations. Figure 8–12 shows the Reserve Room use case, including the Check Room Details use case. The Check Room Details use case is a utility use case that contains a set of flows that are useful for making general queries on rooms, such as checking room availability, checking room rates, checking who is staying in the room at the moment, and checking the outstanding charges for the room. Such flows are included not only by the Reserve Room use case but also by many other use cases in the Hotel Management System, such as Check In Customer and Check Out Customer use cases.

The Check Room Details use case provides the ability to retrieve rooms. Let's assume that this functionality is used often and there is some caching mechanism to make retrieval faster. The realization of the Check Room Details use case comprises two classes: `CheckRoomHandler`, which plays the role of a controller, and the `Room` class, which plays the role of a resource.

Figure 8–13 shows the interaction between instances of the two classes. Let's assume that the `CheckRoomHandler` maintains a local cache containing data values of room details to minimize retrievals from the datastore. When some client invokes the `retrieveRoom()` operation on a `CheckRoomHandler` instance, the latter first tries to get data values from its cache. If the data values are not available, `CheckRoomHandler` instance invokes `retrieve()` on a `Room` instance to retrieve them from the datastore. If local data values are available, it is returned to the client.

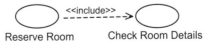

Figure 8-12   *Factoring out common behaviors with use-case include.*

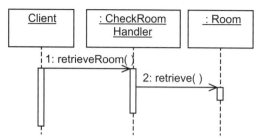

Figure 8-13   *Interaction diagram: Check Room Detail use-case realization.*

Let us see how the include relationship between use cases gets propagated to their use-case realizations and, hence, how the including use-case slice can make use of the included use-case slice. This is modeled as a dependency between use-case slices. Figure 8–14 shows the Reserve Room (i.e., including) use-case slice, including the Check Room Details (i.e., included) use-case slice. We model the include relationship between use-case slices as a dependency stereotyped as «include».

Recall that a use-case slice comprises collaborations, classes, and features specific to a use case in a model. Thus, semantics of the include relationship between use cases gets translated to relationships between these elements.

Collaborations. A collaboration identifies the features required by classes to play the roles in the collaboration. It provides the means to view what is needed by a use-case realization through interaction diagrams. The interaction diagrams in the including use-case slice can reference the interaction diagrams in the included use-case slice. This translates to a dependency from the including collaboration to the included collaboration.

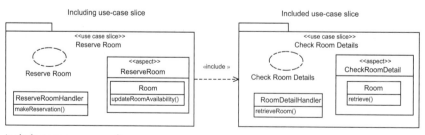

Figure 8-14   *Include across use-case slices.*

Classes. Classes in the including use-case slice can make use of classes in the included use-case slice. For example, the ReserveRoomHandler class can have an association or a dependency to the CheckRoomHandler class. This allows a ReserveRoomHandler instance to make a call such as retrieveRoom() on a CheckRoomHandler instance.

Extensions. Features defined in the included use-case slice are made available to the including use-case slice. This is exemplified by the retrieve() operation defined in the Check Room Details. The Check-RoomDetail aspect extends the Room class with this operation to be used by the ReserveRoomHandler instance defined in the Reserve Room use-case slice.

In this case, there are no dependencies between the aspects in the two use-case slices. They do not make use of each other. Only classes make use of each other, so dependencies between classes suffice.

8.3.2   Generalized Use-Case Slice

Recall that a parent use case has two purposes. First, it defines common behaviors that can be inherited by their children. Second, it acts like a template for their children. Figure 8–15 shows the Reserve Room use case inheriting from a Reserve Facility use case. The Reserve Facility use case is an abstract use case that describes in general terms the sequence of actions leading to the reservation of a facility. The Reserve Room use case specializes the Reserve Facility use case for making room reservations.

The realization of the parent use case is depicted through an interaction diagram in Figure 8–16. It shows the interaction between instances of the two classes. When some client invokes the makeReservation() operation on a ReserveFacilityHandler instance, the latter invokes retrieve() on a Facility and thereafter updates its availability.

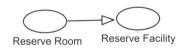

Reserve Room   Reserve Facility

Figure 8-15   *Factoring out common behaviors with use-case generalization.*

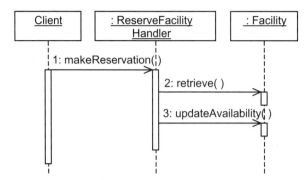

Figure 8-16   *Interaction diagram: Reserve Facility use-case realization.*

Let us see how the generalization relationship between use cases is propagated to their use-case realizations and, hence, how the child use-case slice can utilize the parent use-case slice. Figure 8–17 shows the contents of the two use-case slices. We call the Reserve Room use-case slice the child use-case slice and the Reserve Facility use-case slice the parent use-case slice. For the purpose of discussion, let's assume that both operations, `makeReservation()` and `updateAvailability()`, are abstract and that the `retrieve()` operation is concrete.

Collaboration. The collaborations in both use-case slices occur at different levels of abstraction. The Reserve Facility collaboration describes

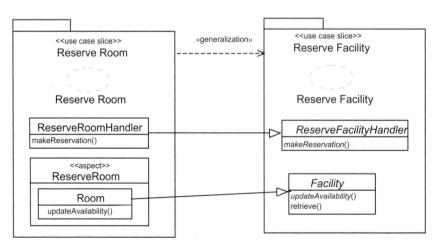

Figure 8-17   *Generalization across use-case slice.*

generic behaviors, and the Reserve Room use-case slice describes more specific behaviors. In general, they are separate (they describe things at different levels of abstraction), so there are no dependencies between them. But a child collaboration can make use of the parent collaboration, in which case there will be a dependency between collaborations.

Classes. A class such as the `ReserveRoomHandler` can have a generalization relationship to the `ReserveFacilityHandler` parent class and inherits the features of the parent class. Through the aspect, you can add a generalization relationship from the `Room` class to the `Facility` class through the aspect in the child use-case slice. These generalizations are depicted in Figure 8–11. Once the generalizations are added, a child can make use of its parent's features.

Features. If the features in the parent are abstract, the child has to make them concrete. In the example above, the `makeReservation()` operation in the `ReserveFacilityHandler` class is abstract. The `Reserve-RoomHandler` class has to provide a concrete definition. The same goes for the `updateAvailability()` operation in the `Facility` class. If the features in the parent are concrete, the child can redefine them.

Let us consider what happens if the `retrieve()` operation in the Reserve Facility use-case slice is also abstract. Since, the Reserve Room use-case slice does not define it, it is incomplete. In this case, the Reserve Room use-case slice must include another use-case slice, such as the Check Room Details, or have a dependency to the non-use-case-specific slice to import the definition.

There can be generalization between aspects, but we discuss them in the next chapter.

8.3.3   Non-Use-Case-Specific Slice

Some classes are part of the problem domain, and they are used in many use-case realizations. The realization of the Reserve Room use case and the Check In Customer use case need the same `Room` class. In fact, this `Room` class us needed by many other use-case realizations, even included use-case slices like the Check Room Details discussed above.

The Room class is part of the domain and is fundamental to the Hotel Management System. Without rooms, there wouldn't be a hotel, let alone a Hotel Management System. Hence, the Room class is not use-case-specific and should not be defined in a use-case slice. Instead, it is part of what we call a non-use-case-specific slice. It is stereotyped as «non-uc specific slice». Other use-case slices will extend it, as depicted in Figure 8–18.

A non-use-case-specific slice is different from a use-case slice in that it contains no aspects. This is because it defines a base and does not need to add to any existing classes. Non-use-case-specific slices usually represent a domain of some kind. It can be a business domain, such as Hotel Management (see Figure 8–18), or it can be used to represent some technical or infrastructural domain, such as user interfaces or communications. These also normally need a set of common classes, which individual use-case slices will add on to. For example, different use-case slices might need to add their respective menu options to a common menu bar. We present many examples of non-use-case-specific slices in Part IV of the book when we discuss how to establish an architecture based on use cases and aspects.

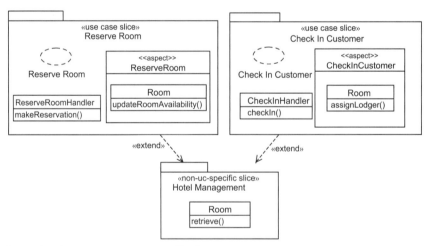

Figure 8-18   *Dependencies on non-use-case–specific slice.*

> **Sidebar 8-2   Instead of Non-Use-Case-Specific Slice, Can We Use an Abstract Use-Case Slice?**
>
> Use-case slices of abstract use cases present possible alternatives to non-use-case-specific slices. If you start to generalize all use cases in a use-case model or a use-case package, you will end up with one or more abstract use cases. The use-case slices for these abstract use cases will contain the domain classes needed by all other use-case slices. This suggests that it might not be necessary to have non-use-case-specific slices and that use-case slices alone are sufficient.
>
> However, using use-case slices of abstract use cases instead of non-use-case slices might have adverse implications when it comes to practice. Practitioners might spend excessive time to find these abstract use cases. So, from a practical standpoint, we allow the use of non-use-case-specific slices for the time being. Indeed, non-use-case-specific slices can be considered a special case of a use-case slice that contains no aspects.
>
> There is another reason why we have non-use-case-specific slices: they contain no aspects and are therefore readily applied in non-aspect-oriented environments today. If you are subject to some project constraints that disallow aspect orientation, you can still apply the concept of slices and overlays advocated in this book. Although you are prevented from using use-case slices, you can still use non-use-case-specific slices. This is an advantage because it provides a gradual path in applying the approach suggested in this book. You first get acquainted with the concept of slices using only non-use-case-specific slices. Thereafter, you apply use-case slices containing aspects.

8.4   Summary and Highlights

In this chapter, we demonstrated how you can keep the realizations of peer use cases separate. This is achieved through a new modularity unit, which we call a use-case slice. A use-case slice contains the collaborations, classes, and features specific to a use-case realization. Table 8–1 summarizes the correspondence between elements of a use-case slice during design (with UML) and during implementation (with AOP).

Table 8.1   *Mapping UML Constructs in to AOP Constructs*

UML Constucts	AOP Constructs
Use-case slice	Package
Collaboration	None
Aspect	Aspect
Class extension	Grouping of intertype declarations for each class

We have to emphasize that use-case slices are not the typical packages you find in a design model. The design model contains a hierarchical element structure in terms of layers, packages, and so on. Even though use-case slices are part of the design model, they are orthogonal to this element structure. Use-case slices are overlays on top of this element structure. Each time you add a use-case slice on top of this element structure, you superimpose the contents of the use-case slice into it. If you remove a use-case slice, all contents in the use-case slice (class and features) are removed from this element structure as well.

In this chapter, we also showed how the include and generalization relationships between use cases in the use-case model are translated to corresponding relationships between use-case slices in the design model. In the next chapter, we show how the extend relationship in the use-case model is propagated into the design model. In this way, we have preserved all use-case relationships existing in the use-case model in the design model.

9

Keeping Extensions Separate with Pointcuts

Extension use cases are a special kind of use case that allows you to keep additional functionality separate from an existing use case. The realization of extension use cases requires additional behavior to be defined into existing operations. This is often intrusive with traditional techniques. Through aspects, use-case slices keep these operation extensions separate from the existing operations. They are subsequently executed at designated points specified by pointcuts during compilation or execution. Pointcuts are parameterizable, which allows you to apply the same extensions on multiple points at once. This parameterization capability can also be used in conjunction with templating to address a wider range of problems. In addition, with abstract pointcuts, you can have prebuilt extensions that can be attached to desired points later.

9.1   Realizing Extension Use Cases

Let us do a quick recap of what we have discussed earlier on extension use cases. Each use case has a set of extension points by which you can extend its behavior. An extension use case will introduce additional behaviors (which we call extension flows) into existing use cases at designated extension points. The designation of extension points is achieved through extension pointcuts. This keeps the separation of the extension and the existing (also known as the base) use case separate during requirements time.

When we discussed the composition of a use-case slice into the design model in Chapter 8, "Keeping Peer Use-Case Realizations Separate with Aspects," we dealt only with complete operations. You had only to overlay complete operations onto existing classes. However, when you realize extension use cases, you need to add behaviors (or what we call operation extensions and what AOP calls advices) into existing operations at precise points designated by pointcuts. This means that to keep the separation of extension use-case realizations from the base use-case realization, you need a more fine-grained composition mechanism than that discussed in Chapter 8.

The discussion in this chapter uses a simple example of a logging extension. More complex examples are available in the next part of the book. The Logging extension use case is an infrastructure mechanism that extends both the Reserve Room and Check In Customer use cases, as shown in Figure 9–1.

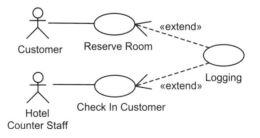

Figure 9-1   *Logging use case.*

The objective of the logging extension is to count the number of requests on enquiries about any room types and whether or not they are successful. This information allows us to subsequently analyze the relative popularity of various room types in our hotel.

9.2   Keeping Modularity of Extension Use-Case Realizations

Let us begin by considering how we will extend the Reserve Room use-case realization with the Logging extension. In the Logging extension, we have two roles. The two roles and the classes that play these roles are depicted in Figure 9–2.

The first role is that of a logger. The class that plays this role saves the number of room requests and their outcomes into some persistent data storage. Most language environments provide data storage capability. In this example, let's assume that we will create a `LogStream` class, which merely encapsulates that capability with a `log()` operation that stores information into a stream (e.g., text file).

With the `LogStream` class, we now have the ability to store information into a file, but we also need to extract the required information in the first place. In the Reserve Room use-case realization, the `ReserveRoomHandler` is the class responsible for making room requests. The `ReserveRoomHandler` class plays the role of a target, and we need operation extensions to be composed onto the target to extract the required information.

We now identify the specific execution point at which the operation extension will be composed onto the target. Figure 9–3 shows the sequence diagram describing the interactions within the Reserve Room use-case

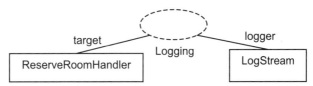

Figure 9-2   *Roles in Logging extension.*

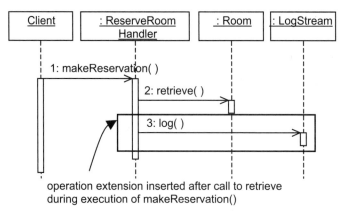

operation extension inserted after call to retrieve
during execution of makeReservation()

Figure 9-3   *Extending existing operation«aspect».*

realization. When a Client invokes `makeReservation()` on a `Reserve-RoomHandler` instance, the latter invokes `retrieve()` on a `Room` instance.

On top of this base interaction, we overlay the logging operation extension. This is framed within a box in Figure 9–3. This box also depicts where the additional behavior is executed. It occurs within the `makeReservation()` operation after the call `Room.retrieve()` is completed. In essence, the operation extension invokes the `log()` operation on the `LogStream` instance to store the required information—whether or not the call to `retrieve()` on a `Room` instance is successful.

9.2.1   Operation Extensions

An operation extension comprises the behavior specific to a use-case realization within an operation. In our example, the operation extension is responsible for simply invoking the `log()` operation on the `LogStream` instance. An operation extension maps to an advice in AOP.

Structural and Behavioral Context. You must note two things when identifying the place to execute the operation extension: the structural context and the behavioral context. The structural context describes where in the design element structure you will be overlaying the operation extension—that is, which package, which class, and which operation you will be executing within. In our example, we are executing the operation extension within the `makeReservation()` operation within the `ReserveRoomHandler` class.

The behavioral context identifies the point in the execution flow where the operation extension extends the existing operation. This point corresponds to what we term in use-case modeling as extension point, and corresponds to the concept of join points in AOP. In our example, we are only interested in calls to `retrieve()` on a `Room` class. You might be interested in which class or operation is calling `makeReservation()` itself, or even in the caller of that calling class. In general, the execution context will refer to the state of the call stack.

In addition, it is also useful to give the operation extension a name that describes what it does.

Operation Extension Declaration. Recall that the name of a class extension describes which existing class in the design element structure we want to overlay. Likewise, the declaration of an operation extension expresses where in the existing operation we will be extending and what the operation extension is doing. Accordingly, the operation extension declaration will have these three segments. We express the declaration in the following form:

```
structural context  + behavioral context + operation extension
```

In Figure 9–3, the declaration of the logging operation extension is specified as follows:

```
makeReservation()  {after call(Room.retrieve()) logData }
```

The first segment, `makeReservation()`, describes the existing operation within which we will be executing. We do not need to express it as something like `ReserveRoomHandler.makeReservation()`, because the operation extension will be placed within a class extension in an aspect, and this identifies the class to which the operation extension belongs.

The second segment, **call**(`Room.retrieve()`), identifies the extension point when a call is made to the operation `retrieve()` in the `Room` class. This expression is what AOP terms a pointcut. The **after** keyword is a modifier to define where that operation extension will be executed relative to the pointcut. The semantics of the operation extension declaration are that we will be executing the operation extension within the execution of the `makeReservation()` *after* `makeReservation()` completes a call to the `retrieve()` operation in a `Room` instance.

Finally, the third segment, `logData`, indicates what the operation extension actually does.

Figure 9–4 depicts the complete Logging extension use-case slice, with the `Logging` collaboration, the `LogStream` class, and the `Logging` aspect. Notice that the `LogStream` class resides outside the `Logging` aspect. This is because, the `LogStream` class is a new class that we created for the logging functionality.

The UML aspect contains class extensions, each containing a subset of features (attributes, operations' and relationships) specific to the use case it realizes. This gives a good representation of the overall effects a use-case realization has on an existing class. As shown in Figure 9–4, an operation extension resides within a class extension. This is useful to identify the structural context of the operation extension—that is, which class and which operation you are extending. This provides a good indication of the overall effect a use-case realization has on an existing operation.

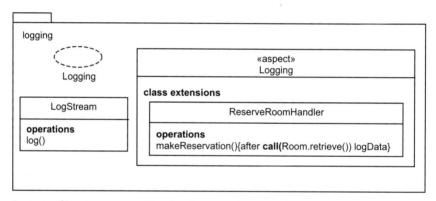

Figure 9-4   *Contents of logging use-case slice showing operation extensions.*

9.2.2   Pointcuts

Let's take a closer look at the expression **call**(Room.retrieve()). It is a direct reference to a specific extension point in the existing makeReservation() operation where a call to the retrieve() operation in the Room class is made. Such direct referencing makes it sensitive to changes. So, for instance, if the retrieve() operation is renamed read(), the referenced extension point will no longer be valid. Therefore, such a direct reference to an extension point is not good.

A better option is to give the extension point a meaningful name that signifies what the existing operation is doing when you need to execute the operation extension. You can then define the actual extension point separately. In our example, we want to track the outcome of calls to the Room class, so a name like roomCall is more meaningful, and you can link this name with the definition of the extension point. This naming of an extension point is known as a pointcut. The operation extension declaration is now:

```
makeReservation(){after (⟨roomCall⟩) logData}
```

The ⟨⟩ indicates that roomCall in the operation extension declaration is a parameter that can be bounded to different values. This can be achieved using a pointcut expression in the aspect. Alternately, the parameter may apply to the entire use-case slice, in which case the use-case slice becomes a template.

Figure 9–5 shows the revised logging use-case slice after using a pointcut to refer to the join point (i.e., execution point) at **call**(Room.retrieve()). A pointcut named roomCall is defined as follows:

```
roomCall = call(Room.retrieve())
```

Note that there are no ⟨ ⟩ brackets in the pointcut definition. This is because using the brackets would have indicated that the name of the pointcut is parameterized, but this is not the case.

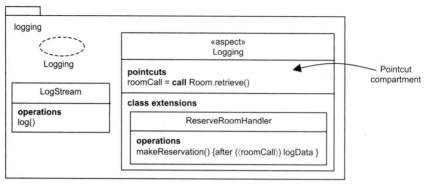

Figure 9-5 *Logging use-case slice with pointcut compartment.*

The implementation of the Logging aspect in Figure 9–5 is shown in Listing 9–1.

Listing 9-1 Logging Aspect in AspectJ: Logging.java

```
1.  package infra.logging;
2.  import app.customer.ReserveRoomHandler ;
3.  import domain.room.Room ;
4.
5.  public aspect Logging {
6.  pointcut roomCall() :
7.     withincode(void ReserveRoomHandler.makeReservation())
8.            && call(void Room.retrieve()) ;
9.
10. after () : roomCall() {
11. // code
12. }
13. }
```

The Logging aspect resides in the logging package within the infrastructure layer (see line 1). Since the aspect references the ReserveRoomHandler, it must import it, and since the pointcut roomCall contains a reference to the Room class, the Room class must be imported. These import statements are in lines 2 and 3. Note that in Chapter 8, we located the ReserveRoomHandler class in the customer package in the application layer and the Room class in the room package in the domain layer, so the Logging aspect has import statements to reference these packages.

The pointcut `roomCall` is defined in lines 6, 7, and 8. The operation extension is implemented as an advice in lines 10, 11, and 12. The keyword `after` indicates that the operation extension extends the existing operation after the join points specified by the pointcut `roomCall`.

The pointcut `roomCall` defined in lines 6, 7, and 8 is a conjunction of two smaller pointcuts separated by a logical `and` operator (denoted by `&&` in Listing 9–1). Let us look at them individually:

- The **withincode**(void   ReserveRoomHandler.makeReserva-tion()) segment refers to all possible join points in the makeReser-vation() operation.
- The **call**(void   Room.retrieve()) segment refers to all calls to the retrieve() operation in the Room class.

The conjunction of these two pointcuts matches all join points within the makeReservation() operation that are calls to Room.retrieve().

Note that we do not explicitly describe the segment **withincode** (void ReserveRoomHandler.makeReservation()) in Figure 9–5. This is because it has already been expressed by the fact that the structural context of operation extension itself. So, you see that the representation in Figure 9–5 emphasizes the context in which operation extensions execute rather than merely listing them as advices in AspectJ.

9.3   Parameterizing Pointcuts

We have just seen how we can extend a single use-case realization. In general, you might want to execute an operation extension at multiple extension points in multiple use-case realizations or even into multiple extension points in the same use-case realization. One of the key attractions of applying AOSD lies in its ease of parameterizing the definition of pointcuts with wildcards and regular expressions, which we discuss in this section.

Note that the parameters we discuss in this section are used to locate and bind the aspect onto existing classes and operations in order to extend them. There is yet another kind of parameter—a template parameter, such as those used for C++ templates. This template capability is also seen in

Java 1.5. Templates are frequently used as a means to generate classes and elements. We discuss template parameters in Section 9–5.

9.3.1   Identifying Parameters

Recall the interaction that occurs when a client class invokes a `ReserveRoomHandler` instance to perform the `makeReservation()` operation (shown in Figure 9–3). The `makeReservation()` in turn invokes the `retrieve()` operation on a `Room` instance. This is sufficient when we want to extend just the one specific `makeReservation()` operation. If we want to extend multiple operations at once, we must introduce some parameterization. Let us replace `ReserveRoomHandler`, `makeReservation()`, and `retrieve ()` with the parameters ⟨RoomAccessor⟩, ⟨roomAccessOperation⟩, and ⟨roomCall⟩ respectively. The sequence diagram shown in Figure 9–3 will now be parameterized as shown in Figure 9–6.

Recall that the objective of the Logging use-case extension is to count the successes and failures of requests made on any `Room` instances. These requests are not limited to the `retrieve()` operation, but any operation in the `Room` class itself. We collectively call these `Room` operations ⟨roomCall⟩. A number of classes may make calls to ⟨roomCall⟩. In our example, we had one class that made these calls: `ReserveRoomHandler`. Assume instead that multiple classes may invoke `Room` operations. We call these classes collectively ⟨RoomAccessor⟩. In these ⟨RoomAccessor⟩

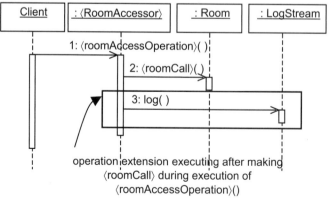

Figure 9-6   *Using sequence diagrams with parameters.*

classes, there will be various operations that will make a ⟨roomCall⟩. We collectively call these operations ⟨roomAccessOperation⟩.

9.3.2   Defining Parameters

After parameterizing the Logging extension in Figure 9–5, we have the result shown in Figure 9–7. In this case, we have defined the parameters as pointcuts. In Figure 9–7, there are three pointcuts, one for each of the three parameters RoomAccessor, roomAccessOperation, and roomCall.

Figure 9–7 shows a hierarchical structural composition. The Logging aspect contains the ⟨RoomAccessor⟩ class extension, which contains the ⟨roomAccessOperation⟩ operation, which makes a ⟨roomCall⟩. Each sets the structural context for the next and gradually narrows down the specific point where the operation extension will be executed.

The pointcut

```
RoomAccessor = ReserveRoomHandler or CheckInHandler
```

restricts the classes to be extended to the ReserveRoomHandler and the CheckInHandler classes.

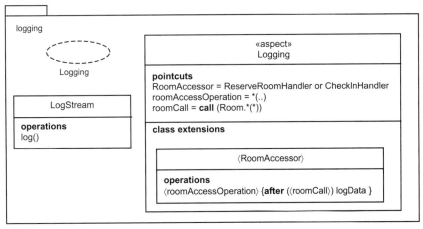

Figure 9-7   *Parameterized logging use-case slice.*

The pointcut

```
roomAccessOperation = *(..)
```

refers to any operation. However, since the parameter is in the context of the `RoomAccessor` class, it means any operation in the `RoomAccessor` class.

The pointcut

```
roomCall  = call (Room.*(..))
```

refers to any calls to any operation in the `Room` class. Together, the three pointcuts refer to any execution point in any operation of `ReserveRoom-Handler` or the `CheckInHandler` classes that make calls to any `Room` operation.

9.3.3   Parameterizing Pointcuts in AOP

Let us see how the `Logging` aspect in Figure 9–7 gets implemented in AspectJ. Since you make no changes to the behavior of the operation extension, it will be the same as what you had previously in Listing 9–1. However, since you are executing the operation extension into multiple points, the pointcuts will be changed, as shown in Listing 9–2.

Listing 9-2   Regular Expressions in AspectJ: Logging.java

```
1.      pointcut RoomAccessor():
2.              within(ReserveRoomHandler)
3.              || within(CheckInHandler) ;
4.      pointcut roomAccessOperation() :
5.              RoomAccessor()
6.              && withincode(* *(..))
7.      pointcut roomCall() :
8.              roomAccessOperation()
9.              && call(* Room.*(..)) ;
```

The pointcuts in Listing 9–2 are a direct mapping from what is in Figure 9–7. However, aspects in AspectJ have no concept of class extensions and are, therefore, unable to make use of the hierarchical context of Figure 9–7. To get around this problem, the logical and operator (denoted by `&&`) is used.

For example, lines 10, 11, and 12 show that the pointcut `roomAccessOp-eration` has two segments joined by the `&&` operator. The first segment sets the context for the second. The pointcut `roomAccessOperation` therefore refers to any operation in the `ReserveRoomHandler` or `Check-InHandler` classes.

The same goes for the `roomCall` pointcut in Lines 13, 14, and 15. It contains two segments. The first segment uses the `roomAccessOperation` pointcut to define the context for the next.

As you can see in Listing 9–2, the use of the `&&` operator makes the pointcut expression slightly lengthy. You can definitely shrink the pointcuts. For example, since the parameter `RoomAccessOperation` refers to all operations, it does not restrict anything and can therefore be left out. Thus, the `roomCall` pointcut can be expressed more compactly as follows:

```
pointcut roomCall()
    : (within(ReserveRoomHandler)||within(CheckInHandler))
    && call(* Room.*(..))
```

However, as you try to make the pointcut expressions more compact, it becomes harder to understand which points your advices are extending.

It is important that you express pointcuts in a manner that highlights the structural and behavioral context by which the advice will be executed. This greatly improves the readability of pointcut expressions.

9.4   Generalizing Extension Use-Case Realizations

Now let's consider how to generalize extensions. We continue with the Logging extension example. Suppose the required behavior for the Logging extension is the same for various existing use cases and can therefore be applied repeatedly on these different existing use cases. However, the extension points are different for these use cases. You can factor out the generic behavior into a Generic Logging aspect in which the pointcuts are deliberately undefined (i.e., they are declared abstract).

When you want to apply the logging extension behavior on an existing use case, let's say the Reserve Room use case, you specialize the Generic Logging use case into a Concrete Logging extension with the pointcuts defined. This is depicted in Figure 9–8.

If you realize the Generic and the Concrete Logging use cases, you find corresponding aspects, as shown in Figure 9–9. For brevity, we do not depict their respective use-case slices in Figure 9–9. We are interested only in the aspects here.

Since the Generic Logging use case is where the behavior is defined, you have class extensions there. However, since you are speaking in generic terms, you deliberately do not define all the pointcuts yet. Instead, you postpone the specification of the pointcuts to the child `ConcreteLogging` aspect.

Recall that the objective of the Logging extension is to count the number of successful or failed requests to the `Room` instance. So, for any given class, we are interested in any of its operations that invoke the `Room` instance. Thus, you have two pointcuts, ⟨roomAccessOperation⟩ defined as `*(*)` (i.e., any operation) and ⟨roomCall⟩ defined as `call`(Room.`*(*))`.

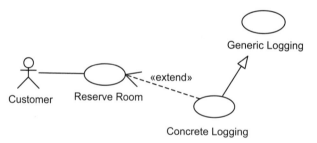

Figure 9-8   *Generalizing Logging extension.*

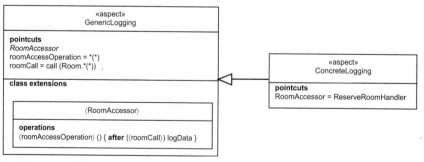

Figure 9-9   *Realizing generalizations.*

The `RoomAccessor` pointcut is deliberately left undefined in the `GenericLogging` aspect. The definition is postponed to the child `ConcreteLogging` aspect. In Figure 9–9, the `ConcreteLogging` aspect defines the `RoomAccessor` pointcut to be `ReserveRoomHandler`. In this way, you overlay the generic logging onto a specific use-case slice, in this case the Reserve Room use-case slice.

The AspectJ mapping for the `GenericLogging` aspect in Figure 9–9 is shown in Listing 9–3, and the mapping for the `ConcreteLogging` aspect is shown in Listing 9–4.

Listing 9-3   Abstract Aspects in AspectJ: GenericLogging.java

```
1.   package infra.logging;
2.   import domain.room.Room ;
3.
4.   public abstract aspect GenericLogging {
5.       abstract pointcut RoomAccessor() ;
6.       pointcut roomAccessOperation() :
7.               RoomAccessor()
8.               && withincode(* *(..)) ;
9.       pointcut roomCall() :
10.              roomAccessOperation()
11.              && call(* Room.*(..)) ;
12. after () : roomCall () {
13. // code
14. }
15. }
```

The `GenericLogging` aspect in Listing 9–3 resides in the logging package. Since these pointcuts have a reference to the `Room` class (see line 9), we need to import the `Room` class (line 2).

The `GenericLogging` aspect has three pointcuts: `RoomAccessor()`, `roomAccessOperation()`, and `roomCall()` (see the UML aspect depicted in Figure 9–9). The `GenericLogging` aspect is abstract because the `RoomAccessor()` pointcut is abstract.

The advice in lines 12, 13, and 14 adds the required behavior to do the logging after the `roomCall` pointcut.

Listing 9-4   Concrete Aspects in AspectJ: ConcreteLogging.java

```
1.  package infra.logging;
2.  import app.customer.ReserveRoomHandler ;
3.
4.  public aspect ConcreteLogging extends GenericLogging {
5.      pointcut RoomAccessor():
6.              within(ReserveRoomHandler) ;
7.  }
```

The ConcreteLogging aspect inherits from the GenericLogging aspect through the Java **extends** keyword. Note that Java extends *is not* a use-case extend but rather a class inheritance (i.e., generalization). The ConcreteLogging aspect defines the RoomAccessor() pointcut to refer to the ReserveRoomHandler class.

9.5   Templating Use-Case Slices

We earlier discussed the use of applying aspects on multiple operations at once by parameterizing pointcut expressions. There is yet another way to apply aspects on multiple operations and classes—through the use of templates.

In UML, a template element (also known as a parameterized element) is annotated by a dashed box on its top right-hand corner. This dashed box contains the parameters for that element. Figure 9–10 shows an example of a parameterized List class with Item as a parameter. In essence, it is a list of items.

You can create different lists—ReservationList, RoomList, and so on—by substituting the Item parameter with Reservation, Room, and so on.

Figure 9-10   *Parameterized list.*

From our discussion, you see that there are three ways for you to define parameters in a use-case slice:

- Identify the parameter as a pointcut and define the pointcut expression.
- Identify the parameter as a pointcut and postpone the definition of the pointcut expression to a child aspect.
- Identify the parameter as a template parameter.

In general, you use a combination of the three techniques. This is illustrated in the parameterized logging use-case slice on Figure 9–11.

In Figure 9–11, you find several parameters, each delimited by ⟨⟩:`roomAccessOperation`, `roomCall`, `RoomAccessor`, `Logger`, and `Resource`. The `roomAccessOperation` and `roomCall` parameter are defined through pointcuts in Figure 9–11. The `RoomAccessor` parameter is defined through a pointcut. But in this case, we are postponing the definition of the pointcut expression to its child aspect.

The `roomCall` pointcut uses a `Resource` use-case slice parameter in its expression, `call (⟨Resource⟩.*(..))`. This `Resource` is a string parameter that will be substituted when the template is applied. The `Logger` is also another parameter for the use-case slice. In our example, we want to log requests to the room resource, so the `Resource` parameter is substituted by the `Room` string. We can also substitute the `Logger` parameter with the `LogStream` class when we apply the logging use-case slice.

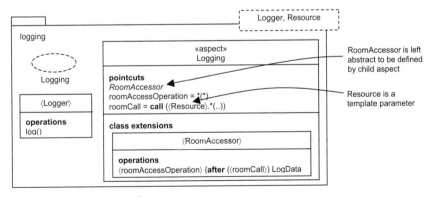

Figure 9-11 *Logging use-case slice template.*

We have just shown you the different techniques for defining parameters in use-case slices. When working with use-case slices, you should begin by identifying the parameters first. Thereafter, you decide which technique is most applicable. You will frequently use a combination of techniques. We provide further examples in Part IV of this book.

9.6   **Summary and Highlights**

In this chapter, we demonstrated how you can keep the realizations of extension use cases separate from that of a base use case. This requires the composition of operation extensions defined in extension use-case slices to be composed into operations defined in the base use-case slice. When defining operation extensions, it is important to clarify its structural context—within which class and which operation you will be executing the operation extension—and also to clarify its behavioral context—when in the execution of the operation the operation extension will execute.

When developing with AOP and AspectJ, your pointcut expressions may become rather lengthy. This is extremely dangerous because you might lose track of which operations you are extending. The solution to the problem is to break the pointcut expressions into segments to explicitly highlight the structural and behavioral context of the pointcut. This makes your pointcut expressions more understandable.

AOP offers a powerful mechanism to apply aspects (specifically advices) on multiple classes (specifically operations) at once by permitting regular expressions to be used to define pointcuts. This is extremely convenient because you find that crosscutting behaviors are generally repetitive. With regular expressions in pointcuts, this repetition is minimized. In addition, through the use of abstract pointcuts, you can even construct prebuilt extensions that can be hooked onto existing operations by defining the pointcuts. This makes extensions highly reusable.

However, an aspect in AOP has a limitation in that it can only add to existing classes. This is overcome by templating capabilities, which can be modeled in UML today as template elements. In fact you can parameterize any element in a use-case slice, including aspects. This makes your use-case slices even more reusable.

10

Building Systems with Use-Case Modules

Software development is about building models. You begin with the use-case model to capture stakeholder concerns; you refine the use-case model into an analysis model, which also formulates a high-level overview of the system; you strategize how the system will run on the execution platform with the design model, and in the implementation model, you have the actual codes and binaries. However, you do not build a system model by model. Instead, you do so use case by use case. You take each use case and refine and realize it progressively through the various models. When you complete the work on a use case, you deliver all artifacts associated with the use case in a single package—we call this a use-case module. A use-case module comprises use-case slices of each model. Use-case modules are developed separately and are composed to yield the complete system.

10.1   A System Comprises Models

As we saw in Part I of the book, the concept of separation helps us deal with complexity. Models are an alternate way to deal with complexity—through abstraction. Instead of separating the problem into smaller parts, you often need to look at the problem in its entirety. For example, when you want to establish an overall structure for your system, you definitely need to consider the entire system. When you want to design user interfaces, you need to consider multiple uses cases for an actor at once. Here, you cannot afford to go into every detail. You work with a high-level abstract description. You achieve this with the help of models.

So, what are models? A model is a description of the system from a particular perspective and from a chosen level of abstraction or detail. In a given model, you want to consider only things that are relevant to that perspective and that level of detail. Thus, you deliberately suppress and ignore details that are not relevant. For example, you might have a user interface model. In this case, you are only interested in how information is displayed, how you navigate from screen to screen, and so on. How information is stored or retrieved is irrelevant to a user interface model, and so is validation checks used on each piece of information.

When working with a model, you must first define a language for it. This language identifies the constructs or element types that you have at your disposal to adequately represent the system from the model's chosen perspective. For example, you might want to describe the user's interaction with the user interface, so you may have such elements as screens, pop-ups, buttons, and so on. The language also defines the different kinds of relationships between these elements. For example, a screen can contain some buttons and labels—so containment will be one kind of relationship. You can also navigate from one screen to some other screen, but not to others—thus, navigation is a kind of relationship that exists in the user interface model. With UML, you can easily define stereotypes to denote the different kinds of elements you are using in each model as well as the relationships between elements across models.

The constructs in a model are organized within containment hierarchies with some namespace. For example, there can be layers containing packages, which contain other packages and classes. A model can have more than one structure. As mentioned in earlier chapters, models other than the use-case model will contain at least two structures—an element structure and a use-case structure.

During development of a system, one of the first things you do is identify a set of models to describe your system adequately. If you have too few models, you might not have a good understanding of the system in its entirety. This happens when you rush into coding too quickly—you get pulled into the details and gradually lose the big picture. There are just too many details within the code, and you need to operate at a higher level of abstraction. So, more often than not, you have more than one model and, as you would expect, a more complex system needs more models. Some models are driven by business processes and application needs; others are driven by technology. But with more models, you must invest some effort to keep the integrity between models. This will certainly be a chore if you were to do it manually. Thanks to more powerful modeling tools, models can be kept synchronized with a click of a button.

The deliverables of a project have a direct relationship with the models you have chosen. The more models you identify, the more work you must do. You should never attempt to over-model. You use a new model only if you are unable to express what you want with the models you already have. If, on the other hand, you have a complex system and choose to have fewer models than necessary, you will end up with loose bits of undigested information. So, from a pragmatic standpoint, you begin with some minimum set of models at the beginning of the project and when they are insufficient, you identify more. Once the models are identified, the whole project life cycle will be about building these models.

In the context of use-case-driven development, there are several basic models: the use-case model, the analysis model, the design model, and the implementation model. Before we proceed further, we want to emphasize that these models are the only models, but they represent a minimum set. In addition, you need a tool that supports multimodels to maintain the integrity between the models. We explain the purpose for each of these models.

10.2   Use-Case Model

The use-case model serves as an agreement between the stakeholders (or customers) of the system and the developers on what the system should do and what qualities the system should have. Since the use-case model is meant for the stakeholders, their specifications are often expressed in the language understandable to the stakeholders. So, you try to describe it in a nontechnical way, and this is normally achieved using plain English.

The use-case model captures the users' and stakeholders' concerns by describing how actors will use the system and the acceptable behaviors that the desired system should produce. It comprises actors and use cases. For a larger system, you may choose to organize use cases within packages. In addition, different use cases may be related through relationships such as include, generalization, and extend. These relationships facilitate the reuse of system behaviors and the addition of new behaviors on top of existing ones, as we discussed in the Part II of the book. Since use cases represent a good way of understanding the system, it is beneficial to preserve the structure of the use-case model in the rest of the models.

10.3   Analysis Model

Use-case specifications describe the system's desired behavior from the external perspective using the end-user representatives' language, which is often in some natural language, such as English. To end-user representatives, this textual description of the system is a lot easier to understand than a more formal representation in UML. But there is a price to pay, because while natural language is intuitive, it is imprecise and there are some details in use-case specifications that one just cannot specify with English. For example, details such as the relationships between information to be captured, how information is to be presented, and conflicts between use cases simply cannot be expressed clearly with textual description. We need a more precise representation. This is possible with the analysis model.

Analysis is a refinement of the requirements with the goal of creating precise specification of requirements. Its purpose also is to find abstractions in the form of classes that make the requirements clearer as compared to plain use-case specifications. In fact, it is possible to formally define the sequence of actions the system performs to realize the use case in precise notation. This is what recent developments such as Executable UML attempt to achieve. Executable UML attempts to extend UML with precise action semantics to make the analysis model executable, as if it were the code itself, although in a platform-independent form. Such formal specifications are too overwhelming for the use-case model.

10.3.1   Language of Analysis

As mentioned earlier, each model has its own language and its own constructs to help you describe the system from that modeling perspective. To achieve this, the analysis model contains two structures:

- **Analysis element structure**. This comprises analysis classes organized in packages and layers. As mentioned earlier, these analysis classes are empty.
- **Use-case analysis structure**. This comprises use-case slices that add the content into the analysis element structure.

The language of an analysis model is a subset of the UML, which is deliberately chosen to be platform-independent so that you need not go into the details. To abstract away low-level details, the analysis model provides three stereotyped analysis classes (or constructs): boundary, control, and entity stereotyped classes.

Boundary. A boundary class is used to model the interaction between the system and its actors (i.e., users and external systems). The interaction often involves receiving and presenting information and requests from and to users and external systems. Boundary classes act as mediators between the system's surroundings (i.e., actors) and the system. It shields the system from changes in its environment. If such changes occur, only boundary classes are affected.

Control. A control class is responsible for the coordination, sequencing, transaction, and control of other objects and is often used to encapsulate control related to a specific use case. An instance of a control class often shares the same lifetime as a use-case instance. Frequently, it is instantiated when the use case is instantiated and is terminated when the use-case instance terminates. Control classes can also represent complex calculations and business logic.

Entity. An entity class is used to model information in the problem domain. Such information is long-lived and often persistent. An entity

boundary   control   entity

Figure 10-1   *Analysis stereotypes.*

class manages and stores such information. It encapsulates changes in the data structure or datastore. An entity class is use-case-generic and often participates in multiple use-case realizations.

These stereotypes are associated with corresponding icons, depicted in Figure 10–1. These icons help us recognize them quickly when they appear in UML diagrams. Stereotypes are extremely powerful tools that help you to quickly understand the responsibilities of a particular class even without looking at its operations or responsibilities.

These analysis stereotypes are now de facto standards in the software development community when conducting analysis. Those of you who are familiar with the OOSE approach in which they were first introduced, or with the Unified Process, should be familiar with these stereotypes.

10.3.2   Conducting Analysis

In creating an analysis model, which is a refinement of the use cases, you also identified the elements (in the form of analysis classes) that realize the use cases as well as their responsibilities. This often reveals reusable elements across use cases. You organize these abstractions into a high-level element structure of the system. The constructs you use in the analysis model are deliberately high level and platform-independent so that you are not pulled into implementation details too early.

At this level of abstraction, you have fewer elements to manipulate, and you can rapidly identify the responsibilities of each of these elements. You can quickly evaluate the system's element structure against some key use cases and scenarios. In addition, analysis constructs (such as analysis classes) help you localize possible changes to the system. These analysis classes are refined as you proceed to design and implementation.

Orthogonal to the element structure is the use-case structure. The use-case structure contains both non-use-case-specific slices and use-case slices. Use-case slices are for the purpose of preserving the separation of use cases from analysis to design and to implementation. Each analysis use-case slice contains the specifics of a use case in the analysis model.

Thus, you see that the purpose of the analysis model is twofold. First, it is a refinement of the use-case model. Second, it is also where you begin to describe the internal structure of the system. This serves as an excellent input to the design model. The boundary, control and entity classes in analysis are candidates to become components during design. Sometimes, one of such classes will evolve into a component by itself during design. Other times, several closely related analysis classes will evolve into a component.

Sidebar 10–1   How Detailed Should Analysis Be?

How detailed your analysis should be depends on several factors. If you are at the beginning of the project, you want to quickly identify the analysis classes and structure for the entire system so you have a good overall understanding of the complexity of the system. In this case, analysis will be extremely light so that you can consider many use cases within a short period of time. Later in the project, you might go into greater detail.

If you are dealing with a simple use case, there is of course nothing much to be analyzed. For example, a simple create, read, update, delete (CRUD) functionality needs little analysis. But if your system is nothing but CRUDs, you might want to revisit your use cases and have a better understanding of your stakeholder concerns. Ask yourself if there are any work processes or other features that you have missed in your analysis. If you are dealing with a complex use case, you definitely need to spend more time in analysis to refine requirements.

The level of detail in your analysis also depends on the generative power of your modeling tool. If your modeling tool provides support to generate much of the design and implementation model, you will of course spend more time refining your analyses. If your modeling tool does not provide that support, then all you need to do when analyzing a use case is to quickly identify the responsibilities of classes and evolve the structure of the system. You leave the detailed work to design and implementation.

10.4 Design and Implementation Models

The design model is a refinement of the analysis model and deals with the specifics of the execution platform. Thus, the design model must plan many important details. It has to address the multitude of implementation languages and technologies. It has to organize the distribution of the system across multiple processing nodes and arrange multiple implementation languages. Even if you decide to use a single platform like J2EE, you still have many languages to work with—Java, JSP, SQL, and more. In addition, there are also different implementation technologies for you to choose from—technologies that deal with persistency, presentation, and so on. Since a design model must prepare many things, it is significantly more complex than the analysis model. Therefore, it is advisable to keep the analysis model and the design model as distinct models. You use the analysis model to define the high-level structure and the design model to refine this structure and incorporate the details.

10.4.1 Language of Design and Implementation

To describe platform specifics, the design model must contain more constructs and, hence, more structures than the analysis model. It contains the following structures:

- **Deployment structure.** The deployment structure comprises processing nodes used in the system, the nodes the system needs to interface to, and the links between these nodes.
- **Process structure.** The process structure comprises active elements such as processes and threads. These processes and threads execute within nodes in the deployment structure.
- **Design element structure.** The design element structure comprises design classes organized into layers, subsystems, and packages. Some elements are refinements of boundary, control, and entity in the analysis element structure. Classes are refined with attributes and operations. Interfaces appear here. Classes are executed in the context of active elements in the process structure.
- **Use-case design structure.** The use-case structure runs orthogonally across the design element structure. It comprises use-case slices, aspects, class extensions, and so on.

Since, the design model is a refinement of the analysis model, you expect the structure of the analysis model to be preserved in the design model.

This means that you find packages in the design element structure corresponding to packages in the analysis element structure. You also find classes in the design model that are derived from the classes in the analysis model. Likewise, the use-case slices you identify during analysis will be refined during design.

Figure 10–2 illustrates what it means to have the design model preserve the structure of the analysis model. In essence, the structures within the analysis model are all platform-independent. The design model comprises structures that are cleanly divided into two parts: one part is minimal design, and the other part is platform-specific.

The minimal design part corresponds to what you find in the platform-independent analysis model. We consider it minimal design in the sense that even though it has a defined implementation language (e.g., Java), it makes no use of platform- or technology-specific calls (e.g., classes specific to J2EE). Thus, the minimal design part in the design model is quite simple, and the elements therein are traced directly from the analysis model (which is platform-independent). This clear separation is crucial in making the design model significantly more understandable without the entanglement of platform specifics. It also improves portability.

In the minimal design part, there are boundary control and entity classes. But to distinguish them from their analysis counterparts, we give them different stereotype icons. These are shown in Figure 10–3.

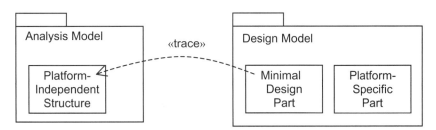

Figure 10-2 *Preserving the structure of analysis model in the design model.*

Figure 10-3 *Stereotyped design classes.*

In addition, there are classes to represent data/messages that get passed between boundary, control, and entity classes, and there are classes for handling exceptions, and so on. Since the design model deals with platform specifics, there are also many other kinds of design elements and probably more stereotypes.

We earlier mentioned that individual boundary, control, and entity classes, or groups of them, will evolve into components in design. These components will have interfaces that are derived from the responsibilities of analysis classes. We call these interfaces *minimal design interfaces*. During design, we also incorporate platform specifics, and consequently, components also have platform-specific interfaces. For example, a component may have a Web-based HTTP interface, or perhaps interfaces for distribution, such as J2EE remote interfaces. We discuss more of these platform-specific interfaces in Chapter 15, "Separating Platform Specifics with Platform-Specific Use-Case Slices."

10.4.2   Conducting Design and Implementation

You usually work on the design model and the implementation model together, so even though they are distinct models, you make changes on them in a single activity. You conduct tests together with design and implementation. Design is not complete until you know exactly how to test the design elements, and implementation is not complete until you pass these tests.

You take each use-case slice in analysis and refine it into design. You also start to incorporate user interface elements and elements to support distribution, persistence, and so on. You keep these elements separate from the boundary, control, and entity classes in both the element structure and the use-case structure. In the element structure, you have subpackages for these elements. Similarly, in the use-case structure, you have sub-use-case slices.

10.5   Use-Case Modules Cut Across Models

When you build a system, you do not build it model by model. Instead, you build it use case by use case. You first identify the use cases for the system. Thereafter, you take each use case, one at a time, to specify it, analyze

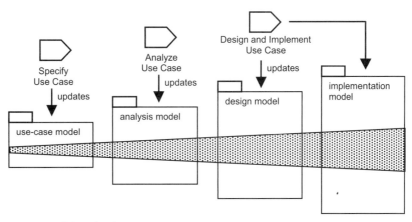

Figure 10-4 *Updating models in development.*

it, design it, and implement it. As you build each use case through the various models, you update the corresponding use-case slice in the respective models. These slices are shaded in Figure 10–4.

As you work on a use-case slice (e.g., the use-case slice in design), you start with the use-case slice upstream (e.g., the use-case slice in analysis), do some refinement, and add a little more. So, as depicted in Figure 10–4, each use-case slice downstream is bigger and more complex than the one upstream. This is the same with models. Downstream models are more complex than upstream models because downstream models must take into consideration more and more issues. This is why in Figure 10–4, each downstream model is depicted larger than the preceding one.

10.5.1   Preserving the Structure of the Use-Case Model

Thus, the way you develop the system is by gradually refining use-case slices through the various models. The structure of the use-case model is essentially preserved throughout all models downstream through the use-case slices of those models. This is useful for several reasons. First, this helps us understand the models downstream. You can easily identify what each use-case slice is doing by looking at the corresponding use case.

Second, software development is not a linear progression from use case to implementation. You frequently need to move back and forth in and update the various models. Preserving the structure of the use-case model helps you move from one model to another seamlessly and in a controlled manner. You do a little bit of the use-case specifications, move to its analysis, explore the interactions, and go back to the use-case specifications to clarify some missing details with the stakeholders. Maybe as you are working on the design, you need to revisit the system structure and go back to the analysis slice. Or maybe you need to clarify some special requirement for the use-case specification. This moving back and forth occurs frequently during the early iterations of the project when you are exploring design options, evaluating risks, and establishing an architecture baseline for the system.

Let us see what happens if you do not preserve the structure of the use-case model downstream. In this case, each downstream model is structured in its own way; it defeats the purpose of spending time structuring the use-case model. It means that you must understand completely different structures and maintain a mapping between these structures. If there are no formal rules for this mapping, it will be difficult to assure consistency between models. Not only that, but it actually removes seamlessness as you progress from one model to the next.

Sidebar 10–2   Does Preserving the Structure of Use-Case Model Introduce Design in the Use-Case Model?

It is important that when you conduct use-case modeling, you should not introduce "design" into the use-case model. Use-case modeling is to help you capture, understand, and structure stakeholder concerns.

So, when we say that you should preserve the structure of the use-case model, are we introducing design into use-case model? Absolutely not. What we are doing here is using the structure that has been agreed upon by the stakeholders and the development team to drive subsequent design of the system. This is the natural thing to do. Put another way, design should reflect how stakeholders perceive the system. Use-cases structure stakeholders' concerns in a manner that they understand. If stakeholders ask for changes, new enhancements, and so on, it must be in terms of what they understand about the system—and that is accomplished through the use-case model. So, the use-case model drives the design model. That is why our approach is called use-case-driven development.

10.5.2   A Use-Case Module Contains Use-Case Slices

Since you work on slices of various models for each use case together, it makes sense to collate all these slices into a single package. We call such a package a use-case module. A use-case module contains a use-case specification slice (of the use-case model), an analysis slice (of the analysis model), a design slice (of the design model), and an implementation slice (of the implementation model), as depicted in Figure 10–5.

In addition, there are slices of the design model and the implementation model for the purpose of conducting tests. Each test slice contains classes and class extensions needed to drive a particular slice through a test scenario. It also has extensions to perform instrumentation to collect test results. The number of test slices you need depends on the types of tests you will perform on the use-case module. For example, you might have a test slice for functional tests and a test slice for performance tests.

The «trace» dependencies in Figure 10–5 indicate that there exist some rules for you to derive elements from one upstream model to an element in the downstream model. Frequently, such rules are described informally by the architect as development guidelines and principles to be adhered to by the development team. However, there are certainly opportunities for you to formalize the derivation rules for possible automation. In fact, there are tools available today that provide some degree of automation to generate the downstream model at least partially. Since the upstream model is more abstract than the downstream one, you definitely need to define additional parameters for this automatic generation to be possible.

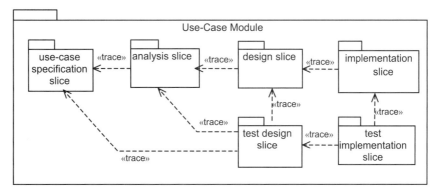

Figure 10-5   *Slices within a use-case module.*

When developing a system comprising use-case modules, you may be able to treat each use-case module as a project that is developed independently, so you might have in your hard disk or some central development repository a root folder for a use-case module and subfolders for each slice in the use-case module.

Sidebar 10–3 Traceability and Preserving the Structure of Models

Traceability is an important concept in software development. In essence, traceability links elements in an upstream model to elements in a downstream model. This helps us determine whether all requirements have been implemented and what the impact is of requirement changes or, in general, changes in upstream elements on downstream elements.

If the upstream and downstream models follow different structural principles, then significant effort must be invested to maintain the traceability between elements. The problem becomes protracted for large projects. However, with our approach of preserving the structure of models, the need to explicitly maintain traceability between elements is reduced significantly. This is because they essentially follow the same structure.

10.5.3   Use-Case Module Relationships

Just as there are relationships between use cases, use-case modules have relationships with each other. The relationships between use-case modules are the same as between use cases: generalization, include, and extend, as exemplified in Figure 10–6.

Use-case module relationships can be used in two complementary ways. First, from a forward engineering perspective, we can use relationships between use cases to drive the relationship between use-case modules. In other words, use-case modules preserve the relationships between use cases. This is illustrated by Figure 10–6, which shows a correspondence between use-case relationships and use-case-module relationships. For example, the Reserve Facility use case is a generalization of the Reserve Room use case, and so the Reserve Facility use-case module is a generalization of the Reserve Room use-case module.

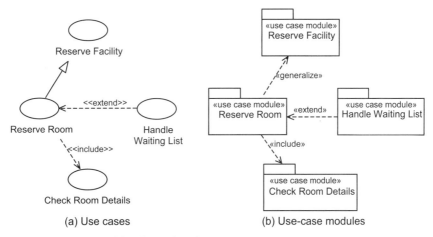

Figure 10-6   *Deriving use-case-module relationships from use cases.*

Second, the relationship between use-case modules can be used as a means to detect access violations in which an element in one use-case module has an illegal relationship with another element in another use-case module. The relationship between two use-case modules is an aggregate of all the relationships between elements of one use-case module to elements of the other. Thus, by aggregating these lower level element relationships, we check if they conform to the relationships at the use-case-module level.

Let us consider the relationship between the Reserve Room and Handle Waiting List use-case modules. In this case, we allow an element in the Handle Waiting List use-case module to extend an element in the Reserve Room use-case module, but not vice versa. We can be stricter by saying that no element in the Handle Waiting List use-case module can be a specialization of an element in the Reserve Room.

By watching the relationships across use-case modules, we can detect any access violations early whenever they occur and make the necessary changes quickly.

10.6   Composing and Configuring Use-Case Modules

After working on individual use-case modules, you compose them into the desired build. Suppose we allocate three use-case modules targeted for delivery in one build. We have a composite use-case module called build1, which is the result of merging the three use-case modules, as shown in Figure 10–7. The UML package «merge» dependency in Figure 10–7 depicts the composition of use-case modules.

The relationships between use-case modules govern how they are composed to form the desired build. When you compose or merge use-case modules, you compose all the corresponding slices within them.

Suppose, for some reason, the Handle Waiting List «use case module», which is responsible for the Handle Waiting List use case, is extremely buggy. Naturally, we do not want to release this defective use-case module at the end of the iteration. All we need to do is remove it from our build, and the actual build is build2, as depicted inFigure 10–8. Since the use-

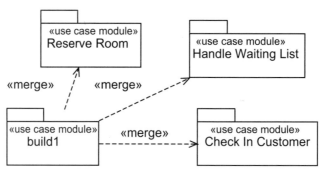

Figure 10-7   *Composing use-case modules.*

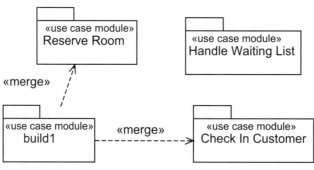

Figure 10-8   *Removing out defective modules.*

case module is not composed into build2, none of the extensions owned by the Handle Waiting List «use case module» will be compiled into build2. It is as if it was not developed in the first place. So, you can release build2 to the stakeholders while you use build1 to do further debugging and testing.

In general, you can mix and match versions of use-case modules at will to yield a desired build. If, on the other hand, you were to use the traditional modularity approach (classes alone), you must have the developers work on classes and add code fragments directly to existing classes, making them extremely cluttered. Suppose there are some defects and you want to remove those code fragments that belong to the defective use case. This is a practical impossibility because it means that you must go to individual classes and undo the work being done. What usually happens is that developers simply leave the dead codes within the system. This adds to the tangling within the existing classes and potentially introduces more bugs.

10.7   Summary and Highlights

As a quick recap, software development is about building models. At the beginning of a project, you have to choose a set of models that adequately describe the system. Each model has its own language and constructs to describe the system from that modeling perspective, and in addition, there are relationships between constructs from one model to another to help maintain consistency among models and to guide the derivation of model elements downstream.

You do not build a system model by model, but rather use-case module by use-case module. Use-case modules are units of software development effort. They localize the elements from different models related to a single use case in a single package. They are developed independently and iteratively. In fact, in Part IV of the book, each chapter is formulated in this way. Each chapter takes a use case and walks through all the activities about that use case, from requirements to code.

PART IV

Establishing an Architecture Based on Use Cases and Aspects

Building good software is like building many other kinds of systems. You start by building a skeleton, and then you add on to that skeleton, making sure that whatever you add to the system later will not impact what you built previously. When it comes to software, you can, after some initial prototyping, design a skinny system that includes the skeleton that you can build upon. To make sure that you can grow the skinny system to become the full-fledged system, you must determine whether the features not yet included in the skinny system can be added later without redesign of the system. In fact, you need to make sure that all risks that may impact the graceful growth of the skinny system can be taken care of without redesign.

The skinny system is developed as an early version of the system, called the architecture baseline. It contains the small but representative parts of the system, including requirements, analysis, design, code, and tests—but only the important ones. Accompanying the architecture baseline is an architecture description that consolidates your decisions.

The quality of the architecture is one of the most significant determinants of the success of the project. The emphasis in the early part of a project is on establishing a resilient architecture, one that systematically keeps concerns separate. Since there are different kinds of concerns, you use different techniques, too. With object orientation, you can keep the specifics of different kinds of objects separate with classes. You apply layering to keep the specifics of the domain separate from those of the application. However, the emphasis of this book is about keeping crosscutting concerns separate, and we spend time on this topic. In particular, we demonstrate how, with use-case slices, you can:

- Keep use-case specifics separate from use-case generics.
- Keep the handling of extensions separate from a base.
- Keep the realization of nonfunctional requirements separate from functional ones.
- Keep platform-specific separate from platform-independent elements.
- Keep test, control, and instrumentation separate from the elements being tested.

You must also consider the composition of multiple use-case slices to evaluate performance and other characteristics. After all, the design model is the sum of all the use-case slices. By tracing through a representative set of use-case slices, you evaluate the architecture baseline for its performance, reliability, and other execution characteristics. Thus, developing architecturally significant use cases early in the project naturally leads you toward an effective architecture that is designed for maintainability, extensibility, performance, and reliability.

Part IV includes the following chapters:

Chapter 11, "Road to a Resilient Architecture"

Chapter 12, "Separating Functional Requirements with Peer Application Use Cases"

Chapter 13, "Separating Functional Requirements with Extension-Application Use Cases"

Chapter 14, "Separating Nonfunctional Requirements with Infrastructure Use Cases"

Chapter 15, "Separating Platform Specifics with Platform-Specific Use-Case Slices"

Chapter 16, "Separating Tests with Use-Case Test Slices"

Chapter 17, "Evaluating the Architecture"

Chapter 18, "Describing the Architecture"

11

Road to a Resilient Architecture

The single most important determinant of the quality of a software system is its architecture. A good architecture keeps concerns of different kinds separate so that a change in one does not affect other parts of the system. You establish this architecture by identifying the critical use cases for the system. By analyzing these critical use cases, you can build a resilient structure—one in which concerns of different kinds are kept separate and changes in one part of the system have minimum impact on the rest of the system. The architecture must also be designed to meet system-level concerns such as performance and reliability. The architecture is manifested in an early and critical version of the system, a version that can be made executable—a version we call the *architecture baseline*. It might take several iterations before you finally establish the architecture baseline, but when you do, you have validated your assumptions, your approach to developing the system, and you have reduced your risks. Based on this architecture, the rest of the development can speed up tremendously.

11.1   What Is Architecture?

Architecture clearly is important, but if you ask five different people what architecture really is, you will probably get five different answers. Architecture, like many other words, is something you cannot really touch. It is in that sense similar to process, use case, project, component. However, these terms are concrete in the form of their descriptions. We can understand a process description, a component description, a use case specification, a project plan and, thus, an architecture description. So, when we talk about architecture, we talk about how we understand the architecture description. Architecture is thus the semantics of an architecture description, which encompasses the major decisions about the system, such as:

- How are the system elements organized?
- How does the system realize the required functionality?
- How does the system meet the desired performance, reliability, and other quality characteristics?
- What technologies does the system require (e.g., Web client, rich client, a particular messaging middleware)?
- Are the internals of the system structured to be resilient to changes in functionality, technology, platform, and so on?
- Are standards in place to ensure that the system is developed consistently? For example, what design patterns will be used? What guidelines will be used to handle exceptions?

Definitely, there are important, project-specific decisions to consider. For example, you may have to interface to a particular legacy system. Or maybe the system has to be configurable and you need a way to define system parameters. Perhaps the system has to be remotely installed and managed. Possibly the system is to deal with the complexities of a particular business domain. The list goes on. But the architecture is not everything. It is just the top 20 percent of the most important things about the system.

11.2   What Is a Good Architecture?

So, a good architecture is important. But what constitutes a good architecture? Of course, a good architecture meets systemwide concerns such as performance and reliability. It must be understandable so that you can easily trace which part of the architecture realizes which requirement or use case. Each class—and consequently the packages it resides in—plays clearly defined roles and performs a set of responsibilities that fulfill those roles and nothing else. There is little or no duplication of responsibilities between classes.

A good architecture keeps concerns separate, which means that changes in one part of the system do not propagate to other parts of the system. Even if they do, you can clearly identify what changes are to be made. If there is a need to extend the architecture, the impact should be minimal. Everything that already works should continue to work. For a system that applies aspect orientation, the different concerns about a system can be kept separated effectively.

Separating Functional Requirements. In general, you want to keep functional requirements, whether expressed as features, use cases, or in other terms, separate from each other. After all, they address different end-user concerns and will evolve separately. You do not want changes in one to impact the other. The functional requirements are often expressed on top of the problem domain (e.g., hotel management, logistics, banking, insurance, etc.). You naturally want to keep what is specific to the functionality of the system separate from the domain. In this way, you can easily adapt a system to a similar domain. In addition, some functional requirements are defined as extensions of other functional requirements: you must keep these separate from each other as well.

Separating Nonfunctional from Functional Requirements. Nonfunctional requirements usually specify the desired quality attributes of the system: security, performance, reliability, and so forth. These are provided by some infrastructure mechanisms—for example, you need some authorization, authentication, and encryption mechanisms to achieve security; you need caching and load-balancing to achieve performance. Frequently, these infrastructure mechanisms require small bits of behavior that must be executed within many classes. This means that a change in the realization of an infrastructure mechanism often implies huge repercussions, so you want to keep these separate.

Separating Platform Specifics. Today's systems need to execute on top of many technologies. Even for a single infrastructure mechanism such as authorization, you still have many technologies (e.g., through HTTP cookies, session identifiers, etc.) to choose from. These technologies are often platform- and vendor-specific. When a vendor upgrades its technologies to a new and better version, it is not easy to upgrade your system accordingly if your implementation has been tightly coupled with the previous version of that technology. You most certainly do not want to be tied down to a particular technology. Thus, you need to keep platform specifics separate.

Separating Tests from the Units Being Tested. As part of implementing a test, you must perform some control and instrumentation (e.g., debugging, tracing, logging, etc.). Control is for the purpose of forcing the execution flow of the system to follow some test sequences. Instrumentation is for the purpose of extracting information to verify that the system does indeed follow the desired test sequence. Control and instrumentation usually require some behavior that must execute within the context of the system under test. Such control and instrumentation behavior have to be removed after the test is conducted. Thus, you want to keep the implementation of tests separate from the system under test.

11.3   Steps to Establish an Architecture Baseline

A good architecture should be established as early as possible. Even in theory, it is very difficult to change a poor architecture into a good one with incremental techniques such as refactoring. In practice, it is extremely difficult. This is not to say that refactoring is not useful, but it is much better to begin with an initial structure that is relatively good. Otherwise, the cost of refactoring is too high for any business-oriented manager to accept, and he or she will typically opt for quick fixes instead. So, a good architecture needs to be created when the cost of creating it is small or even nonexistent. Prioritization of architectural work has a good return on investment. It reduces the need for redesign and minimizes throwaway work during the remainder of the project. Having achieved a good initial structure, you can continually evaluate the architecture and make the necessary refinements and refactorings.

Architecture Baseline. The architecture is manifested as an early version of the final system known as an architecture baseline. The architecture baseline is a subset of the entire system, so we call it the skinny system.

This skinny system has versions of all the models that the full-fledged system has at the end of the project. It includes the same skeleton of subsystems, components, and nodes, but not all the musculature is in place. However, they do have behavior, and they are executable code. The skinny system evolves to become the full-fledged system, perhaps with some minor changes to the structure and behavior. The changes are minor because, at the end of the elaboration or architectural iterations, we have by definition a stable architecture; otherwise, the elaboration phase must continue until we know that this goal has been achieved. There is a systematic way to do this.

Even though the skinny system (the architecture baseline) usually only includes 5 to 15 percent of the final code, it is enough to validate the key decisions you have made. More importantly, you need to be assured that the skinny system can grow to become the complete system. The skinny system is accompanied by a paper product called the architecture description. But now, this paper product is verified and validated through the architecture baseline.

Use Cases Drive the Architecture Baseline. The establishment of the architecture baseline is driven by a critical subset of use cases. We call this subset the architecturally significant use cases. Before you can identify the architecturally significant use cases, you must first identify all the use cases for the system—at least to the best of your knowledge with the available information. Please note that identifying use cases is not the same as specifying use cases. Identifying is about scoping and exploring and finding what the system needs to do. Specifying use cases is about detailing the flows and the steps in the use case. Specifying use cases is allocated across the project lifecycle. However, identifying the use cases can and must be done early.

From these identified use cases, you determine which among them are important—important in the sense that together they cover all the key decisions you need to make:

- They exercise key functionalities and characteristics of the system.
- They have a large coverage in terms of the various risks that you face concerning functionality, infrastructure, platform specifics, and so on.
- They stress some delicate or risky parts of the system.
- They are the basis for the rest of the system to be developed.

Architecturally significant use cases involve use cases of different kinds. After all, each use case captures a different set of stakeholder concerns and requires different decisions to be made. Your list of architecturally significant use cases will therefore involve a combination of both application and infrastructure use cases. You might find this in your system use cases that are technically similar and have similar interaction patterns. In that circumstance, you need to choose just one use case as a representative, since the moment you can solve one of them, you can solve the others. For example, the Check In Customer and Check Out Customer use cases are similar, so you choose just one of them to serve as an architecturally significant use case.

Once you have identified the architecturally significant use cases, you can explore the critical scenarios within them. As you analyze the use case scenarios, you get a better understanding of what the system needs to do and how the elements in the system should interact with each other. Through that understanding, you define and evaluate the architecture. This proceeds iteratively until you achieve a stable architecture. By stable, we mean that key risks in the system have been resolved, and the decisions made are a sufficient basis for you to develop the rest of the system.

The architecture is influenced not only by the architecturally significant use cases, but also by the platform, legacy systems that the system needs to be integrated to, standards and policies, distribution needs, middleware and frameworks used, and so on. Even then, use cases are still useful for evaluating the architecture. You analyze each use case in the context of the chosen platform, the chosen middleware, the chosen distribution structure, and so on. In this way, you can evaluate whether the choices you have made are sufficient and discover where improvements need to be made.

Establish the Architecture Baseline Iteratively. For a complex system, it takes several iterations before you finally establish a stable architecture. Since these iterations focus on developing the architecture, they are also called the architectural iterations. In Unified Process terminology, these iterations are known as elaboration iterations.

You must address all architectural concerns in each architectural iteration. You may not be successful at resolving all of them in each architectural iteration, but you need to consider all of them. Each architectural iteration produces an increment that resolves some of these architectural concerns.

The iterations proceed until all architectural concerns have indeed been resolved. At the end of these architectural iterations, you have an early version of the system (a skinny system) that is executable. It is supported by test and execution results, so it is verified and validated.

The version of the system at this point is the architecture baseline. Thus, the architecture is an early version of the system that demonstrates how architectural concerns are resolved. Since the system comprises a set of models, the architecture baseline is also represented by a version of these models. The architecture baseline is accompanied by an architecture description, which is an extract of the models.

The architecture description serves as a guide for the whole development team through the lifetime of the system. The architecture description is the reference to be followed by the developers in subsequent iterations of the project.

The architecture description is also reviewed by stakeholders to determine if the architecture is indeed feasible. Attached to the architecture description (and basically to every artifact) is a history sheet that explains the system's evolution. It may also explain important decisions.

You normally find the architecture description developed concurrently, often ahead of the activities that result in the versions of the models that are parts of the architecture baseline. It is to be updated in iterations following the architecture baseline.

During architectural iterations, progress is relatively slow because you need time to make decisions. Once you have gone past the architectural iterations, productivity will shoot up significantly, so the time devoted to iterations is well spent.

Before we discuss architecture description, we need to present the concepts that will help you understand it. Since the architecture description is such an important artifact, we devote an entire chapter to it (see Chapter 18, "Describing the Architecture").

11.4   Begin with a Platform-Independent Structure

The way you structure the system is an important architectural decision. You structure the system such that concerns are kept separate. You achieve this structure first from a platform-independent perspective and then refine it with platform specifics. A platform-independent structure is driven by functional requirements (as modeled with use cases).

The tools you use to achieve a resilient structure are classes and use cases. Classes help you keep the elements in a system separate, and use cases help you keep the tasks of each element separate. Accordingly, there are two orthogonal structures in the system—the element structure and the use case structure.

- The element structure identifies where elements of the system are located in the element namespace. It structures the elements hierarchically in terms of layers, packages, classes, and the features within these classes.
- The use case structure defines how you overlay functionality onto the element structure. It comprises slices—both use-case slices and non-use-case-specific slices—that add the actual classes and class features onto the element structure.

You want your structure to be resilient along both structures. This means that if there are changes in requirements, their impact should be localized to a few packages and classes in the element structure. Their impact must also be localized to a few use-case slices. Localized means that there are few changes, and the changes do not propagate beyond those packages or use-case slices that require change.

11.4.1   Element Structure

The element structure for a model is a hierarchical structure of packages and classes. It uniquely identifies each element. Since the goal is to achieve resilient structure, you naturally locate classes that are used for the same purpose together.

Layers. You normally use layers as the first-level partitioning in a model. Layers are used to group software elements that are on the same level of abstraction. You place more abstract and reusable elements in lower layers and more concrete or less reusable elements at the top. Normally, two high-level layers are sufficient to refine the functional requirements for the system: the application layer and the domain layer.

Application Layer. The application layer contains elements that realize workflows in the use cases supporting the primary actors of the system. The elements in this layer normally use the elements in the domain layer to realize use cases. You can organize packages in the application layer according to the following criteria.

• Classes that support one or more particular actors.
• Classes that are involved in one or more particular use cases.
• Classes that are involved in some functional area in the system.

Domain layer. The domain layer contains elements representing significant domain concepts. They capture information to be maintained, tracked, or manipulated by the system and the associated behaviors for doing so. These elements are normally shared across use case realizations. They are more reusable and so reside in a lower layer than the application layer. However, since they are shared by use-case realizations, use-case realizations frequently cut across domain elements.

Figure 11-1 depicts the initial structure of the Hotel Management System that realizes the functional requirements of the system. The packages in the application layer are grouped according to actors—the customer, the hotel counter staff, and the management. The packages in the domain layer group classes related to rooms and classes related to reservations.

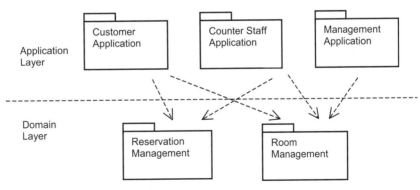

Figure 11-1   *Initial layers and packages in the element structure.*

The structure in Figure 11-1 is an initial one. It is refined further into classes and so forth as you analyze the use cases for the system.

Sidebar 11-1   How Use Cases Help to Structure the Application Layer

We mentioned earlier that classes that are involved in a particular use case can be placed within packages in the application layer. Figure 11-1 shows a relatively simple case of identifying packages in the application layer. For larger systems, you can partition your application layer based on the principles illustrated by the figure below. Before we go on, we want to emphasize that this is but one way for you to structure the application layer.

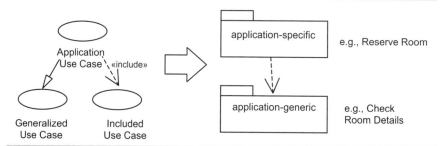

In the example above, we split the application layers further—application-specific and application-generic. Classes participating in peer use case realization are allocated to application-specific packages. Classes that participate in generalized or included use cases are allocated to application-generic packages. There is a dependency from application-specific packages to application-generic packages. This preserves the relationship from the use case model into the analysis element structure.

Note that there is a limit to how much you can keep the realization of the use cases separate in the element structure. That is why we need the use case structure that defines overlays on the element structure.

Sidebar 11-2   How to Organize the Domain Layer

In Figure 11-1, we show only two domain-layer packages. You definitely expect more from larger systems. The example below shows how you can structure packages in the domain layer.

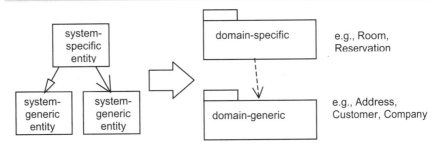

In essence, you organize entities that are common across industry domains within domain-generic packages. For example, classes like `Address`, `Customer`, and `Company` are used in many industry domains and are, therefore, highly reusable. Domain-specific entities can then either specialize these entities or reference them through associations. Again, we like to emphasize that this is but one way for you to organize your domain layer. The key idea is to distinguish between what is domain-specific and what is domain-generic or independent. This is a way to achieve understandability and also reuse.

11.4.2   Use-Case Structure

As mentioned, the element structure is simply about identifying elements in a namespace. It is the slices in the use-case structure that overlay the actual content for each element. There are two kinds of slices: use-case slices and non-use-case-specific slices.

The convention is to depict the element structure (comprising layers, packages, and classes) vertically such that at the top you find application-specific layers and packages, and at the bottom you find application-independent ones (as per Figure 11-1). To emphasize the orthogonality of the use case structure, we depict the use case structure horizontally with the non-use-case-specific slices on the left and the use-case–specific slices on the right (see Figure 11-2). The arrows in Figure 11-2 show the dependencies between the use-case slices and non-use-case-specific slices.

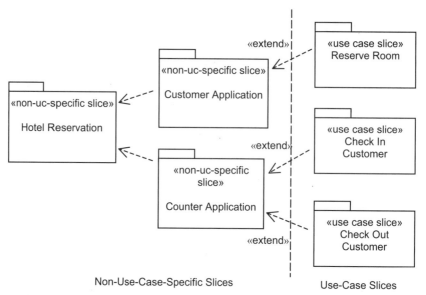

Figure 11-2 *Use-case structure.*

Non-use-case-specific slices are derived by exploring the commonalities between use-case realizations. They normally have a close correspondence to the element structure, especially to the lower layers. After all, lower layers in the element structure and non-use-case-specific slices are for the purpose of grouping things that are shared—though shared from a different perspective. This is exemplified by the slices on the left of Figure 11-2. The Hotel Reservation slice adds the domain packages into the element structure. The slices Customer Application and Counter Application add classes to the corresponding packages in the element structure.

The use case slices in Figure 11-2 are derived directly from use cases in the use-case model. Thus, on the right of Figure 11-2, there are use-case slices for Reserve Room, Check In Customer, and Check Out Customer.

Note that the Customer Application and the Counter Application non-use-case-specific slices do not extend the Hotel Reservation non-use-case-specific slices. The former contains classes that depend on or makes use of classes contained in the latter. The former do not extend the latter. Hence, there is no «extend» relationship between them.

> ### Sidebar 11-3   How Use Case Slices Improve Reuse
>
> Without aspect orientation, you normally attempt to achieve reuse by pushing reusable things into lower layers. For example, if a class is reusable, you push the class down to a lower layer or a lower package. If some operations in a class are reusable, you may factor the common operations into a generalized class and push this down to a lower layer or package. This seems to work well, but the problem is this: you need to push down complete operations or complete classes.
>
> On your project team, you may find a good programmer. Every boss likes her and gives her different things to do. Soon, she has so many different things to do that she ceases to be effective. Working with reusable elements is similar. As you attempt to make these elements more reusable, you inevitably get them to do more things, and they quickly become heavyweight and entangled.
>
> This problem is solved with aspect orientation and use-case slices. In the use-case structure, you can push only those reusable extensions into lower slices—not the entire class. For example, the Hotel Reservation non-use-case-specific slice contains partial elements that are needed by all slices that are on top of it. In this way, you achieve reuse without the heavyweight problem.

11.5   Overlay Platform Specifics on Top

At the end of the day, the system you are building must execute on some target platform. You must incorporate some user interfaces. If you need to offer high processing capacity, you must distribute the processing across processing nodes. Distribution is platform-specific. You must provide persistent storage for information managed by your system. You might need to integrate with a legacy system. Thus, you see that platform specifics occur throughout the realization of a use case whether this is an application use case or an infrastructure use case.

11.5.1   Choosing the Platform

The platform specifics for a system are based on the deployment structure and process structure chosen by the architect. In this case, we assume that the architect has chosen a J2EE-based solution. Figure 11-3 depicts the deployment structure for the Hotel Management System. It is annotated with the architect's choice of communication mechanisms, implementation languages, and technologies.

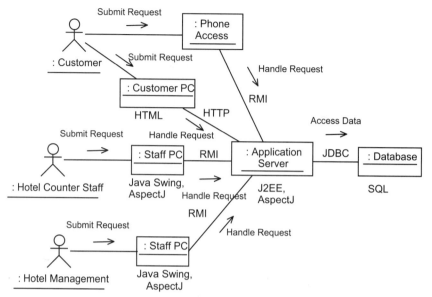

Figure 11-3 *Deployment structure for Hotel Management System design model.*

Figure 11-3 depicts actors so you can readily see how the deployment structure relates to the use-case model. The customer accesses the system through a phone or his own PC. The customer PC interacts with the application server over a wide area network over HTTP. The application server accesses that database to retrieve records, update records, and so on. Access to the application server is through Remote Method Invocation (RMI). Hotel counter staff and hotel management access the system through their PCs. Staff PCs uses Java Swing, which is a GUI framework for Java. For those nodes that use Java as a programming language, AspectJ is used as the composition technology.

Zooming into each deployment structure, you find active elements (i.e., processes and threads) executing. This is depicted in Figure 11-4, which shows the customer PC running a browser, whereas the staff PC runs a thick client. The application server runs a Web container and an EJB container. The staff PC communicates using HTTP with the Web container, which in turn communicates with the EJB using RMI. The thick client communicates with the EJB container directly. The EJB container communicates with the relational database using Java Database Connectivity (JDBC).

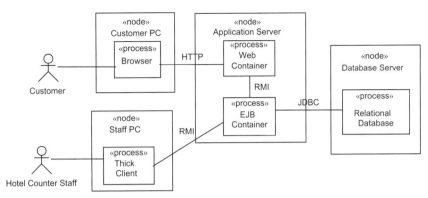

Figure 11-4 *Process structure for Hotel Management System design model.*

11.5.2 Keeping Platform Specifics Separate

Even with a chosen deployment and process structure, there are still many platform-specific implementation technologies to be chosen. You most definitely do not want to be tied down to a particular execution platform or even to a particular vendor. Platform-specific technologies evolve, and a new and better version becomes available regularly. It would be disastrous if you had to modify the design just to keep up with the changes in these technologies. Thus, you would like to keep platform specifics separate.

If you strip away the platform specifics from the design of a use case, what remains is a minimal use-case design. This minimal use-case design has the following characteristics:

- It is executable and is implemented in a default programming language such as Java.
- It is activated through a program interface. A separate program triggers the minimal use case. In this way, all concerns on user interface, presentation of information, and data input mechanisms is kept out of the minimal use-case design.
- Concerns about distribution, interprocess communication, and platform-specific messaging are kept separate from it. So, the minimal use case design *appears* to run on a single node, a single process, and a single thread, when in fact it is running on the chosen platform described earlier.

- Every piece of information it needs is assumed to be in memory. In this way, all persistency concerns are not present in the minimal design. Likewise, each action from the actor instance is an atomic action.

Everything else (user interface, distribution, etc.) is considered platform-specific and is designed separately and overlaid on top of this minimal use-case design.

Figure 11-5 shows a use-case design slice decomposed into the minimal use-case design slice plus several platform-specific slices for the use case. There is a platform-specific slice to modularize the user interface design for the use case, another platform-specific slice to modularize the distribution of the use case, and yet another to handle platform-specific persistency. There could be potentially other platform-specific slices, depending on what kinds of platform specifics you want to overlay on top of the minimal use-case design slice.

The benefits of separating the platform-specific parts from the minimal use-case design are many. First, the minimal use-case design is significantly simpler. Anyone who knows the designated programming language can develop it without knowing all the platform specifics. The minimal use case design is easy to design and develop, and you can produce an executable quickly. It is also much easier to test because it does not require any platform-specific test environment.

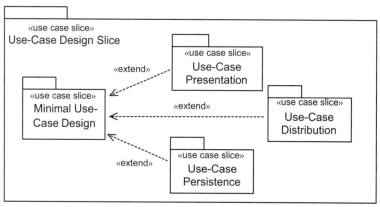

Figure 11-5   *Use-case design slice with platform specifics kept separate.*

Sidebar 11-4   How Aspect Orientation Relates to Model-Driven Architecture (MDA)

Perhaps you are familiar with research on model-driven architecture (MDA) [Kleppe et al. 2003]. Model-driven development recognizes the need to keep business and application specifics separate from the infrastructure and environment specifics. Thus, in MDA, a platform-independent model (PIM) is distinguished from a platform-specific model (PSM). The analysis model in use-case–driven development corresponds to the PIM, and the design model corresponds to the PSM.

The idea behind MDA is to define a set of transformation rules to map a PIM into a PSM automatically. This is quite attractive because a sizeable portion of software development work is about dealing with platform specifics. There are common solutions to deal with platform specifics, and they apply to many parts of the system. Developers who incorporate the platform specifics find such work repetitive, laborious, and also error prone. It also means that they must learn about the platform specifics, too, not an easy task considering the regular and frequent updates to technologies. An architect also wants the transformations from platform-independent to platform-specific to be made in a consistent manner. Thus, the possibility of automating the transformation process is quite attractive.

In practice, you do not transform complete models; you transform part by part, since real projects have different members working on different parts of the models in parallel. In addition, breaking down the models into smaller parts simplifies the transformation process. After all, transforming a smaller model is much easier than transforming a larger model. However, this necessitates two mechanisms: one to separate the model and the other to compose the result. Use-case modularity is advantageous in this situation because it provides both the separation criteria and the composition mechanism. You work on the models use-case module by use-case module, and through aspect technology, you compose the use-case modules.

As mentioned, with MDA you get a lot of code generated for you automatically into the classes in the PSM, provided that you have a good and sufficient set of transformation rules. But, what if the transformation rules are not comprehensive enough? This means that you must at times work on the PSM itself. This creates two major problems. First, much tangling results from all the code generated using different transformation rules, different parts of the PIM, and so on. This makes understanding and debugging difficult. Second, if you make changes to the PSM itself, you worry that if you were to regenerate the codes from the PIM, it might overwrite what you have done on the PSM. Alternately, you may attempt to write your own transformation rules. However, such effort is attractive only if you can apply the transformation rules many times in your project. If your transformation rules can be applied only once or twice, it is definitely much easier to work on the PSM directly. In this case, you again worry about whether other transformation rules will overwrite your work, but you can choose a powerful MDA tool that can ensure that your changes to the PSM do not get overwritten.

In our opinion, use-case slices and aspects provide an effective solution to the problem. In the PSM (i.e., the design model), you have minimal use-case design slices that contain platform-independent parts and additional slices that have platform specifics. This means that the platform specifics are kept separate even in the PSM. In this way, you do not worry about your work being overwritten. Moreover, since the platform specifics are kept separate, what you have in the PSM is much easier to understand and maintain. You can use the same code-generation techniques in MDA to generate the platform-specific slices. Moreover, since the minimal use-case design has few platform specifics, it is much easier to generate it from the PIM than from the complete PSM. Thus, aspects dramatically solve the many problems faced by MDA.

Furthermore, aspects are a more general technique. Whereas MDA attempts to keep platform specifics separate, aspects keep crosscutting concerns in general separate—not just platform specifics, but also functional requirements, nonfunctional requirements, and tests. Aspects can benefit from MDA approaches too. By assimilating the code-generation technologies to generate platform-specific use-case slices, you can speed up aspect-oriented software development tremendously.

In short, you get exceptional leverage if you apply a combination of aspect orientation and MDA. The use case–driven approach provides the methodology to unify these technologies.

Definitely, aspect technologies today cannot transform a language-independent analysis model to a language-specific design model as MDA attempts to do. This is not a big drawback for aspects because many projects today do choose an implementation language upfront in the project.

11.6   Summary and Highlights

Establishing resilient architecture early in the project is critical. The goal is to make the system robust and reduce the impact of requirement changes and changes elsewhere in the system. It also make the system easier to understand. From an aspect orientation point of view, a resilient system makes your pointcuts easier to define because all the classes and responsibilities you need to extend are localized.

The way you establish the structure of models that describe the system is iterative. You start with some initial platform-independent structure. You then analyze the architecturally significant use cases one by one. As you do so, you add on and refine the existing structure and incorporate platform-specific elements onto the structure. After going through all the architecturally significant use cases, you will have established a fairly resilient architecture.

In the subsequent chapters, we explain how to handle different kinds of crosscutting concerns with different kinds of use cases. This will help you understand the general approach to aspect-oriented software development.

12

Separating Functional Requirements with Application Peer Use Cases

A system must meet many functional requirements. To support parallel development, you need to keep different concerns about the functional requirements separate. This separation is also needed to ensure that the system is understandable and easily maintained. Since the functional requirements are about what users can do with the system, an effective way to separate them is through use cases—specifically, through application use cases. But separation does not end with requirements; it has to go all the way to code if your developers are to work on different parts of the system separately. Thus, you have to analyze the use cases to determine what is use-case-specific and what is use-case-independent, what is application-specific and what is application-generic, what is domain-specific and what is domain-generic. This provides the basis for you to separate classes into their respective layers, packages, and class extensions and into respective slices and modules. Once you have achieved this separation, developers can design, implement, and test their respective use-case modules in parallel. The value of being able to work like this cannot be overexaggerated. This is the only way you can meet project deadlines.

12.1   Analyzing Application Use Cases

This chapter deals with a special case of functional requirements that we call peers. Two functional requirements are peers when their realizations touch the same classes. In our Hotel Management System, the Reserve Room use case, the Check In Customer use case, and the Check Out Customer use case are peers to one another. They have no modeled relationship between them, but they share some classes that participate in their realizations. Such overlap becomes apparent when you conduct analysis and design.

In this chapter, we demonstrate how to keep the specifics of a peer application use case separate all the way down to code, using the Reserve Room use case as an example. The essential steps to conduct analysis and design of a use case are as follows:

1. Consider the use-case specification and update it if necessary.
2. Analyze the use case by identifying analysis classes that participate in the realization of the use case and allocating the behavior of the use case to these analysis classes).
3. Organize the classes into layers and packages within the element structure and both classes and class extensions into slices within the use-case structure (see Section 12-2).
4. Design the use case by mapping the analysis elements to design elements, identifying interfaces and additional design elements (e.g., exception classes and transfer objects, which we discuss shortly), and subsequently refining these elements (see Section 12-3).

We walk through the steps above in this chapter to illustrate how concerns are kept separate. In subsequent chapters, we walk through similar steps of analysis and design. However, since we are dealing with different kinds of use cases, there will be slight variations in the steps listed above. Nevertheless, the approach remains the same.

You may refer back to Part II, if necessary, to review how to identify and specify use cases. For your convenience, we list the specification for the Reserve Room use case in Listing 12–1. Note that Listing 12–1 covers only the basic flow.

Listing 12-1 Use-Case Specification: Reserve Room

The use case begins when a customer wants to reserve a room or rooms. The customer selects to reserve a room. The system displays the types of rooms the hotel has and their rates. The customer selects his desired room type and indicates his period of stay. The system computes the cost for the specified period. The customer makes the reservation for the chosen room. The system deducts the number of rooms available for reservation for the specified room type for the specified period. The system creates a new reservation with the given details. The system displays the reservation confirmation number and check in instructions. The use case terminates.

12.1.1 Identifying Classes

The first step when analyzing a use case is to identify the participating analysis classes. The analysis class stereotypes provide guidance to identify these classes. You can apply the following rules.

- For each actor that interacts with the use case, you have one boundary class.
- For each use case, you can begin with one control class to coordinate other classes to realize that use case.
- From the use-case specification, you identify the entities that are needed.

Based on the rules above, classes participating in the realization of the Reserve Room use case are identified as depicted in Figure 12–1.

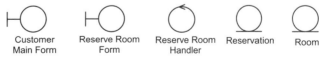

Customer Main Form   Reserve Room Form   Reserve Room Handler   Reservation   Room

Figure 12-1 *Participating analysis classes in Reserve Room use-case realization.*

If you follow the above rule, there should be only one boundary class (i.e., Reserve Room Form). We added the Customer Main Form to show how the customer actor can invoke the reservation functionality from the main form. We want to demonstrate how to resolve a particular kind of overlap between use-case slices. This is discussed shortly.

Since this is the first use case you are analyzing, there is no structure defined as yet. This means that the classes you have identified have yet to be organized into packages. After identifying the requirements and responsibilities of these classes, you organize them. If, on the other hand, you have already analyzed several use cases, the structure of the system will already have begun to take shape. In this case, you can locate the packages to which the classes belong immediately.

12.1.2   Allocating Use-Case Behavior to Classes

Once you have identified the participating classes, you proceed to the second step, which is to describe how their instances collaborate to realize the use case. This is achieved by walking through the steps of a use-case flow and describing how participating class instances interact (i.e., invoke each other) at each step. You can describe these interactions with UML through a number of means, using the following:

- Communication diagrams showing how instances interact and the messages that pass between them.
- Interaction diagrams showing the chronological sequence of events that emerge as you step through a use-case flow or a use-case scenario.
- Class diagrams showing the responsibilities and relationships between classes.

You must apply some rules when describing the interaction between the class instances. These rules apply whether you are using communication or interaction diagrams.

- Actors can interact only with boundary classes. Otherwise, other kinds of classes will be dependent on changes in the environment—user interfaces, external interfaces. and device interfaces.
- Instances of entity classes should not send messages to boundary or control classes. Entity classes are part of the domain and should not

be dependent on the use of the system or on how the interfaces are designed.

- For simple interactions—such as database record create, read, update, and delete—there may be no need for a control class. In such cases, it suffices for the boundary class to interact with the entity class directly.

There are different levels of detail you can use when conducting analysis. How detailed you want analysis to be depends on your tool support. If you have very little tool support and you only want an outline of class and package responsibilities, then a high-level, rough description suffices. If, on the other hand, you have powerful analysis tools that can interpret and execute the analysis model (i.e., executable UML), you must be detailed. If you want to automatically transform the analysis to design, such as through model-driven architecture (MDA), your analysis must be detailed.

Using a Communication Diagram. A communication diagram in UML 2.0 was previously known as a collaboration diagram. It shows the instances as icons. Instances interact by passing messages to one another, as indicated by the arrows. These messages travel over links denoted by lines joining class instances. These links imply that an instance has a reference to another object. In analysis, the preference is to use communication diagrams, since the primary focus is on finding the requirements and responsibilities on instances and not on finding detailed and chronological sequences of interactions. If you want such details, an interaction diagram, which we describe later, is more appropriate.

Figure 12–2 depicts the communication diagram for the Reserve Room use-case realization. It is derived by stepping through the use-case flow of events. At each step of a use-case flow, you consider what each instance is supposed to do and how it passes control to another instance by sending messages. You frequently find that an actor (Customer) instance will have the initial control. This is passed over to the boundary instance (either the Customer Main Form or the Reserve Room Form) when the actor instance interacts with the system. The boundary instance then gets a control instance (Reserve Room Handler) to handle the actor's request according to what is described in the use-case flow of events. This normally implies accessing or updating information through some entity instances (Reservation and Room).

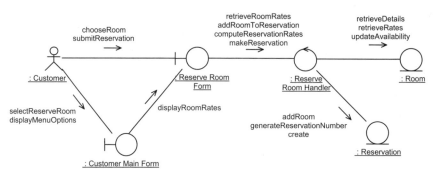

Figure 12-2   *Communication diagram: Reserve Room use-case realization.*

After stepping through the whole use-case flow of events, you have a communication diagram like that shown in Figure 12–2. The name of the message should denote the intent of the calling instance when interacting with the called instance.

Interaction Diagram.   If you want to analyze the use case in greater detail, an interaction diagram is usually more appropriate. An interaction diagram shows how instances interact with each other in a chronological sequence from top to bottom. Figure 12–3 describes the chronological sequence of interactions for the Reserve Room use-case realization. To improve readability, we have added the use-case flow description on the left-hand side of Figure 12–3.

The chronological nature of an interaction diagram is useful when timing details are important for the use case. The chronological nature of interaction diagrams makes it easy for you to identify pointcuts, which we discuss in Chapter 13, "Separating Functional Requirements with Application Extension Use Cases."

You normally use one interaction diagram to describe one use-case scenario or use-case flow. Now, with enhancements in UML 2.0, you can systematically describe alternate paths in interaction diagrams. Nevertheless, as you describe more paths, interaction diagrams become longer. With communication diagrams, however, you can use one communication diagram for multiple scenarios or flows in the same diagram without lengthening it. This is because you can simply add messages on top of communication diagrams.

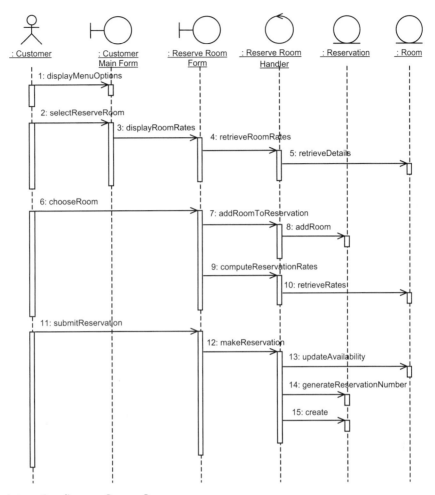

Figure 12-3 *Interaction diagram: Reserve Room.*

Class Diagrams. After considering the interactions between the participating class instances, you can collate the responsibilities and relationships required for each class in the context of that use case. In essence, each message sent to an instance in a communication diagram or an interaction diagram translates to some responsibility for the corresponding class. You can summarize the result on a class diagram, as shown in Figure 12–4.

During analysis, the purpose is not to go into details of classes. You should refrain from detailing operations. Instead, focus on identifying key

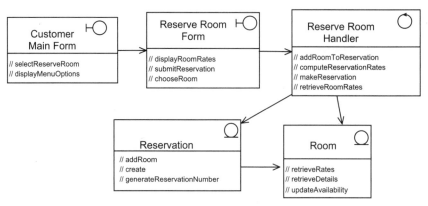

Figure 12-4   *Reserve Room use-case realization: class diagram.*

responsibilities of each class. At this point, you should not be focusing on whether you are retrieving a room by customer name, by room type, by availability, and so on. You will be doing that in design and implementation. Our convention is to prefix the name of responsibilities with / /.

Note that the classes shown are only partial definitions. Each class will likely have responsibilities and relationships that are identified from other use-case realizations. You have to analyze at least several more use cases before you get a good idea of the complete set of responsibilities for each analysis class. Thereafter, you will have a better idea of which classes or features of classes are reusable. These will be the inputs for the structure of the system in both dimensions—element structure and use-case structure.

Analyzing Multiple Use Cases. What we explained above is really just walking through the analysis of one use case. At the beginning of the project, when you are trying to outline the architecture, you analyze several use cases simultaneously, switching back and forth between different kinds of diagrams, as we discussed above. You basically start by quickly going through a couple of important use-case specifications, then suggest a class diagram like the one in Figure 12–4. You then describe each use case through a collaboration of class instances and consider what messages flow between them. Thereafter, you summarize the responsibilities of classes on class diagrams.

12.2   Keeping Application Use Cases Separate

Analysis is about getting a better idea of the requirements for the use case. With that understanding, you can define the structure of the system by putting them into packages, and so on. This structure is platform-independent and is preserved during design. Recall that the analysis model comprises two orthogonal structures: the analysis element structure and the use-case analysis structure.

- The analysis element structure defines the namespace for elements in the model. It defines the hierarchical organization. It comprises packages in which classes and their features will eventually reside.
- The use-case analysis structure defines how you overlay functionality on top of the analysis element structure. It comprises slices—non-use-case-specific slices or use-case slices—which will overlay the actual classes and class features onto the element structure.

You want your structure to be resilient, and this resilience must be along both structures. Changes are normally made in terms of the problem domain (i.e., abstractions or entity classes) of the system or in terms of use cases. For example, you might want the `Reservation` class to capture certain details. Such a change concerns an entity. There might be changes to the way a reservation is made. In this case, the change is about the Reserve Room use case. You make the analysis model (and the system) resilient by ensuring that each class performs a clear and cohesive set of responsibilities, and each use case deals with a particular use of the system. By having a clear separation between classes and between use cases (and between use-case slices), you get a resilient structure. This means that if there are changes in requirements, their impact should be localized to a few packages and classes in the element structure. Their impact must also be localized to a few use-case slices. Localized means that there are few changes, and the changes do not propagate to the surrounding elements.

12.2.1   Element Structure

Since the idea of a resilient structure is about localizing changes, you naturally try to put classes that will change together in the same package. So, for instance, you may find that classes that support a particular actor (i.e., the customer) may change together. Thus, you package the Customer

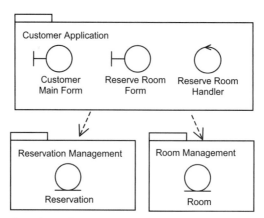

Figure 12-5   *Structuring the analysis classes for a use-case realization.*

Main Form, the Reserve Room Form, and the Reserve Room Handler in a Customer Application package, as shown in Figure 12–5.

You also try to factor out reusable classes into a package For instance, you find that the Room and Reservation classes are part of the domain and are reusable across many packages in the system. Figure 12–5 places the Reservation and the Room classes in separate packages. This is because the Room class is used in multiple functional areas in the system: it is used in room reservations and perhaps also used to manage the inventory of the hotel. Thus, the Room class is placed in a separate package from the Reservation class.

12.2.2   Use-Case Structure

The purpose of the element structure is to keep concerns about the abstractions or other elements within the system separate. The purpose of the use-case structure is to keep the specifics of each use case separate from one another. The use-case structure comprises both use-case slices and non-use-case-specific slices. Recall that use-case slices are for the purpose of keeping extensions and elements specific to a use-case realization together, and non-use-case-specific slices are to hold parts that are shared.

Non-Use-Case-Specific Slices. Figure 12–6 depicts the non-use-case-specific slices that are needed in the realization of the Reserve Room use case. The Room and Reservation classes are fundamental to the system. They

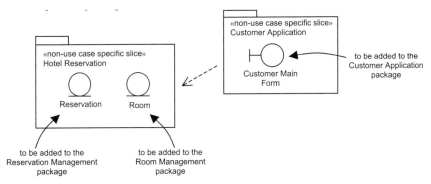

Figure 12-6 *Non-use-case-specific slices overlay initial classes and features.*

represent the domain of the system and will most probably be used in more than one use-case realizations; that is, they are not use-case-specific. Thus, there will be in the Hotel Reservation a non-use-case-specific slice that overlays the `Room` and `Reservation` classes into the respective packages within the element structure.

On top of the Hotel Reservation base slice, there is a Customer Application non-use-case-specific slice. It is used to contain common user interfaces for the Customer actor. For simplicity, we show only a main form from which a Customer actor can navigate to other forms to invoke the various use cases to reserve room, check in, check out, and so on.

If you want to extend the domain, for example, to hotel asset management, you will have another non-use-case-specific slice for hotel asset management entities. This introduces new classes to a new package with new classes in the domain-specific layer within the element structure. Normally, as you extend the domain, you also provide more functionality to the end users (i.e., there are additional use cases.) Accordingly, you overlay use-case slices that make use of and extend the classes you have just added through the non-use-case-specific slices.

Use-Case Slices. For every use case, there is one use-case slice in the analysis model. The use-case slice for the Reserve Room use case is depicted in Figure 12–7. It is a package containing a collaboration named Reserve Room that describes the realization of the Reserve Room use case in terms of communication diagrams, interaction diagrams, class diagrams, and so on.

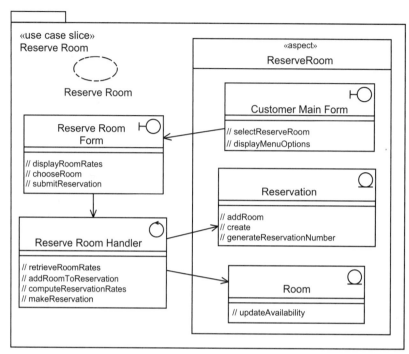

Figure 12-7   *Use-case slice contents: Reserve Room.*

The Reserve Room use-case slice contains classes that are specific to the Reserve Room use-case realization. These are the `ReserveRoomForm` and `ReserveRoomHandler` classes.

The Reserve Room use-case slice also contains class extensions that overlay onto existing classes: `CustomerMainForm`, `Reservation`, and `Room` classes. By existing, we mean that these classes have been defined in some non-use-case-specific slices or some other use-case slices that this usecase slice depends on. However, the Reserve Room use-case realization requires some specific responsibilities on these classes. These are added through the `ReserveRoom` aspect, as depicted in Figure 12–7.

As you can see, the total number of responsibilities in the use-case slice (Figure 12–7) is less than that in the use-case realization (see Figure 12–4). After all, the use-case slice contains only that which is specific to the use case. Thus, the responsibilities `retrieveRates` and `retrieveDetails`, which appear in Figure 12–4, do not appear in Figure 12–7.

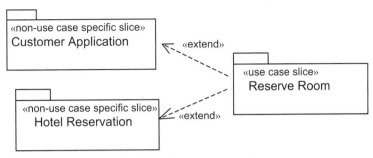

Figure 12-8 *Use-case structure context for the Reserve Room use-case slice.*

It is useful to describe the context of a use-case slice—that is, what a use-case slice depends on and what depends on it. This is helpful in understanding the use-case structure. It also tells you which use-case slices you will develop together. As an example, the use-case slice context for the Reserve Room use case is depicted in 12–8. Here, you see that the Reserve Room use-case slice has to be overlaid on top of both Customer Application and Hotel Reservation non-use-case-specific slices.

You have now separated the classes in their respective packages and specifics of each use-case realization into use-case slices.

12.3 Designing Application Use Cases

In the preceding section, we showed how to analyze an application use case, how to organize the classes that are involved in the use-case realization into layers and packages, and how to keep the specifics of a use case in use-case slices. What you have now is a high-level structure based on the analyzed use case. In this section, we describe how you proceed to design and implementation.

The basic steps in design are as follows:

1. Identify design elements.
2. Identify component and interfaces.
3. Refine the design elements.

We walk through each step in the following sections.

12.3.1   Identifying Design Elements

The first step in design involves identifying design elements. These design elements can be derived from analysis elements, or they can be new ones. We look at both cases.

Identifying Design Elements from Analysis Elements. Recall that the design model preserves the structure in the analysis model. Consequently, for each layer in the analysis model, you find a counterpart in the design model, and likewise in the packages. However, the design model must take into account some implementation considerations, such as the naming restrictions imposed by the compiler as well as naming conventions.

We use the Customer Application package in the application layer of the analysis model to illustrate the mapping. This is depicted at the top of Figure 12–9.

You will find boundary control and entity classes in design, but to distinguish them from their analysis counterparts, we give them different stereotype icons (i.e., squarish in design as opposed to circles in analysis). These are shown in Figure 12–9. The dashed arrows stereotyped «trace» indicates the analysis elements from which the design elements are derived.

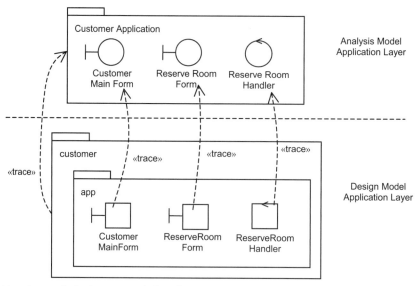

Figure 12-9   *Mapping analysis elements to design elements.*

During design, you will start to incorporate platform-specific elements into the design element structure. You want to keep these platform-specific elements separate. This is achieved, as shown in Figure 12–9, by putting the design boundary and control classes in an app package. Any change in platform should not affect the contents of this app package. Note that these design classes make use of minimal platform specifics. In Java, they are also known as Plain Old Java Objects (POJOs). In fact, the design elements that we describe in this chapter are all POJOs. We discuss how to incorporate platform specifics in Chapter 15, "Separating Platform Specifics with Platform-Specific Use-Case Slices."

As shown in Figure 12–9, the Customer Application package in the analysis model is now mapped to the customer package. We use Java as an example. The Java naming convention uses small letters for package names and does not allow spaces. In addition, during implementation, the normal convention is to have package names prefixed by `com.<company name>.<project name>`. So, for instance, if we take the company name to be aosd and the project name to be hotel, then the fully qualified name for the `ReserveRoomForm` can be as follows:

```
com.aosd.hotel.application.customer.app.ReserveRoomForm
```

The mapping of analysis use-case slices to design use-case slices is the same. Just as the classes in the analysis package are localized into an app package, the contents of the use-case slice in analysis are mapped into the minimum use-case design slice in the use-case design structure. This is illustrated in Figure 12–10.

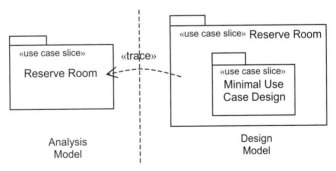

Figure 12-10 *Mapping analysis use-case slices to design use-case slices.*

The reason for having the minimum use-case design slices is precisely to keep the platform specifics separate from the platform-independent, as discussed in the previous chapter.

*New Design Elements.*There will be design elements in addition to those that are mapped from the analysis elements. You will frequently find that you must pass information between boundary, control, and entity classes. Instead of passing small data bits like customer name, customer identifier, and room description, you should pass entire objects. These are known as Transfer Objects. There are also container classes (e.g., `Lists`) to manage Transfer Objects.

Figure 12–11 depicts examples of Transfer Objects, namely, the `RoomTO` and the `ReservationTO`. The `ReservationTO` class has an association with the `RoomTO` class, and `RoomTO` has the role named room in the association.

Please note that they are not entity classes. They are just passed between boundary, control, and entity classes. Since the system is potentially distributed, they are made serializable (by implementing the `Serializable` interface in Java).

You normally have Transfer Objects in the domain layer because they are shared across application-layer classes. So, let's take a look at how a domain layer package (e.g., Room Management) in the analysis model maps to its counterpart (i.e., the room package) in the design model. The result is depicted in Figure 12–12.

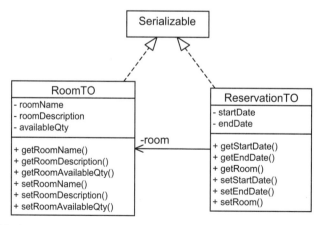

Figure 12-11 *Transfer Objects.*

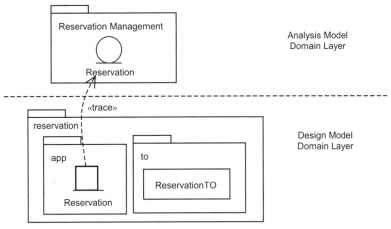

Figure 12-12 *Mapping domain-layer packages from analysis to design.*

The `Reservation` design entity is derived from its counterpart in the analysis model. In addition, a Transfer Object (`ReservationTO`) is located in a nested package within the reservation package.

12.3.2   Identifying Components and Interfaces

When you identify boundary, control, and entity classes and packages in analysis, you are taking the first step toward identifying components. Some of these analysis classes individually evolve to become design components. Sometimes groups of these classes evolve into design components. For each of these components, you must identify interfaces so that the components can be developed in parallel and can be easily replaceable.

Figure 12–13 shows the design elements participating in the Reserve Room use-case realization. Figure 12–13 further shows the packaging of these design elements into components. We named the components with the same name as the design elements and the interfaces to these components are named in a similar way but prefixed with an `I`.

Even though each of the components in Figure 12–13 is depicted as containing only one class, in reality there are several. These additional classes are identified as we refine the design of each component. To facilitate parallel development, you must define the interface operations clearly. The interface operations can be easily found from the analysis

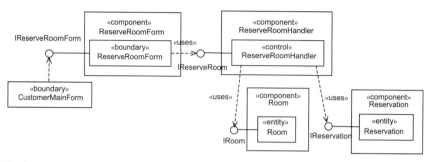

Figure 12-13 *Design components participating in the Reserve Room use-case realization.*

use-case realizations. In addition, you must define the return types and parameter types clearly.

Let's look at the `ReserveRoomHandler` component in greater detail.

Figure 12–14 depicts the component with the notation specified in UML 2.0. The `ReserveRoomHandler` component realizes the `IReserveRoom` interface. This is shown on the right of Figure 12–14. In UML 2.0, this is known as a *provided interface*—that is, this interface is provided by the component. For the `ReserveRoomHandler` to execute, it «uses» two interfaces to be realized: `IRoom` and `IReservation`. From the perspective of the `ReserveRoomHandler` component, these are called *required interfaces*. Provided and required interfaces help us think about a component's substitutability. To plug a component into a system, the component's provided and required interfaces must match those defined in the system. In Chapter 13, we discuss how the use of interfaces helps us achieve extensibility.

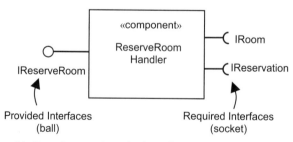

Figure 12-14 *Component provided interfaces and required interfaces.*

Note that at this point you are still considering the design of the system from a minimum design perspective, so the interface operation declarations should not have any parameters that use, for example, IP addresses, platform-specific database classes, and so on. If such parameters are included, you will find it extremely difficult to separate the platform specifics later. In short, the interfaces you identify here are from a minimum design perspective. In Chapter 15, we discuss how to incorporate platform specifics. Accordingly, the components will be endowed with platform specifics. It also means that components will have additional platform-specific interfaces.

12.4   Refining Design Elements

As you add more behavior into use cases with alternate flows, your classes grow. You will start to see more overlap between classes. One way to resolve the overlap is through use-case slices and aspects. There are other alternatives as well, which we discuss in this section. When exploring alternatives, your knowledge of object orientation and design patterns [Gamma et al. 1995] will come in handy.

12.4.1   Keeping Class Extensions Separate

Let's consider the case of the `Room` class. Assume that during analysis we found that the `ReserveRoom` class needs two operations: `updateAvailability()` and `retrieveDetails()`. Assume that `updateAvailability()` is specific to the Reserve Room use case and that `retrieveDetails()` is common across use cases. Figure 12–15 depicts different alternatives to deal with the overlap.

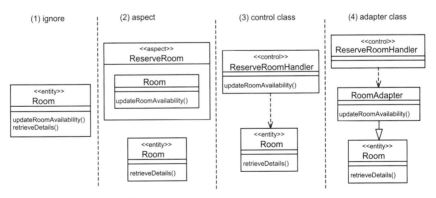

Figure 12-15 *Alternatives for dealing with overlap.*

Ignore. The most obvious way to deal with overlap with object orientation is simply to ignore it. This technique is shown on the left side of Figure 12–15. In this case, the `Room` class simply collates all responsibilities from different use-case realizations. In the absence of aspect orientation, this is the approach most practitioners take.

Aspect. The second technique is, of course, to apply aspects to keep the `updateRoomAvailability()` operation separate within the `Reserve-Room` aspect. The `ReserveRoom` aspect has a class extension to the `Room` class through intertype declarations.

Control Class. The third technique is to relocate the `updateRoomAvail-ability()` operation to the control class, `ReserveRoomHandler`. Since control classes are mostly specific to some use case, this seems like a good alternative in the absence of aspects. However, the operation `update-RoomAvailability()` might need frequent access to `Room` attributes. Since these attributes do not belong to the `ReserveRoomHandler`, programming will be awkward.

Adapter Class. The fourth technique is to create an adapter for the `Room` class. In Figure 12–15, this is achieved by creating a child of the `Room` class called `RoomAdapter`. The control class will now call this `RoomAdapter` class. For this example, this is a better approach than the previous technique (using the control class) because the `RoomAdapter` has access to all the `Room`'s attributes.

Applying aspects and the adapter class are comparative but have subtle differences. They are comparable because, in both cases, you have access to the attributes of the `Room` class directly. With aspects, however, no subclass is created, and the `updateRoomAvailability()` operation introduced by the `ReserveRoom` aspect is available to all instances of the `Room` class. In the case of adapter technique, `updateRoomAvailability()` operation is accessible only to instances of `RoomAdapter`.

In our example, we have only one use-case-specific operation, so it is simpler just to put the `updateRoomAvailability()` operation within the `ReserveRoom` aspect. Note that the `ReserveRoom` aspect may introduce features to other classes as well. Thus, it is certainly more convenient. Moreover, aspects can add operation extensions to existing classes and it is a more generic and preferred solution. However, if the number of use-case-specific operations added to a particular class is large, you may wish to consider using the adapter technique for that class.

Our discussion shows that there is indeed more than one way to solve a problem. Although aspect orientation is a new technique available to us, we have a history of existing techniques as well, and we should not abandon them. Instead, you should always weigh the pros and cons and choose the most appropriate technique for your problem. You may need to apply a combination of techniques.

12.4.2 Keeping Operation Extensions Separate

Overlaps are not limited to complete operations. Sometimes they occur within parts of operations. In particular, we highlight two forms of overlap that appear between peer use-case realizations. We call them *summation* and *selection*.

Summation. Summation occurs when two use-case slices expect different outcomes from the same operation, and the responsibility of the operation is to provide the union of the two outcomes. Let's consider the responsibilities in the Customer Main Form to display `MenuOptions`. Since we are realizing the Reserve Room use case, this will display menu options for reservations. Another use-case slice might need to display its own menu options. The composed result is to display the menu options for *both* use-case slices. If there are more use-case slices that need to display their menu options, then the composed result is to display menu options for *all* use-case slices shown in Figure 12–16. The result is a sum of all operation extensions from different use-case slices into the `display-MenuOptions()` operation.

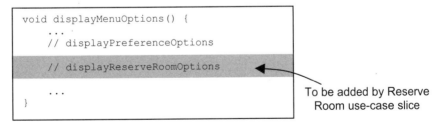

```
void displayMenuOptions() {
    ...
    // displayPreferenceOptions

    // displayReserveRoomOptions          ◄──── To be added by Reserve
                                                 Room use-case slice
    ...
}
```

Figure 12-16 *Summation of operation extensions.*

To add the operation extension, you define its declaration as follows for the `ReserveRoom` use-case slice.

```
displayMenuOptions(){ after(execution) displayReserveRoomOptions }
```

Recall that an operation extension declaration comprises three segments:

* The structural context indicates which operation you are adding onto. In this case, it is the `displayMenuOptions()` operation.
* The behavioral context indicates when the extension will be executed. In this case, it is just after the execution of the `displayMenuOptions()` operation.
* The final segment indicates the additional behavior, which is simply to `displayReserveRoomOptions`.

Selection. Selection occurs when use-case slices expect different outcomes from the same operation and the desired composed result is such that only one outcome is possible. In essence, only one is selected. Let's consider again the Customer Main Form, which allows the user to select a particular menu option. In this case, depending on which menu option the customer (the user) selects, the corresponding outcome is initiated. Without aspect orientation, you get a long list of if-statement blocks or a long list of case statements, as shown in Figure 12–17.

With aspect orientation, you can keep each of the if-statement blocks together with the use-case slice. This is achieved by the Reserve Room use-case slice with the operation extension shown below.

```
selectMenuOption(option:String){after(execution)handleReserveRoom}
```

```
void selectMenuOption(String option) {
    ...
    if(option=="Modify Preference") {
        // Handle Modify Preference
    }
    if(option=="Reserve Room") {
        // Handle Reserve Room
    }
    ...
}
```

To be added by Reserve Room use-case slice

Figure 12-17 *Selecting the handling of a use case.*

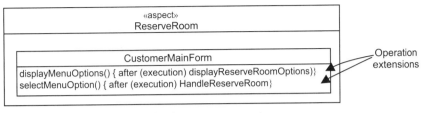

Figure 12-18 *CustomerMainForm class refined with operation extensions.*

Again, the operation extension has three segments. `selectMenuOp-tion(option: String)` is the operation being added onto—the structural context of the operation extension. The behavioral context, `after (execution)`, refers to *the end of the execution* of `selectMenuOp-tion()`. The additional behavior `HandleReserveRoom` is added just after the execution of the `selectMenuOption()` operation.

Figure 12–18 summarizes the resulting `ReserveRoom` aspect. It contains a `CustomerMainForm` class extension. This class extension contains two operation extensions, described above.

12.4.3   Keeping State Transitions Separate

So far, our discussion has been about modularizing operations and operation extensions into use-case slices and non-use-case-specific slices. We now discuss attributes.

If an attribute of a class is updated by one use-case slice, then there is no contention. It is part of that slice. For example, when reserving a room, you might keep track of the reservation creation date. This is specific to the Reserve Room use-case slice.

If an attribute of a class is updated by multiple use-case slices, then there is contention between use-case slices. Consider the case of the `Reserva-tion` class, and let's assume that it has a status attribute. This attribute has many possible values. The value of the status attribute tracks the state of a `Reservation` instance from the time it is created, submitted, confirmed, cancelled, and even when the customer checks into the hotel. The transition of a reservation instance from one state to another is triggered by different use cases or different use-case flows. Now the attribute must be pushed down to some non-use-case-specific slice, and if you follow the discussion above, this attribute should be in the Hotel Reservation slice as an attribute of the `Reservation` class. It should not be overlaid by any use-case slice.

Let's consider the operations that update the `Reservation` status by looking at how the values of a `Reservation` instance status evolve. You depict this using a state chart in UML, as shown in Figure 12–19.

Each rounded rectangular box in Figure 12–19 shows a possible state of a `Reservation`, in this case, one possible value of the `Reservation` status. Each arrow is a transition from one state to another and represents an update to the `Reservation` status. The transitions Create, Confirm, Cancel, and Expire are part of the Reserve Room use-case slice. The CheckIn transition is part of the Check In Customer use-case slice. The dashed line attempts to separate the states that results from the two use cases. This separation is, of course, dependent on your use-case specifications.

The transitions are accompanied by actions such as notifying the customer of the reservation status. Such actions are use-case-specific. Thus, you implement each state transition as either operations or operation extensions in the respective use-case slices.

If you choose to lump the transitions into a single `updateStatus()` in the `Reservation` class, then you have corresponding operation extensions in the respective use-case slices. Each operation extension is of the form similar to Figure 12–20. Each transition is an if-statement block that checks the current state and identifies the event, and based on these, performs the transition and updates the status attribute.

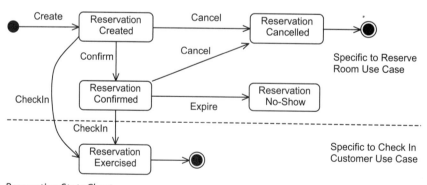

Figure 12-19 *Reservation State Chart*

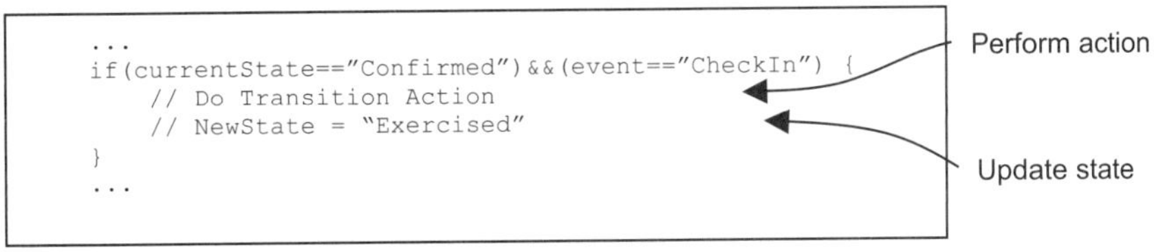

```
...
if(currentState=="Confirmed")&&(event=="CheckIn") {          ———— Perform action
    // Do Transition Action
    // NewState = "Exercised"
}
...                                                          ———— Update state
```

Figure 12-20 *Operation extensions in update status.*

This follows the same selection pattern we explored in our discussion of what happens when the customer actor selects a menu option.

If you implement the transitions as separate operations, then you have operations like `create()`, `confirm()`, `cancel()`, and `expire()` in some class (possibly the control class) within the Reserve Room use-case slice. These operations may be in different aspects within the Reserve Room use-case slice because they correspond to behaviors specified in different use-case flows. For example, the operation `checkIn()` will be in some class within the Check In use-case slice. There might be an alternate flow in the Reserve Room use case to let the customer cancel the reservation, so the cancel operation will be in a `ReserveRoomCancellation` aspect. But granularity is important, so it is likely that you have a group of related alternate flows implemented as an aspect.

12.5 Summary and Highlights

In this chapter, we walked through the steps from use-case analysis to design, keeping the specifics of use cases separate all the way. This represents a technique that is new to most of you, so let's briefly compare aspect-oriented analysis and design to object-oriented analysis and design.

With aspect-oriented analysis, you have an additional step of identifying use-case slices and separating classes and extensions across slices. This step is very important because you keep concerns between use cases separate early instead of leaving it to programming. You have progressed from aspect-oriented programming to aspect-oriented software development. You get tremendous payback because developers can now implement and test each use-case slice in parallel. Since each use-case slice deals with only one use case, it is much easier to understand and maintain. During design, you make an explicit attempt to keep platform specifics separate from the minimum design. This practice is useful regardless of whether you apply object-oriented analysis and design or aspect-oriented analysis and design. But with aspect orientation, the separation of platform specifics is achieved in a more elegant way. You can subsequently overlay platform specific use-case slices later, which we discuss in Chapter 15. Other than these two key differences, what you already know in object-oriented analysis and design applies.

13

Separating Functional Requirements with Application-Extension Use Cases

You build a system from a core and gradually add more functionality on top of it over iterations and releases. This functionality that you add must be well modularized and separated from existing functionality. By that, we mean that the added extensions must realize different concerns than existing ones realize. This modular separation is important, otherwise, the increments will be like patchwork. Application-extension use cases provide the means to separate functional requirements into such modular extensions. Such extensions can be used to modularize enhancements to provide richer functionality, or they can be used to factor out complexities to make the core of a system simpler and more reusable. With use-case slices and aspects, you maintain the modularity of use-case extensions during design and implementation. Through the use of appropriate design techniques, you limit the impact that changes in the core can have on the extensions.

13.1   Analyzing Application-Extension Use Cases

A key benefit of aspect orientation is the ability for you to add extensions onto an existing system. This is extremely advantageous, especially for building large systems [Jacobson 1986]. In fact, it is the only way to go.

However, a word of caution: you have to make sure that each extension represents some modular unit of stakeholder concerns. Otherwise, you end up repeatedly patching the system in an ad hoc manner. This results in tangling and scattering of another kind and makes the system impossible to understand.

The use-case technique provides the means to modularize functional extensions to the system through application-extension use cases. An application-extension use case represents a modular unit of functionality defined on top of a core that is represented by some other application use case.

In this chapter, we describe how to analyze an application-extension use case and drive it all the way to design and implementation. While the underlying principles are the same, you have an additional step of identifying pointcuts and operation extensions (i.e., advices in AOP).

We use the Handle Waiting List use case as an example in this chapter that extends the Reserve Room use case (see Figure 13–1).

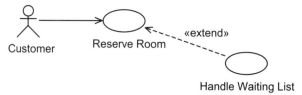

Figure 13-1   *Extension use cases.*

The Handle Waiting List use case has an extension flow, Queue for Rooms. It lets the customer queue up for rooms if none is available. The brief description of this extension flow is shown in Listing 13–1.

Listing 13-1 Handle Waiting List: Queue for Room Extension Flow

This extension flow occurs after the pointcut `UpdatingRoomAvailability` yields No Rooms Available.
The system creates a pending reservation with a unique identifier for the selected room type. The system puts the pending reservation into a waiting list. The system displays the unique identifier of the pending reservation to the customer. The base use case terminates.

Extension Pointcuts
UpdatingRoomAvailability = Reserve Room.UpdateRoomAvailability

---

13.1.1   Identifying Classes

As in the case of analyzing peer use cases, you first identify the classes that participate in the use-case realization. The required classes are depicted in Figure 13–2. Since the Handle Waiting List use case extends the Reserve Room use case, you expect to see the classes in the Reserve Room use-case realization to be involved.

The waiting list capability is potentially an optional service. Take it away from the system and what remains is still a functioning hotel management system. The recommended practice according to the Unified Process is to

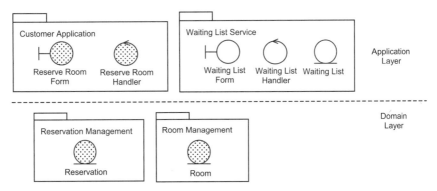

Figure 13-2   *Identifying participating classes: Handle Waiting List.*

put the classes that provide such optional services into in a separate package by themselves. Such packages are known as *service packages*.

The Waiting List service package is overlaid onto the application-specific layer. It contains three classes:

- A boundary class named Waiting List Form for hotel counter staff to view the waiting list.
- A control class named Waiting List Handler to coordinate the classes that are involved in the realization of this extension use case.
- An entity class named Waiting List to manage and store the contents of the waiting list. The waiting list is, in essence, a list of pending reservations.

13.1.2 Identifying Pointcuts

You now determine how the waiting list capability will be attached into the Reserve Room use-case slice. More specifically, you must identify the specific classes and responsibilities that will invoke the Waiting List Handler to put the customer in the waiting list. The extension pointcut in the use-case specification gives an idea where you ought to extend the base use-case realization.

```
UpdatingRoomAvailability = Reserve Room.Update Room Availability
```

Recall that when defining where operation extensions will execute, you need to specify the operation extension's structural and behavioral context. Use-case specifications describe system behaviors but do not define the internals. Thus, you can derive the behavioral context from the pointcuts defined in the use-case specification. However, you cannot derive the structural context from use cases, since the use-case model does not describe the internal structure of the system (i.e., the element structure).

Identifying the Structural Context. The interaction diagram in Figure 13–3 describes the behavioral context at the time when the system detects that there are indeed no rooms of the selected type available. This interaction diagram is an excerpt from Figure 12–3 in Chapter 12, "Separating Functional Requirements with Peer Application Use Cases," where we demonstrated how to analyze a use case.

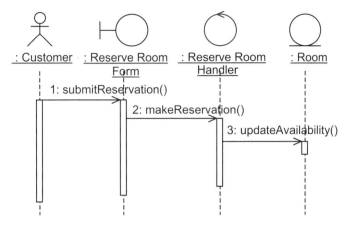

Figure 13-3   *Interaction diagram: realization of base use case.*

You must decide where you want to execute the operation extension to invoke the extension. The `NoAvailableRoom` condition is detected at `Room.updateAvailability()`. If you trace this message back to the actor, there are a total of only three messages (see Figure 13–3) where this condition can be handled. Technically, we are tracing up the call stack. Now, in design, you need to consider more extension points because you have more classes then. But for now, there are only three operations in the call stack and hence only three possible extension points for you to execute the operation extension.

Room.updateAvailability. Let's first consider the `Room` class because that is where the system first detects that no rooms are available. The `Room` class resides in a lower layer than the other two classes. This means that it will be called more frequently than the other two classes. Do you want to put the customer into a waiting list every time you find that there are no rooms available? Probably not, because you may invoke the `updateAvailability()` for other purposes. For example, if a customer cancels a reservation, the availability of the room must be updated; if a customer checks out, the availability of the room must be updated, and so on. Thus, there are many reasons to update room availability, but only when a reservation is being made is it necessary to put the customer on the waiting list. Hence, if you want to execute this operation extension to put the customer on the waiting list, you need to check the execution context of this operation—that is, the reason this operation is called. Although AOP gives you the ability to check the execution context during implementation, it just makes things complicated. In short, the `Room` class is not a good place to execute the operation extension.

Operations in Reserve Room Handler and Reserve Room Form. Let's move up the call stack and consider whether you should extend the operations in the Reserve Room Form or the Reserve Room Handler. The same reasoning applies: Do you want to add the customer to the waiting list whenever a call is made to the Reserve Room Form to `submitReservation()`, or whenever a call is made to the Reserve Room Handler to `makeReservation()`?

In addition, you must consider the information needed by the extension. The Waiting List Handler needs to put the customer into the waiting list, and this waiting list is for each room. Hence, it needs a reference to the `Customer` instance and a reference to the `Room` instance. You must consider whether the Reserve Room Form and Reserve Room Handler have references to these instances.

13.1.3   Allocating Use-Case Behavior to Classes

Let's assume it is the Reserve Room Handler that has a reference to the `Customer` instance. Thus, you extend the Reserve Room Handler class and specifically the `makeReservation` responsibility to invoke the Waiting List Handler. Now that you have made this decision, you can describe the class interactions, as shown in Figure 13–4.

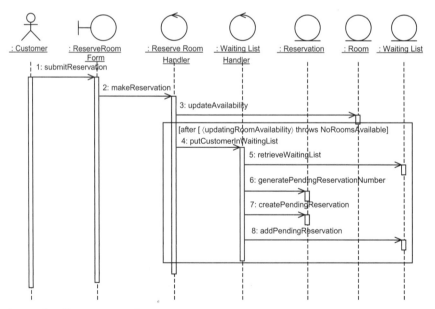

Figure 13-4   *Interaction diagram: queue for room.*

Behavioral Context. Now that you have identified which responsibility you want to extend, you define where within the responsibility you want to invoke the Waiting List Handler. This behavior executes at the point when the call to `Room.updateRoomAvailability` fails, specifically when a `NoRoomAvailable` exception is thrown. This is depicted in Figure 13–4 as a guard condition:

```
[after (⟨updatingRoomAvailability⟩) throws NoRoomsAvailable]
```

In UML, a guard condition is simply a Boolean expression, and in this case it determines whether the following messages in Figure 13–4 will execute. The pointcut `updatingRoomAvailability` refers to the point when the responsibility `Room.updateAvailability` is called. It is defined as follows:

```
updatingRoomAvailability = call (Room.updateAvailability())
```

Note that the pointcut identification during analysis is still at quite a high level. When you proceed to design and implementation, your responsibilities will be refined into operations, and your analysis classes may be refined into multiple design and implementation classes. Since you do not have sufficient detail in analysis, you should not be too detailed about the pointcuts. So long as you know the structural context and have some idea about the behavioral context, you have done your work.

Describe Class Responsibilities. After identifying the responsibilities of participating class instances and the pointcuts, you can consolidate the class responsibilities in a class diagram, as shown below in Figure 13–5. In Figure 13–5, you can see that the operation extension to invoke the Waiting List Handler is added to the Reserve Room Handler class. The rest of Figure 13–5 is just plain old class diagram.

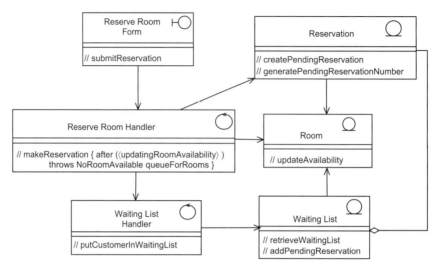

Figure 13-5   *Participating classes in Handle Waiting List use-case realization.*

13.2   Keeping Application-Extension Use Cases Separate

Having analyzed the extension use case, you can now update the structure of the analysis model (and that of the system). You once again consider which of the responsibilities you have identified are specific to the extension use case you are analyzing. You present the results in the use-case slice. This is exemplified for the Handle Waiting List extension use-case slice as shown in Figure 13–6.

As before, since the Handle Waiting List use-case slice shows only the specifics of the use case, you might also like to show what it needs to complete the entire use-case realization. To do this, you describe its dependencies on other slices, as depicted in Figure 13–7.

Figure 13–7 shows the Handle Waiting List use-case slice as an extension of the Reserve Room use-case slice. From Figure 13–6, you can see that the Handle Waiting List use-case slice extends the Reservation class in the Hotel Reservation non-use-case-specific slice. This translates to an extended dependency from the Handle Waiting List use-case slice to the Hotel Reservation non-use-case-specific slice.

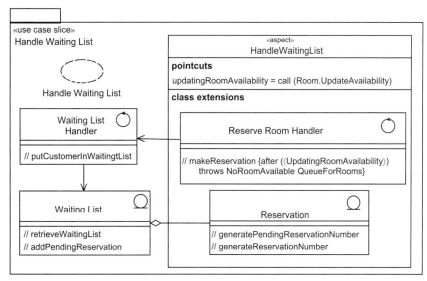

Figure 13-6 *Use-case slice: Handle Waiting List.*

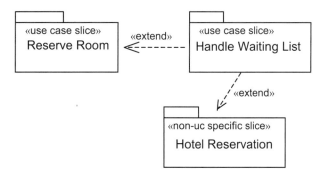

Figure 13-7 *Use-case slice context: Handle Waiting List.*

13.2.1   Structuring Alternate Flows

In the discussion above, we explained how to analyze and structure extension flows. The operation extensions that are involved in the extension flow are modularized within an aspect. Extension flows are a special case of alternate flows. You analyze an alternate flow in the same way as you analyze extension flows, discussed earlier in this chapter. You identify pointcuts and allocate the behavior of the alternate flows to the participating classes, and so on.

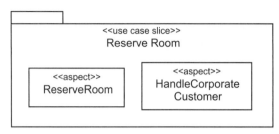

Figure 13-8   *Multiple aspects in use-case slices.*

You normally group alternate flows according to variables, as discussed in Chapter 7, "Capturing Concerns with Use Cases." For example, for the Reserve Room use case, you have variables such as different customer types and different reservation periods. You might have a group of alternate flows for handling corporate customers, a group of alternate flows to handle registered customers, and so on. The groups of alternate flows are analyzed together and realized as an aspect. Hence, you have multiple aspects in a use-case slice, as exemplified by Figure 13–8.

Of course, the Reserve Room use-case slice will contain classes that are specific to the Reserve Room use case, but since they are not important to this discussion, we do not show them in Figure 13–8. To find these classes, you simply walk through the same steps we discussed in Section 13.1. What we want to highlight here is this: good use-case models and well-organized use-case flows help you identify good aspects.

13.2.2   Keeping Alternate Flows Separate

Although alternate flows and groups of alternate flows are helpful in identifying aspects, they do not have a one-to-one mapping to operation extensions. Therefore, even though there is usually one pointcut for each alternate flow, you may have more than one pointcut in analysis and in design. This is because the use cases model the system from the external perspective, whereas analysis and design deals with the internals. Let's consider the case when an alternate flow exists in the Reserve Room use case for the customer to add his reservation preference (e.g., smoking/nonsmoking, high floor/low floor, etc.). The analysis of this alternate flow is depicted in Figure 13–9. The customer indicates that he wants to select preferences. He enters his preferences and then submits the reservation.

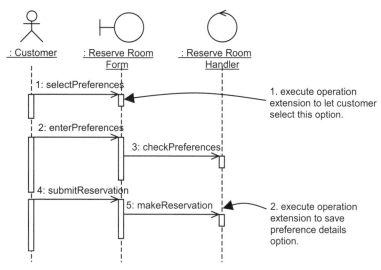

Figure 13-9 *Entering reservation preferences.*

It is evident from 13–9 that you need at least two operation extensions:

1. An operation extension to let the customer select the preference option.
2. An operation extension to save preference details.

You will likely find more operation extensions when you proceed to design—for example, validation checks on preferences.

Note that the minimal use-case design does not care about user interfaces—that is a separate concern. You usually model user interfaces concurrently for several use cases, even for extension use cases, to achieve some consistency between them. But user interfaces are not be just about look and feel, colors, and fonts—they are also about navigability. For example, the sequence of actions arising from the Customer actor will change your user interface flow, so you need to consider how these sequences of actions will be overlaid and what user interface mechanisms are provided to achieve this.

13.3   Designing Application-Extension Use Cases

The use-case analysis steps described above help you establish a high-level organization of the analysis elements. During design, you map these analysis elements into design elements, identify further design elements, and refine the packages and design elements themselves. The approach you apply for designing extension use cases and peer use cases is very much the same. Since they are so similar, we need not repeat the discussion. Instead, we discuss design issues specific to extension use cases:

- Designing operation extensions (i.e., advices)
- Identifying interfaces from use-case extensions
- Achieving extensibility

13.3.1   Designing Operation Extensions

A well-designed operation extension follows the same principle of well-designed operations in classes. You should avoid long parameter lists in operations. Likewise, you should avoid using long parameter lists in operation extensions and advices. Each operation should be single-minded in performing a particular action. Likewise, each operation extension should be single-minded in providing the crosscutting behavior.

Crosscutting extensions are just that—they are extensions. They should be small and they should delegate as much as possible the crosscutting behavior to additional classes that they invoke. In this way, the crosscutting behavior is localized within these additional classes and consequently is more reusable.

Operation extensions act like glue code to invoke crosscutting behaviors. They are subject to changes in the base code. Changes in the base should be prevented from propagating to the classes that perform the actual crosscutting behavior.

To keep the operation extension simple, it must execute within an appropriate context. The same principles we discussed in Section 13.1.2, Identifying Pointcuts, regarding the considerations for choosing the structural context and the behavioral context of the operation extension, apply when you proceed to design and implementation.

13.3.2   Identifying Component Interfaces from Use-Case Extensions

As mentioned in the previous section, operation extension ought to be small. Most of the behavior should be delegated to a new class that realizes the extension flow. In the Handle Waiting List extension use-case example, the WaitingListHandler is the new class. So, the Reserve-RoomHandler class extension makes calls to the WaitingListHandler.

To limit the impact of changes in the WaitingListHandler on the ReserveRoomHandler class extension, you can encapsulate the behavior of the WaitingListHandler class behind an interface. This is depicted in Figure 13–10; the interface is named IWaitingListHandler. The IWaitingListHandler is the required interface for the ReserveRoomHandler. The same IWaitingListHandler interface is the provided interface from the WaitingListHandler.

You can see that there is indeed a systematic approach to achieve extensibility with both the use-case structure and the design element structure. Briefly, the approach is described as follows:

1. **Identify extension points to existing use case:** In the Handle Waiting List example, the extension point is Update Room Availability.
2. **Identify the interfaces between components:** In this example, the interface is named IWaitingListHandler.
3. **Overlay existing component with extension use-case slice to invoke new component:** The Handle Waiting List use-case slice adds an extension to the ReserveRoomHandler component to call the WaitingListHandler.

These three steps are depicted in 13–11.

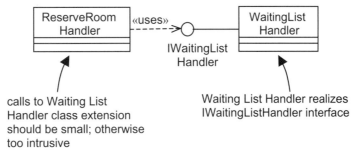

Figure 13-10 *Interfaces for extensions.*

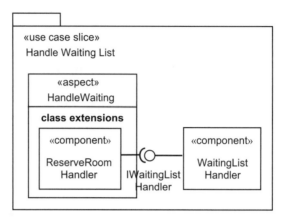

Figure 13-11 *Component interfaces for use-case extensions.*

In the following sections, we discuss how these basic steps can help you achieve extensibility under two scenarios: extending a use case with multiple extension use cases and extending multiple existing use cases with a new use case.

13.3.3   Dealing with Multiple Extensions to a Use Case

An extension point in a base use case can be extended by potentially many extension use cases, each introducing a different behavior. For example, one way to handle the unavailability of rooms is through a waiting list, as we discussed in detail. Another alternative is to find a room elsewhere, perhaps in a different hotel. This implies another extension use case, which we call Find Room, depicted in Figure 13–12.

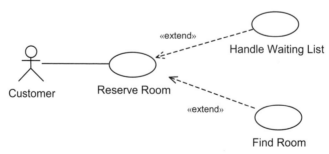

Figure 13-12 *Reserve Room use case extended by Find Room use case.*

Both Handle Waiting List and Find Room use cases extend the base Reserve Room use case at the same extension point. This means that the interface named `IWaitingListHandler` described in Figure 13–10 is no longer suitable, since the name `IWaitingListHandler` restricts the realization to having something to do with a waiting list. A better interface name would be `INoRoomAvailableHandler`, as shown in Figure 13–13. This interface can be realized by the `WaitingListHandler` or another class, which we call `RoomFinder`. The purpose of `RoomFinder`, as the name implies, is to find an available room in another hotel.

In Figure 13–13, we have introduced another class, called `NoRoomAvailableDelegate`. This class is responsible for determining whether to invoke the `WaitingListHandler` or the `RoomFinder`. It simplifies the operation extension for the `ReserveRoomHandler`.

Figure 13-13 also shows the components identified for the Hotel Management System. The `ReserveRoomHandler` component was first introduced in Section 12.3.2. In Section 12.3.2, we only presented one class.

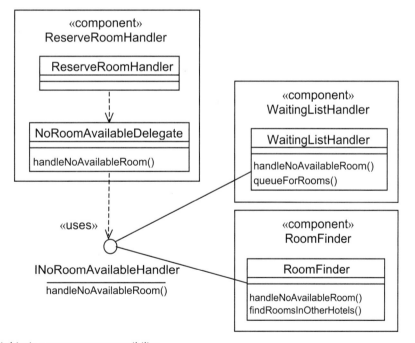

Figure 13-13 *Achieving component extensibility.*

Now we have introduced another class to the `ReserveRoomHandler` component, the `NoRoomAvailableDelegate`. Figure 13–13 also shows two additional components: `WaitingListHandler` and `RoomFinder`.

It may seem that we are using object-oriented concepts (e.g., delegates and interfaces) to achieve extensibility. Where does aspect orientation come into play? Aspects are used to introduce class extensions onto the `ReserveRoomHandler` to invoke the `NoRoomAvailableDelegate`. The `NoRoomAvailableDelegate` class determines whether it will invoke the `WaitingListHandler` or the `RoomFinder`. If another realization of `INoRoomAvailableHandler` interface is added to the system, the `NoRoomAvailableDelegate` class should be able to call this new realization. This can be achieved through some configuration file that describes how the new realization can be instantiated and invoked.

Thus, what you have now is an extensible Reserve Room use-case realization, which you can easily plug in to a new realization of the `INoRoomAvailableHandler` interface. This is depicted in Figure 13–14, which shows the `ReserveRoomHandler` component having a required interface `INoRoomAvailableHandler`. This can be plugged in by either the `WaitingListHandler` or the `RoomFinder` component.

Note that the original `ReserveRoomHandler` component does not have the `INoRoomAvailableHandler` required interface. This interface and

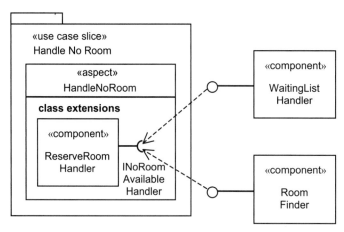

Figure 13-14 *Achieving extensibility through use-case slices.*

the `NoRoomAvailableDelegate`, which we mentioned earlier, are introduced by the Handle No Room use-case slice. Thus, the extensibility mechanism for you to plug in the `WaitingListHandler` component or the `RoomFinder` component is kept separate from the base `Reserve-RoomHandler` behavior.

Figure 13–14 differs from Figure 13–11 in that the components realizing the extension use case (i.e., the `WaitingListHandler` and `RoomFinder` components) are outside the extension use-case slice. This is because the purpose of the Handle No Room use-case slice is to introduce the extensibility mechanism, not the components to be plugged in.

13.3.4   Extending Multiple Use Cases

In the above example, we have extension use cases extending only one use case. Let's look at another situation in which an enhancement affects multiple use cases. For example, you want to add a new and special kind of room, like a penthouse or an executive suite for businessmen. This kind of extension affects many use cases. You identify the extension points for each of these use cases. The extension points are mapped to required interfaces to existing components that realize the existing use cases. A use-case slice then introduces this extensibility mechanism.

Figure 13–15 describes how you can design extensibility into the system one new capability at a time. In this case, you want the system to handle a new and different room type.

Designing an extensibility mechanism starts with modeling concerns—with use cases. You identify the use cases that are affected by the introduction of the new room type and the extension points in these existing use cases. As an example, the Handle New Room Type use case extends three existing use cases: Reserve Room, Check In Customer, and Check Out Customer. These are shown on the left-hand side of Figure 13–15.

The right-hand side of Figure 13–15 shows the Handle Different Room Type use-case slice. In essence, it extends the components realizing the use cases on the left with the ability to call the new room type component through the required interfaces.

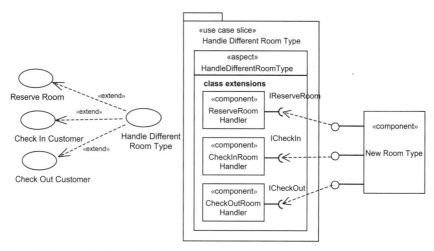

Figure 13-15 *Introducing extensibility mechanism with use-case slices.*

In Chapter 7, we highlighted the need to consider the variability of your system. For example, the Hotel Management System needs to handle different kinds of reservation schemes, different kinds of customer types, and so on. You can treat each case as an extension use case and go through the steps in Figure 13–15. After doing that, you will have a set of extensibility use-case slices offering a set of required interfaces. What you have achieved now is a domain-specific framework (i.e., a Hotel Management System framework) by which you can plug in components to deal with different kinds of variations. In short, you have an extensible architecture.

13.4   Dealing with Changes in the Base

At this point, we want to discuss a specific issue on designing extensions. Extensions are specified on top of a base. In this chapter, we discuss an extending use case on top of a base use case, or an alternate flow on top of a basic flow. This is a technique for keeping extensions separate. Changes from the extension do not impact the base. However, changes to the base do affect the extensions.

What you want to do is limit the impact of any changes to the base on the extension. We briefly discuss some techniques to deal with possible changes in the base.

In simplistic terms, each step of a use case involves moving object attribute values from the database to the actor (i.e., retrieval of information) or moving information from the actor to the database or performing some computation on objects. This is exemplified in Figure 13–16.

You frequently need to traverse through structures of some kind, as shown in Figure 13–16.

1. You must populate the data values in the user interface structure with values from the object structure. You might need to set the values of elements in the object structure based on the inputs provided by the user interface structure.
2. You must traverse the object structure to perform computation. For example, to compute the bill for a customer, you might need to loop through the reservations she has made and, for each reservation check, how many rooms she has reserved, and so on.
3. You must populate values of the object structure elements with the values held in the database structure or vice versa.

Since you will be spending the bulk of the development effort on traversing structures, it makes sense to take the effort to keep traversals separate from computation. These structures are frequently part of the same base that other use-case slices depend on. Keeping traversal separate from computation has two benefits. First, if there are changes to the structures, only the traversals get affected. The impact on the computation is limited. There are several ways to make a system resilient to such changes. We discuss them briefly. Second, even if changes to the structures do impact the computation, keeping traversal separate from the structure makes your implementation more easily understandable.

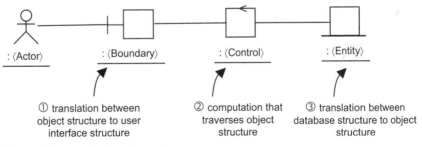

Figure 13-16 *Effects of changes in element structure.*

Before we go on, we like to highlight again that the minimal use-case design is not concerned with user interfaces and the database itself. User interfaces and databases are platform-specific. We explain how you overlay these on top of the minimal use-case design in Chapter 15 when we discuss keeping platform-specifics separate. Nevertheless, the minimal use-case design does have an object structure and is subject to changes in this object structure. That is why we discuss how to deal with such changes here.

13.4.1   Applying Reflection

One technique is to use some kind of runtime identification. The ability to find out information about objects at runtime is called *reflection*. Instead of hardcoding the traversal based on the data structure, you discover the data structure through reflection. Hence, if there are slight changes to the data structure, the traversal code is still valid.

Applying reflection, however, has runtime-performance penalties. Another approach is to use reflection-based code-generation techniques. Code generators reflect on the data structure and generate code based on the data structure and some template. For example, you can have templates and tools to generate database queries and present the results. So, if the underlying structure changes, then all you need to do is to regenerate the codes. Of course, anything that depends on the generated code may be affected, but at least you can generate the code automatically. With aspect orientation, since different slices are kept separate, you do not need to worry about the potential of the code generator overwriting other parts of the system, because you can keep them in separate slices.

13.4.2   Applying Design Patterns

Another technique is available through the Visitor and Strategy design patterns. We highlight this technique because it underpins adaptive programming—one of the research areas in aspect orientation.

To make the discussion concrete, let's consider the example of bill computation, as illustrated in Figure 13–17 and shows the cost of the bill is the total of all reservation costs multiplied by the tax. The operation `computeCost()` in the `Bill` class sums up the costs of the individual `Reservations` items.

The cost of a reservation is the cost of the associated room multiplied by the duration of the reservation (i.e., how many days a person is staying multiplied by the price per day). This is computed through the `compute-Cost()` operation in the `Reservation` class.

The cost of the room is by default its price. If there is any promotional discount associated with the room in the duration of the reservation, the cost of the room will be the discounted price. This is computed through the `computeCost()` operation in the `Room` class.

As you can see in Figure 13–17, three operations are added into the respective classes. This is not a good idea, because bill computation is now scattered across the classes.

The Visitor and Strategy patterns provide a useful technique. A strategy class defines how you would traverse or walk through the class instances that are connected according to the relationships defined in the element structure. A visitor class defines the actions at each point in the traversal. If you apply the Visitor and Strategy patterns to the bill computation example, you need both a visitor class and a strategy class. We named them `CostComputationStrategy` and `CostComputationVisitor`, as shown in Figure 13–18.

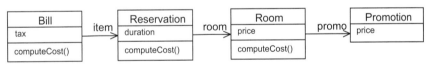

Figure 13-17 *Computation of bill cost.*

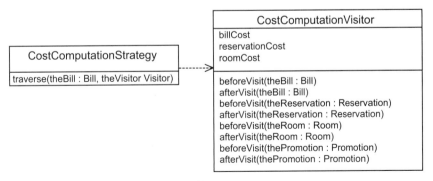

Figure 13-18 *Computation of bill cost using Visitor and Strategy pattern.*

The purpose of the `CostComputationStrategy` is to traverse the `Bill` containment structure. The `CostComputationStrategy` has an operation `traverse()`, which accepts a `Bill` instance and a `Visitor` instance as an input. The purpose of this operation is to walk through the items within the `Bill`. The relationships between these items is depicted in Figure 13–17. The `traverse()` operation calls the `CostComputationVisitor` instance to perform the actual bill computation.

Figure 13–19 depicts the pseudocode for the `traverse()` operation. In essence, it loops through the items in the `Bill` instance. Each time the `traverse()` operation visits an item, it calls the `beforeVisit()` operation with that item as a parameter, and each time it departs from the item, it calls the `afterVisit()` operation with the same parameter.

As you can see in Figure 13–19, the `CostComputationStrategy` contains no computation code. Computation is all left to the `CostComputationVisitor` class. It contains several attributes to hold temporary values during computation:

- The `billCost` attribute accumulates the total reservation cost as the strategy class loops through the reservations in the bill.
- The `reservationCost` attribute is a temporary variable for the cost of the reservation being processed.
- The `roomCost` attribute is a temporary variable for the room being processed. It takes the value of the cost of the room or the promotion value if applicable.

```
void traverse(Bill theBill, Visitor theVisitor) {
    theVisitor.beforeVisit(theBill) ;
    for each reservation in theBill {
        theVisitor.beforeVisit(theReservation) ;
        for each Room in theReservation {
            theVisitor.beforeVisit (theRoom) ;
            for each Promotion in theRoom {
                theVisitor.beforeVisit(thePromotion) ;
                theVisitor.afterVisit(thePromotion) ;
            }
            theVisitor.afterVisit(theRoom) ;
        }
        theVisitor.afterVisit(theReservation) ;
    }
    theVisitor.afterVisit(theBill) ;
}
```

Figure 13-19 *Pseudocode illustrating traversal.*

Table 13–1 describes what occurs in each operation within the `CostComputationVisitor` class. Basically, it is the algorithm for computing the bill value. Each operation updates the attributes in the `CostComputationVisitor` class accordingly. After completing the traversal, the final bill value is stored in the `billCost` attribute.

Table 13-1   *Computation Rules Expressed in Visitor Class*

Operation	Description
beforeVisit(theBill)	Set billCost = 0
beforeVisit(theReservation)	Set reservationCost = 0
beforeVisit(theRoom)	Set roomCost = theRoom.price
beforeVisit(thePromotion)	Do nothing
afterVisit(thePromotion)	If thePromotion is applicable Set roomCost = thePromotion.price
afterVisit(theRoom)	Set reservationCost = reservation.duration × roomCost
afterVisit(theReservation)	Set billCost = billCost + reservationCost
afterVisit(theBill)	`Set billCost = billCost × theBill.tax`

As you can see, the Visitor and Strategy patterns help you keep concerns separate in several ways. If there are changes to the `Bill` item structure, you only need to modify the strategy class. If there are any changes in computation rules, you just need to modify the visitor class. Even if changes affect both the strategy and visitor classes, keeping traversal in the strategy and the computation in the visitor makes the implementation more readable and understandable. In addition, temporary variables are only added to the visitor class, not to any class within the bill item structure, so it does not complicate the bill structure in any way. For this example, this technique is definitely more appropriate than using use-case slices and aspects to overlay use-case behavior onto existing classes.

13.4.3   Applying Adaptive Programming

The adaptive programming technique makes use of the Strategy and Visitor design patterns together with reflection. Recall that the goal of a

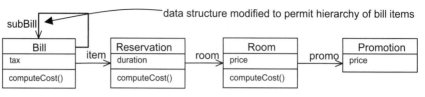

Figure 13-20 *Computation of bill cost.*

strategy class is to traverse a data structure. For the bill computation example, the strategy class has to traverse the bill item structure. shown again in Figure 13–20.

Instead of hardcoding the traversal as a series of loops, adaptive programming uses a strategy string, which in this case is "from Bill to Promotion." Based on this string, and using reflection, the strategy class will be able to traverse the items in the bill structure. Even if you modify the bill item structure, such as by permitting sub-bill items as shown in Figure 13–20, the traversal will still work. Basically, the strategy class will find, based on the string "from Bill to Promotion," all possible paths from a `Bill` instance to a `Promotion` instance.

The technique of adaptive programming is a special case of aspect-orientation that attempts to separate the class structure from computation. The visitor class in adaptive programming makes use of before, after, and even around semantics, much as AOP does. Whereas AOP uses these with reference to an execution point, adaptive programming uses it with reference to a data structure traversal.

13.5   Summary and Highlights

In this chapter, we deal with a class of functional requirements called extensions. Extensions can be enhancements to existing requirements, or they can be factored out just to make the essence of a functional requirement more understandable. You keep these extensions separate from the base during requirements time, as alternate flows or extension use cases. These are gradually refined during analysis and design when you give them structural context—which class, which operation the pointcut will refer to, and so on. In this way, you keep extensions separate from the base all the way to code.

Extensions (extension use cases, class extensions, operation extensions, component extensions) are a very important concept. Extensions are used to keep additional behavior separate from the base. They ensure that the base is easy to understand and maintain. Concerns between the base and the extension have to be kept separate. With use-case slices and aspects, you keep changes in the extension from affecting the base. At the same time, you want to minimize how changes in the base impact the extension. In this chapter, we discussed how this can be achieved through various techniques such as reflection and adaptive programming.

Our discussion was limited to functional extensions. In the next two chapters, we describe how extension use case are used to introduce infrastructure and platform specifics.

14

Separating Nonfunctional Requirements with Infrastructure Use Cases

A system needs to meet a set of nonfunctional requirements such as security, reliability, performance, and supportability. These are provided by a set of infrastructure use cases. Traditionally, the realization of application use cases tends to be tightly coupled with the infrastructure because the former makes direct calls to the infrastructure. As an implementation technique, you can use aspects and pointcuts to factor out the infrastructure. On top of that, you need a way to modularize infrastructure concerns. You achieve this with infrastructure use cases. It is common to find the same infrastructure use case being attached to different parts of the application. To improve reusability of infrastructure use cases, you model them as extensions to an application use-case pattern. You first define the pointcuts generically with reference to this application use-case pattern. Thereafter, you specialize and parameterize the pointcuts for the actual application use cases. This two-step approach keeps both the application and the infrastructure separate from one another.

14.1 Analyzing an Infrastructure Use Case

A resilient system attempts to separate the infrastructure from the application. This separation must begin with requirements and be preserved through analysis, design, and implementation. In Chapter 7, "Capturing Concerns with Use Cases," we discussed the treatment of infrastructure use cases as extensions to application use cases. This makes the application independent of the infrastructure. At the same time, you want to minimize the dependency from the infrastructure to the application. So, you describe infrastructure use cases as extensions to some application use-case pattern. We have such a use-case pattern known as the ⟨Perform Transaction⟩ use case. As an example, in Figure 14–1, we show the Handle Authorization infrastructure use case as an extension of the ⟨Perform Transaction⟩ use case.

As can be seen in Figure 14–1, the application and the infrastructure are separated from a use-case-modeling perspective. Now we want to maintain that separation when we realize the system. We demonstrate briefly how this is achieved through the Handle Authorization as an example.

Infrastructure use cases may have basic flows, which means that actors can initiate them directly. For example, the Handle Authorization use case depicted in Figure 14–2 has basic flows for defining user permissions.

The infrastructure is an important part of a system, and much of the technical complexities in a system lie in the infrastructure. Therefore, you need to spend time analyzing its requirements and establish a resilient struc-

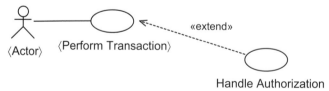

Figure 14-1 *Infrastructure use cases as extensions to application use cases.*

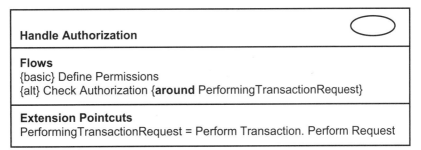

Figure 14-2 *Handle Authorization*

ture, as you did for application use cases. In the discussion to follow, we use analysis stereotypes—boundary, control, and entity—as the constructs to conduct analysis. We do not advocate jumping straight to the platform specifics when dealing with infrastructure (i.e., crossfunctional or nonfunctional) requirements. If you do so, you will be quickly swarmed by the platform specifics and lose sight of the requirements you have to meet. Instead, you ought to proceed from a platform-independent perspective. You will find the analysis stereotypes extremely useful to hide the implementation details. Furthermore, at this level of abstraction, it is easier for you to define a structure for the lower layers of the system. It is also easier for you to borrow from your past experience on the infrastructure (which could be on a different platform altogether).

Analyzing infrastructure use cases is similar to analyzing application use cases. The analysis of the Define Permissions use-case flow is simple, and we do not need to describe it further. The analysis of the Check Authorization extension flow, however, needs further discussion, which is the goal of this section. Unlike a normal extension use case in the application layer, which usually extends a single base use case, an infrastructure use case may extend or crosscut many application use cases. Thus, you analyze extension flows (e.g., Check Authorization in Figure 14–2) with reference to an application use-case pattern. As mentioned earlier, such a generic use case can be modeled through the reference ⟨Perform Transaction⟩ use case. The ⟨Perform Transaction⟩ use case serves as a template and a reference by which other application use cases are modeled and analyzed.

14.1.1 Identifying Classes

Let us identify the classes that participate in the realization of the Check Authorization extension flow. This will comprise the parameterized

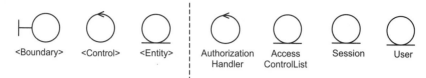

Figure 14-3   *Candidate classes: Handle Authorization.*

classes: ⟨`Boundary`⟩, ⟨`Control`⟩, and ⟨`Entity`⟩, which realize the ⟨Perform Transaction⟩ use-case pattern. These classes are shown on the left of Figure 14–3. We put these classes in brackets, ⟨ ⟩, to indicate that they are parameters to the Handle Authorization use-case slice. We subsequently bind these parameters using pointcuts.

In addition, you need classes to provide the authorization capability. These classes are listed on the right-hand side of Figure 14–3. The Authorization Handler coordinates the interactions between classes that are involved in this use-case realization. The Access Control List class keeps track of which user is able to do what with the system. The `Session` class tracks the user actions from the time she logs in to the time she logouts.

14.1.2   Identifying Pointcuts

You normally start the analysis of a use-case flow at the point when the use-case flow is triggered. For basic flows, the triggering event is typically the result of some actor initiation. For alternate flows, or for that matter, extension flows, the triggering point occurs at the point designated by the pointcut. Thus, the first step in analyzing an infrastructure use-case extension flow is to determine where the pointcut will be pointing to in the realization of the ⟨Perform Transaction⟩ use case.

The basic flow of the ⟨Perform Transaction⟩ use case is shown in Listing 14–1. It describes the pattern involving how an actor retrieves and displays some data on the form. Please note that Listing 14–1 describes only a general and simple case. There are, of course, many variations to this simple case, and you can describe them if necessary using alternate flows or extension flows in a separate infrastructure use case.

Listing 14-1 ⟨Perform Transaction⟩ Use-Case: Basic Flow

The use case begins when an actor instance performs a transaction to access or manipulate the values of an entity instance. The system prompts the actor instance to identify the desired entity instance. The actor instance enters the values and submits his request. The system accesses the entity instance and displays its values. The use case terminates.

The realization of the ⟨Perform Transaction⟩ use case is shown in Figure 14–4. It contains actor instances and class instances, each parameterized with brackets. The interaction between the instances is described simply, as follows: the actor instance performs a request through a ⟨Boundary⟩ instance, which delegates the processing to a ⟨Control⟩ instance. This ⟨Control⟩ instance invokes some data-access operations on an ⟨Entity⟩ instance. The ⟨Boundary⟩ instance then displays the results.

You now identify the context for executing the authorization check. This is based on the Check Authorization extension flow in the Handle Authorization use case (Listing 14–2).

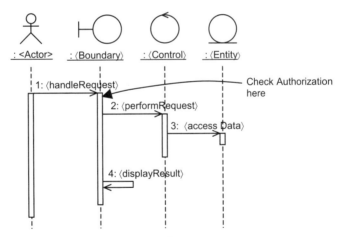

Figure 14-4   ⟨Perform Transaction⟩ use case: interaction diagram.

Listing 14-2 Check Authorization Extension Flow

This extension flow occurs around the pointcut
PerformingTransactionRequest.
The system checks if the actor has sufficient authorization for the request to be
performed. If the actor has sufficient authorization, the system proceeds with the
request. Otherwise, an error is raised.

Extension Pointcut

PerformingTransactionRequest = ⟨Perform Transaction⟩.Perform
Request.

Operation Extension. You now map the extension flow to analysis. This
means you have an operation extension that is responsible to checkAuthorization. You also need to identify the structural and behavioral
context whereby this operation extension executes—that is, you must
map the extension pointcut in the extension flow to the pointcut in the
operation extension.

Structural Context. You choose a class and responsibility (which will be
refined into operations during design) where you can get information
about the user or the session conveniently. Let's assume that you have
access to such information at the ⟨Boundary⟩ class. You execute the operation extension there—more specifically, within the ⟨handleRequest⟩
operation.

Behavioral Context. You now decide where within the ⟨handleRequest⟩
operation the checkAuthorization operation extension will execute
and how it will execute (i.e., the behavioral context). This occurs when a
call to the ⟨performRequest⟩ operation in the ⟨Control⟩ instance is
made. Thus, you have a pointcut:

    performingRequest = **call** (⟨Control⟩.⟨performRequest⟩)

In addition, you want to gain control of the ⟨performRequest⟩ operation
in the ⟨Control⟩ instance—control in the sense that the checkAuthorization operation extension will determine if ⟨performRequest⟩ can
proceed. You achieve this using the **around** modifier, because if the
checkAuthorization fails, the entire ⟨performRequest⟩ operation
will be bypassed; that is, execution will go *around* the whole ⟨performRe-
quest⟩ operation. If checkAuthorization passes, the whole ⟨per-
formRequest⟩ operation will *proceed*.

You now have the complete operation extension declaration in analysis, which is formulated as follows:

⟨handleRequest⟩ { **around** (⟨performingRequest⟩) checkAuthorization}

Since the ⟨Perform Transaction⟩ use case is not an actual use case but a pattern or template, the pointcut ⟨performingRequest⟩ is also a parameter. You must bind the parameters to actual use-case realizations subsequently. We demonstrate that in Section 14.3.

14.1.3   Allocating Use-Case Behavior to Classes

Now that we have identified where the checkAuthorization extension needs to be executed within the ⟨Perform Transaction⟩ use-case realization, we can describe the interaction between the participating class instances as shown in Figure 14–5. Figure 14-5 contains two frames. The first is labeled as follows:

around (⟨performingRequest⟩) checkAuthorization

It represents the operation extension inserted into the ⟨handleRequest⟩ operation of the ⟨Boundary⟩ class. This operation extension gets the ⟨Boundary⟩ to check authorization through the AuthorizationHandler. The AuthorizationHandler instance gets the user from the Session instance. You can assume that the user details have been associated with the Session instance when the user logs in to the system. This is achieved through the realization of the Login basic flow of the Handle Authorization use case. Based on the user details (i.e., user Id, user role), it checks the user's privileges through the Access Control List. If the user has the required authorization, the rest of the ⟨handleRequest⟩ proceeds. Otherwise, an error is raised.

Proceeding with the rest of the ⟨handleRequest⟩ in the ⟨Boundary⟩ is represented by the second frame. AOP provides a **proceed** keyword to achieve this.

The way you describe the interaction between the instances participating in an infrastructure use case is the same as that for a normal application use case. The usual practice applies. For example, an entity instance should not invoke a boundary instance (unless the boundary instance

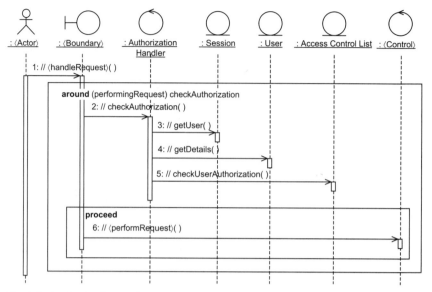

Figure 14-5   *Check Authorization interaction.*

subscribes to changes in the entity instance). In general, you should let a control instance do most of the coordinating work.

Describing Class Responsibilities. From the messages between the instances, you can identify the responsibilities of the participating classes. You can summarize the class responsibilities and the pointcut definitions in a class diagram, as shown in Figure 14–6.

Each box in Figure 14–6 represents a partial definition of classes relevant to the realization of the Check Authorization flow. You must explore the complete set of flows to find all responsibilities of each participating class. This takes place iteratively across the project life cycle. Note that the pointcut is not shown in the class diagram below. It is shown later when we define the aspect that contains the class extensions specific to the Handle Authorization use case.

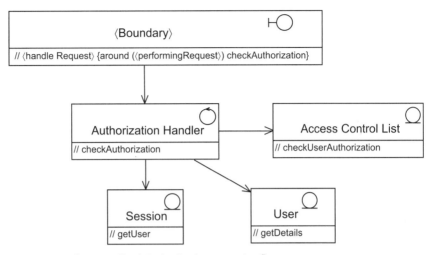

Figure 14-6   *Participating classes in Check Authorization extension flow.*

14.2   Keeping Infrastructure Use Cases Separate

Continuing with the Handle Authorization use case, you refine the model structure to keep the concerns about authorization separate from the application use cases it extends. This means refining the element structure and the use-case structure.

Refining the Element Structure. Consider if there are classes that are functionally related to each other. By functionally related, we mean that they are expected to evolve and change together. You put these classes in a service package. Since you are now dealing with the infrastructure, we call such packages *infrastructure service packages.*

Consider if there are reusable classes. If so, you can put them in a package in a lower layer. These packages support different infrastructure service packages, and we call them *infrastructure support packages.* Infrastructure services and infrastructure support form two layers in the infrastructure.

Frequently, infrastructure support packages are provided by the underlying platform in the form of some middleware. This means that you will seldom need to develop them. Instead, you will just make use of them through the infrastructure service packages. These packages are like the glue that binds the application to the underlying infrastructure.

After making these considerations, you can package the infrastructure classes as shown in Figure 14–7.

The Authorization Handler and the Access Control List are for the sole purpose of handling authorization and are closely related. Hence, we put them in an Authorization infrastructure service package. The `Session` and `User` classes are used by other infrastructure services, such as auditing and profiling. Since they are reusable, we put them in an infrastructure support package.

Keeping Infrastructure Separate in Use-Case Slices. Now that you have determined where the classes that realize the Handle Authorization use case should reside in the element structure, you must determine how they are added. The Session Management classes are fundamental to several infrastructure services and are therefore added through a non-use-case-specific slice named Session Management, as depicted in Figure 14–8. The Authorization Handler and the Access Control List are added through the Handle Authorization use-case slice.

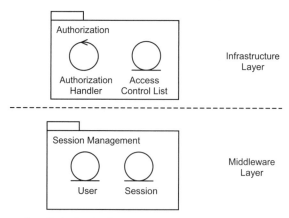

Figure 14-7   *Candidate classes: Handle Authorization.*

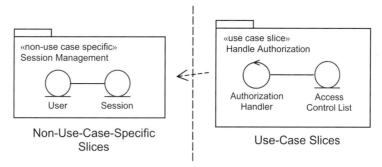

Figure 14-8 *Slices of the infrastructure layers.*

Let us take a closer look at the Handle Authorization use-case slice (see Figure 14–9). It comprises the classes and features that are specific to the realization of the Handle Authorization use case. It contains a collaboration (also named Handle Authorization) that describes the interaction between the participating classes. It contains the Authorization Handler and the Access Control List.

The Handle Authorization use-case slice also contains an extension of the ⟨Boundary⟩ class that it extends. This class extension is housed within an abstract aspect, HandleAuthorization (depicted in italics). It is abstract because the pointcuts, though identified, are not defined; that is, the pointcuts are named but no expression is spelled out.

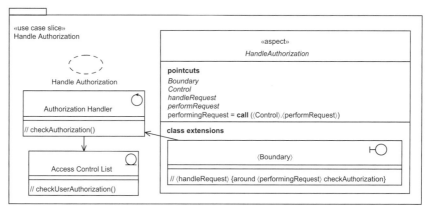

Figure 14-9 *Use-case slice: Handle Authorization.*

The Handle Authorization use case has been analyzed with reference to a ⟨Perform Transaction⟩ use-case pattern. Thus, you find that a number of parameters are currently unbound. These parameters are `Boundary`, `Control`, and `HandleRequest`. Recall in Chapter 9, "Keeping Extensions Separate with Pointcuts," we described two ways to express parameters:

- Through the pointcut mechanism in AOP.
- Through template parameters.

Both are possible, but in this case, we want to take advantage of the first method by using aspect-generalization capability. Thus, the parameters `Boundary`, `Control`, and `HandleRequest` are expressed as abstract (depicted through italics) in Figure 14–9. Accordingly, the `HandleAuthorization` aspect is also abstract. Thus, you have a prebuilt use-case slice waiting to be specialized and attached to an actual use-case slice. The next section demonstrates how you can specialize the `HandleAuthorization` aspect.

14.3   Designing Infrastructure Use Cases

In the previous section, we demonstrated how you can analyze infrastructure use cases using Handle Authorization as an example. The result is a Handle Authorization use-case slice that contains an abstract `HandleAuthorization` aspect. You now have a generic authorization component that is being attached to a generic or fictitious ⟨Perform Transaction⟩ use case. The next step is to attach an authorization component into some concrete application use cases.

As an example, we demonstrate how you can attach the infrastructure use-case slice (e.g., the Handle Authorization use-case slice) to an actual application use case (e.g., Reserve Room use-case slice). We also recognize that there are alternatives to AOP during implementation. We demonstrate how an infrastructure use-case slice maps to object-oriented frameworks (e.g., J2EE). Specifically, we consider J2EE Servlet Filter as an alternative means to keep infrastructure separate.

We complete this discussion by demonstrating how you can componentize the infrastructure and integrate these infrastructure components with application components through aspects or object frameworks.

14.3.1   Applying the Infrastructure Use-Case Slice with Aspects

As an example, let's assume that you want to apply the Handle Authorization use case to the customer package. Thus, you can specialize the abstract `HandleAuthorization` aspect in Figure 14–9 into a concrete `CustomerApplicationAuthorization` aspect.

Let's look at how you can define the pointcut expressions for the `CustomerApplicationAuthorization` aspect. Suppose you want to subject all the boundary classes to authorization checks. You can define the `Boundary` pointcut as follows:

```
Boundary = customer.app.«boundary» *
```

We have just introduced in the pointcut value expression a matching criteria based on the stereotype: «boundary». Thus, `customer.app.«boundary»*` refers to all classes within the `customer.app` package that are of the stereotype «boundary» of any name. You can see that the matching criteria need not be restricted to element names. In general, you can use element names, stereotypes, and tag values. In fact, you can use any modeling mechanism that distinguishes one element from another.

Since most programming languages currently do not have constructs for stereotypes and tag values, the naming convention during implementation must have some prefix or suffix to indicate the kind of stereotype and tag values the element is mapped from.

In AspectJ, pointcut expressions can use the + character to refer to all the children of a particular class. You can define the `Boundary` pointcut as follows:

```
Boundary = Form+
```

This means that you are applying the aspect on all children of the `Form` class in the customer package. You can likewise define the pointcut to bind `Control` to all `Handler` classes as follows:

```
Control = Handler+
```

In this particular case, we do not restrict which package `Control` classes belong to. This is because `Control` classes might not be limited to the

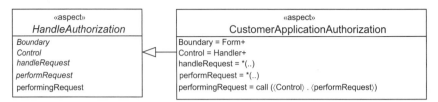

Figure 14-10 *Specializing the HandleAuthorization aspect.*

customer.app package. They may reside in the lower domain-specific layer as well as in the application-specific layer.

You can now summarize the pointcut expressions for the CustomerApplicationAuthorization aspect, as shown in Figure 14–10.

In 14–10, the responsibilities ⟨handleRequest⟩ and ⟨performRequest⟩ are bound to wildcards. This means that the authorization will be checked for every request that the actor initiates. In reality, you may want to impose restrictions on the kind of request you want to check. These restrictions will be project-specific.

14.3.2   Applying the Infrastructure Use-Case Slice with Filters

AOP is but one technique for you to keep infrastructure use cases separate. Object-oriented frameworks such as J2EE provide an alternative solution. In J2EE, a servlet is a Java program that executes on a HTTP Web server. It handles requests from an HTTP client (e.g., a Web browser) and generates responses typically as HTML output. The J2EE servlet specification provides a filtering mechanism that allows you to implement crosscutting concerns such as authorization at predetermined points. A *filter* dynamically intercepts requests to a servlet and responses from a servlet. The filter can modify requests or responses or both. Typically, filters themselves do not create responses, but instead provide universal functions that can be "attached" to any type of servlet.

Simplistically, the operation of the filtering mechanism for J2EE servlets works as shown in Figure 14–11.

Instead of getting the servlet to process a request from an actor directly, the filtering mechanism passes the request through a series of filters

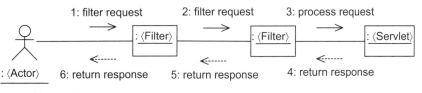

Figure 14-11 *Servlet filter mechanism.*

before it reaches the servlet. The response from the servlet then passes through the same series of filters in the reverse direction. Each filter can act based on the request and even modify the request and response parameters. It can also prevent the request from flowing downstream and return the result immediately. As you can see, the filters are lined up like a chain, so in J2EE, they are collectively called a *filter chain*.

This servlet-filter mechanism is an example of the Composition Filters approach to separate concerns [Bergmans et al. 2001]. The servlet-filter mechanism can be used to implement the authorization use-case slice. In this case, you can map the abstract `HandleAuthorization` aspect we discussed earlier (see Figure 14–10) to an abstract filter. This abstract filter deals with user requests. In addition, you need a corresponding concrete filter to deal with authorization specific to the customer application as a counterpart to the `CustomerApplicationAuthorization` aspect (see Figure 14–10).

Figure 14–12 shows how this is achieved. The left-hand side shows two interfaces provided by the J2EE servlet library. Simplistically, the `Filter` interface defines a `doFilter()` that accepts a request and produces a request.

The `FilterChain` interface defines an operation with the same name, `doFilter()`. This operation gets the next filter in the filter chain to perform `doFilter()`.

The right-hand side of Figure 14–12 shows the classes you will implement. They are both counterparts of the `HandleAuthorization` and `CustomerApplicationAuthorization` aspects respectively. The `HandleAuthorization` filter has two operations: `doFilter()` is abstract, and the `checkAuthorization()` operation performs the actual authorization checks. It accepts the names of the `Boundary` and `Control` classes and

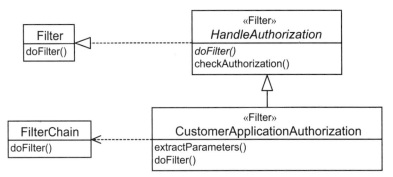

Figure 14-12 *Classes participating in HandleAuthorization implemented using servlet-filter mechanism.*

the use-case operation being initiated by the actor as input. Based on these three inputs, it determines if the actor has sufficient authorization.

The detailed sequence of events for the `doFilter()` operation in the `CustomerApplicationAuthorization` class is depicted in Figure 14–13. It first extracts parameters from the filter request. The request contains strings indicating which boundary class, which control class, and which action the actor is initiating. The `CustomerApplication-Authorization` instance calls the `checkAuthorization()` operation defined in its parent. If authorization passes, it calls the next filter in the filter chain.

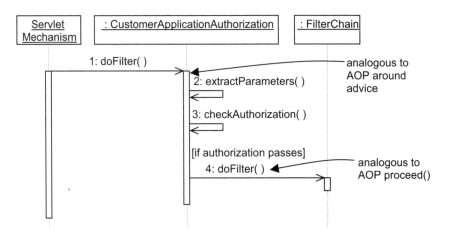

Figure 14-13 *Interaction diagram for HandleAuthorization implemented using servlet-filter mechanism.*

Thus, the `HandleAuthorization` filter provides generic authorization, and the `CustomerApplicationAuthorization` filter attaches it to actual application classes. This mirrors the approach we presented earlier using AOP. Specifically, the `doFilter()` operation is analogous to an `around` advice in AOP, and the `doFilter()` operation on the `Filter-Chain` is analogous to the `proceed` keyword in AOP.

What you see here are two ways for you to design and implement infrastructure use case. Let's compare the solutions you can achieve AOP with servlet filters. Both are able to keep authorization concerns separate in an unintrusive manner. The servlet filter defines a fixed execution point (known as a join point in AOP) whereby additional behaviors can be executed, specifically by implementing the `Filter` interface and the `doFilter()` operation.

AOP is more general, and with powerful primitives to express join points, it can be used to extend different parts of the system with additional behaviors. Thus, AOP is more flexible. But flexibility must be supplemented with guidelines. You do not want the owner of different use cases to add authorization behaviors at different places without architectural control. The ⟨Perform Transaction⟩ use-case pattern gives you a reference to anchor the pointcuts for your infrastructure use cases.

Whichever way you choose, whether AOP or filters, you still go through the same steps of use-case specification, use-case analysis, and refinement of the element structure, which we discussed earlier in this chapter. When it comes to design and implementation, you choose the most appropriate technique. Consider if a fixed-point extension offered by servlet filters is sufficient. If not, choose AOP techniques to find a better extension point.

14.3.3   Identifying Components in the Infrastructure Layer

Handling authorization is a common capability needed by most systems, so it makes sense to develop a component for it. Your system should also provide the means for you to plug in this authorization component. This is achieved through the Handle Authorization use-case slice, which is depicted in Figure 14–14.

The Handle Authorization use-case slice has a `HandleAuthorization` aspect, which can extend existing components with a required interface,

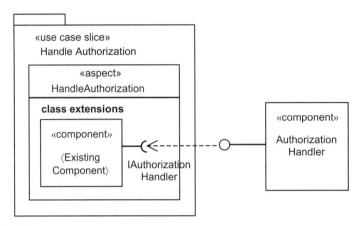

Figure 14-14 *Authorization component.*

`IAuthorizationHandler`, whereby you can plug in a `Authorization-Handler` component. We have shown two approaches to extending components: through AOP (specifically use-case slices) and through filters.

With the AOP approach, you can extend each component individually. With the filter approach, you extend many component at once, since all calls to these components go through the filter mechanism first. This filter mechanism can of course be introduced into the system through a use-case slice.

14.4   Dealing with Multiple Infrastructure Use Cases

In general, there will be a number of infrastructure use cases for your system. Not only do you want to keep the infrastructure use cases separate from the application use cases, you want to keep infrastructure use cases separate from each other. In fact, you should keep concerns and use cases of all kinds separate from each other. So, if there are any changes in the use cases, such changes will have minimum impact on other use cases. If you can achieve that, you have a very resilient system.

The fact that infrastructure use cases are analyzed with reference to a ⟨Perform Transaction⟩ use-case pattern is useful. Through the ⟨Perform Transaction⟩ use case, you can easily consider how to overlay multiple

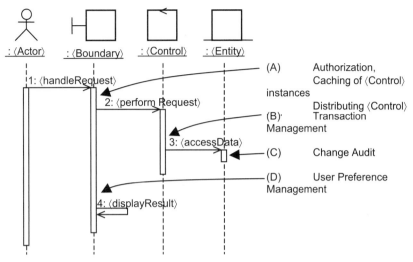

Figure 14-15 *Consider multiple infrastructure use cases.*

infrastructure use cases simultaneously. They are, after all, extensions of the same ⟨Perform Transaction⟩ use case.

To make the discussion concrete, we consider the ⟨Perform Transaction⟩ use case being extended by Authorization, Caching, Distribution and Transaction Management, Change Audit, and User Preference Management. Figure 14–15 shows where they may be potentially executed within the ⟨Perform Transaction⟩ use-case realization.

In Figure 14–15, arrows indicate the execution points where some exemplary infrastructure use cases are added:

- At execution point A, which occurs at the beginning of the ⟨handleRequest⟩ responsibility, you can execute an authorization extension, which we discussed earlier. You can also execute extensions that provide the caching and distribution of ⟨Control⟩ instances here.
- At execution point B, which occurs before any ⟨accessData⟩, you can execute a transaction management extension. This helps provide atomic updates to datastore, handle concurrency issues, and so on.
- At execution point C, which occurs with the ⟨accessData⟩ operation, you can execute the logging extension to save changes to a datastore.

- At execution point D, which occurs just before the ⟨Boundary⟩ instance ⟨displayResult⟩, you can execute an extension to track user inputs and to change the display according to his or her preferences.

We now explore the possible dependencies between the infrastructure use cases and discuss how to deal with them.

Multiple Extensions at a Single Execution Point. Sometimes, infrastructure use cases (specifically, their extension flows in use cases, which are translated to operation extensions) are attached to the same execution point. Execution point A is such an example. In such cases, you must determine whether they are indeed attached to the same execution point. Figure 14–15 is, after all, a relative high-level depiction of the interactions between instances. You need to zoom in further to uncover more detailed interactions. Thus, Figure 14–15 is expanded into Figure 14–16.

In Figure 14–16, the ⟨handleRequest⟩ operation has two steps:

- A call to the ⟨Control⟩ classifier to getInstance(); the purpose of getInstance() is to get an instance of the ⟨Control⟩ class.
- A call to the ⟨Control⟩ instance to ⟨performRequest⟩.

This refinement shows that the authorization extension is executed at a different execution point than in the other two infrastructure use cases. The authorization extension occurs at the beginning of the ⟨handleRe-

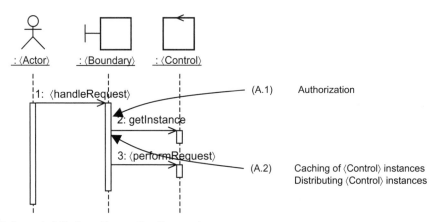

Figure 14-16 *Expanded ⟨Perform Transaction⟩ interaction.*

quest⟩ operation, whereas caching and distribution extensions occur around the getInstance() operation.

The objective of caching is to reduce the need to create ⟨Control⟩ references every time a ⟨Control⟩ instance is needed. The objective of distribution is to hide the fact that the ⟨Control⟩ instance is in reality executing on a different processing node. Though they have distinct purposes, they execute around the getInstance() operation.

Extension of Extension. In conventional programming, you can indicate the order in which infrastructure use cases are attached by simply ordering your programming statements in the existing code. However, with aspect orientation, you are overlaying operation extensions on top of existing operations, so you must define how overlaying is conducted. For example, you might want the distribution to be overlaid first and caching of remote instances on top of that. In this case, you have distribution as an extension of the ⟨Perform Transaction⟩ use case and caching of remote references as an extension of distribution. In use-case modeling, this is modeled as shown in Figure 14–17.

Please note that extensions of extensions do not necessarily lead to having aspects of aspects or operation extensions of operation extensions (i.e., advices of advices). This is because operation extensions are meant to be small. They should delegate the actual work to other classes, and you subsequently overlay on top of these classes. This is illustrated in Figure 14–18.

On the left, you see the ⟨Boundary⟩ class that participates in the realization of the ⟨Perform Transaction⟩ use case. To the right of the ⟨Boundary⟩ class is a Handle Distribution slice. It has an aspect named Distribution, which contains a ⟨Boundary⟩ class extension. This contains an

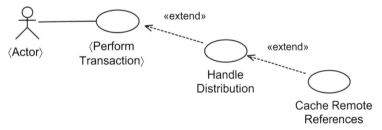

Figure 14-17 *Extension of extension.*

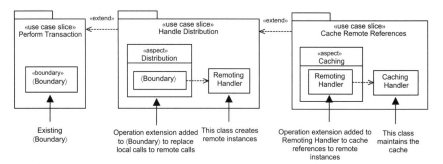

Figure 14-18 *Use-case slices extending use-case slices.*

operation extension that replaces local calls with remote calls in the original ⟨Boundary⟩ class on the left. Now, the operation extension in the ⟨Boundary⟩ class extension does not create the remote instances. Instead, it delegates the responsibility to a class named RemotingHandler.

To the right of RemotingHandler, you see the Cache Remote References use-case slice. In the same manner as above, it has a Caching aspect that adds an operation extension into the RemotingHandler to cache remote instances. This is achieved using the CachingHandler class. Thus, you see that in this case, you can avoid overlaying aspects on top of aspects. The implementation is much easier to understand.

Separate Extensions. Sometimes, you do have extensions at the same exact point. For our example, we have a Logging extension use case and a Handle Distribution use case on the ⟨Perform Transaction⟩ use case, as depicted in Figure 14–19.

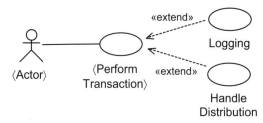

Figure 14-19 *Extensions that are separate.*

Let's say both extensions occur at the same point. They need to be independent and there should be no ordering between them, otherwise, the design becomes complicated. The situation becomes worse when you want to parameterize pointcuts to cover a large number of classes and operations. Thus, you should have either extensions of extensions realized, as shown in Figure 14–18, or extensions where order is not important, as shown in Figure 14–19.

Handling Variations in the Application Use Cases. In addition to considering multiple infrastructure use cases on top of the ⟨Perform Transaction⟩ use case, you also need to consider the variations that may occur in the application layer. The interaction in Figure 14–15 considers only the basic flow of the ⟨Perform Transaction⟩ use case. The variations can be effectively modeled as alternate flows of this basic flow.

You must consider what are the acceptable behaviors of the infrastructure use cases to such variations and handle them accordingly. This may result in:

- Identification of other infrastructure use cases.
- Identification of additional alternate flows in existing infrastructure use cases.

Both will lead to identification of more operation extensions and pointcuts for the infrastructure use cases. To resolve potential conflicts, you need to consider multiple use-case slices and aspects at once, as we demonstrated in this chapter. The benefit you get with use-case modeling is that you can quickly get an overview of the possible conflicts and refactor them with a use-case diagram such as in Figure 14–17 and Figure 14–19.

14.5   Summary and Highlights

In this chapter, we showed you how to keep the infrastructure separate from the application and how to keep each infrastructure services separate from each other. This prevents changes to one infrastructure service from propagating to another. Thus, resilience is achieved. You keep extensions separate by treating infrastructure use cases as extensions to application use cases. Use-case modeling gives you an added advantage—you have a high-level view of how you structure them effectively.

Central to our approach is the use of the ⟨Perform Transaction⟩ use-case pattern as a reference for analyzing infrastructure use cases. The result is a generic infrastructure use-case slice that you can specialize to attach to actual application use-case slices. The ⟨Perform Transaction⟩ use case also acts as a base on top of which you can consider the possible dependencies between infrastructure use cases. You can then either keep infrastructure use cases separate or merge them if appropriate.

AOP represents one way for you to keep infrastructure use cases separate. It is not the only technique. The filter approach is an example of another technique. In fact, AOSD is about systematically applying a host of techniques to solve the problem of separation of concerns and achieving better modularity. You apply AOP, you apply filters, you apply design patterns. Even object-oriented frameworks are techniques available to you.

15

Separating Platform Specifics with Platform-Specific Use-Case Slices

A system ultimately needs to execute on a target platform, so at some point in time, you must incorporate platform specifics into your design. This work is often repetitive, as platform specifics cut across many use cases. You want to be shielded from changes in the platform, since this affects many parts of the system. You want to introduce specifics as late as possible without ever doing anything twice. In this chapter, we demonstrate how this is achieved using the J2EE platform as an example. In particular, we show how processing tiers—presentation tier, business tier, and integration tier—are modeled as parameterized infrastructure use cases. These are subsequently mapped into parameterized use-case slices, which are overlaid on existing, platform-independent use-case slices. We demonstrate not only how you can keep platform specifics separate, but also how you apply both aspect orientation and architectural frameworks side by side. After all, both are techniques to achieve separation of concerns, and in a typical project, you need to apply both of them.

15.1   Keeping Platform Specifics Separate

Up to this point, we have discussed the realization of use cases (application or infrastructure) deliberately from a platform-independent perspective because our intent is indeed to keep platform specifics separate. Nevertheless, at some point in time, you must deal with them and incorporate them into each use-case slice.

Incorporating platform specifics into each use case is achieved is by treating each platform-specific concern as a special kind of infrastructure use case. As in the case of infrastructure use cases, discussed in Chapter 14, "Separating Nonfunctional Requirements with Infrastructure Use Cases," you design the platform specific use case generically with reference to a ⟨Perform Transaction⟩ use-case pattern. This yields a use-case slice pattern template. You then apply the pattern template on the existing use-case slices as needed.

Keeping platform specifics separate in this way is extremely beneficial if your team has designated specialists in each platform-specific area (security, distribution, user interfaces, etc.): you can have these specialists work on the platform-specific slices separately from other use cases.

15.1.1   Three-Tier Systems

Today, many systems are distributed according to a three-tier structure such that the presentation logic, business logic, and integration logic can be neatly separated. However, components no longer communicate directly over a programming interface, but over the network through some communication interface. This makes the implementation of the system significantly more complicated. A developer must understand not only what the application needs to do, but also the low-level details of such distribution mechanisms. It is a great benefit to keep such platform specifics separate from the realization of application use cases. In this chapter, we demonstrate how this can be achieved through a special kind of infrastructure use case—one that introduces processing tiers into the system.

We use the Java 2 Platform Enterprise Edition (J2EE) to demonstrate how to keep platform specifics separate from application-use-case realizations. J2EE comprises a set of technologies to perform session management, object management, communication, persistency, and other tasks. It is widely adopted by many organizations, and much literature has been devoted to it. One of the most important works that provides best practices and recommendations on the appropriate use of J2EE is documented in *Core J2EE Patterns* [Alur et al.]. It categorizes design patterns according to the above mentioned tiers.

Presentation Tier. The presentation tier encapsulates all presentation logic required to service the clients that access the system. It intercepts the client requests and provides authorization and session management. It controls access to the business services and delivers responses to the client. The main technologies in this layer are servlets and Java Server Pages (JSPs). Servlets and JSPs are themselves not user interface elements, but they do generate user interface elements such as HTML that are rendered on client browsers.

Business Tier. The business tier encapsulates business services required by the application clients. It contains the business data and business logic. Usually, most business processing for the system is centralized into this tier. The main technology in this tier is Enterprise Java Beans (EJBs).

Integration Tier. The integration tier is responsible for communicating with external resources and systems such as databases and legacy systems. The main technologies in this tier are Java DataBase Connectivity (JDBC) and J2EE Connector to integrate with legacy systems.

In this chapter, we discuss how the specifics in each tier are overlaid on top of minimal use-case design. We also provide examples to demonstrate different techniques to design slices, and we demonstrate how aspect orientation and object-oriented frameworks such as J2EE can coexist. This is important because you will likely be developing systems that use a combination of these techniques. After all, both are techniques to achieve separation of concerns, and you must find a balance between the two.

In the discussion that follows, we describe some of the J2EE core patterns and demonstrate how they are designed as parameterized use-case slices. Specifically, the J2EE core patterns help to identify the parameters in these slices. Our discussion on the J2EE core patterns is brief, since this is not an AspectJ, Java, or J2EE book. If you want to know more about J2EE and the J2EE core patterns, we suggest that you refer to the relevant literature [Alur et al.].

15.1.2 Tier Packages

In the previous chapters, we described how to identify the contents of the app package: The analysis classes (boundary, control, and entity) are mapped into design boundary, control, and entity. These design elements are meant to have minimal platform specifics. In Java, they are known as POJOs—Plain Old Java Objects. These classes are located in the app package of each design package (see Figure 15–1).

With the incorporation of distribution (i.e., the various tiers identified above), you need additional classes, which are application-dependent. For example, you need a class to handle Web requests for a use case; you need a class to provide distribution of a control class; or you need a class to access the database. Thus, while these classes are application-dependent, they are not POJOs. Instead, they must make calls to the underlying middleware. To keep these classes separate from the minimal design app package, we create one package for each tier. We call them *tier packages*. A tier package represents a subset of a logical tier in the design model, such as web, ejb, and db, as shown in Figure 15–1. A tier package is both application- and platform-specific. The Web tier package contains elements to provide classes to introduce Web presentation for a use case. The ejb tier package contains elements to support EJB-based distribution for a use case. The db tier package contains elements to support persistency, such as accessing a relational database or an XML datastore for a use case.

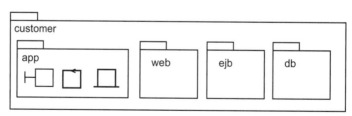

Figure 15-1 *Tier packages.*

We named the tier packages web, ejb, and db within Figure 15–1. This is just one way of naming tier packages. If there are more tiers in your system, you may have more tier packages.

Sidebar 15–1 How Do Use Cases Relate to Tiers?

1. The realization of a use case cuts across tiers. For each use case, you find some parts of the realization in the presentation tier, some parts in the business tier, and some parts in the integration tier. Likewise, in the presentation tier, you find parts of many use-case realizations. So, the question is, what primary decomposition will you choose for your system—use cases or tiers? Our choice is to take use cases as the primary decomposition. Thus, we have packages derived from use cases (e.g., Customer Application package in Figure 15–1), and within these packages, we have tier packages (e.g., web, ejb, db in Figure 15–1).

2. Keeping tier packages on a per-use-case basis follows our principles of slicing the system in terms of use cases. When you realize a use case, you first identify classes in the element structure. These classes are initially empty. Next, you determine the extension to these classes and possibly new classes. You then use use-case slices to overlay these class extensions and the new classes onto the element structure.

3. You do the same with the various tiers in the system. You begin with some empty tiers, and extend them on a per-use-case basis. For each use case, you identify what classes need to be added to the various tiers. You then put these classes into a use-case slice. Thus, you have parts of tiers in use-case slices. This also implies the use of tier packages within each design element package (such as the customer package).

Sidebar 15–2 Why Do We Keep POJOs in Separate Packages?

It is a frequent practice today to have tier packages. However, most practitioners do not explicitly organize POJOs into a minimal design package: they mix these POJOs (i.e., minimal design classes) within tier packages.

On the surface, mixing POJOs into tier packages does not seem to matter, but from a practical standpoint, it has several negative consequences. First, modularity is poor. A developer may mistakenly add platform-specific calls within a POJO. This violates the principle of having POJOs. Moreover, if the implementation of a tier changes, POJOs may accidentally be affected. It is like an innocent bystander in a crime scene. To be safe, the innocent bystander should avoid potentially dangerous places. Thus, you should keep POJOs separate from platform-specific classes.

15.1.3   Modeling Tiers with Infrastructure Use Cases

We have established that there is a need for tier packages to organize the design elements. So, how do we find these design elements? The way to achieve this is to start with use cases—what are the use cases for each tier? What is the value the tier brings? From this use case, you can then start to identify classes, find the responsibilities of these classes, and so on.

The top of Figure 15–2 shows the infrastructure use cases for each processing tier. They are all modeled as extensions to the ⟨Perform Transaction⟩ use-case template. In Figure 15–2, there is one infrastructure use-case template per tier: the ⟨Handle Presentation⟩ template use case, the ⟨Handle Distribution⟩ template use case, and the ⟨Handle Persistence⟩ template use case.

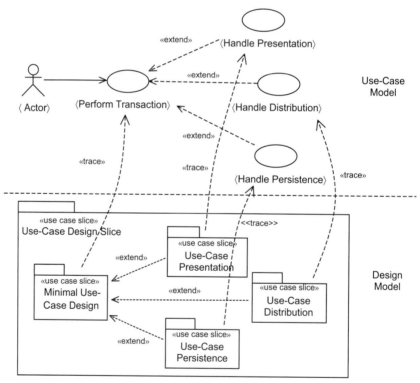

Figure 15-2   *Preserving the use-case structure.*

In essence, each infrastructure use case extends the base ⟨Perform Transaction⟩ use-case template with the specifics of a processing tier. The concerns of the ⟨Perform Transaction⟩ use case is kept separate from platform specifics. In Chapter 11, "Road to a Resilient Architecture," we introduced the concept of a minimal use-case design slice. The contents of a minimal use-case slice adhere to the realization of the ⟨Perform Transaction⟩ use case. The other slices keep the concerns of each tier separate. The use-case presentation slice keeps the presentation behaviors specific to a use case separate. The use-case distribution slice keeps the distribution behaviors specific to a use case separate. The use-case persistence slice keeps the persistence behaviors specific to a use case separate. Thus, you have one of these use-case slices for each use case.

In the remainder of this chapter, we discuss each infrastructure use case in Figure 15–2. For each of them, we briefly describe the use case, and we describe two realizations—one without the infrastructure use case, the base ⟨Perform Transaction⟩ use-case template—and another one with the incorporation of the infrastructure use-case pattern. Thereafter, we describe how you apply the infrastructure use-case pattern.

Sidebar 15–3   How Can We Automatically Incorporate Platform Specifics?

As you can see in Figure 15–2, you have one use-case presentation slice per use case, one use-case distribution slice per use case, and one use-case persistence slice per use case. So, you have three platform-specific use-case slices per use case. If you have 10 use cases, it means that you need to incorporate 30 platform-specifics slice. This seems like a lot of repetition and a lot of work. In fact, this is what most developers do today. It is quite tedious. However, with our approach, we keep the platform-specific use-case slices from the Minimal Use-Case Design slice. This gives us a safe means to generate the platform-specific parts and boost reuse significantly.

15.2   Overlaying User Interfaces

Let us look at how you can incorporate user interface specifics (i.e., the Web tier in this case) onto the minimal use-case design slices. We begin with the ⟨Handle Presentation⟩ use case, depicted in Figure 15–3.

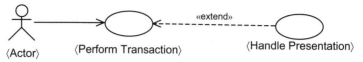

Figure 15-3 *Handle Presentation use case.*

Listing 15–1 briefly describes the ⟨Handle Presentation⟩ use case. The binding of the ⟨Handle Presentation⟩ use case cannot be instantiated directly. It is a pure extension. It has an extension flow to introduce presentation specifics into the ⟨Perform Transaction⟩ use case.

Listing 15-1 Brief Description of ⟨Handle Presentation⟩ Use Case

Extension Flow: ⟨Handle Presentation⟩
This extension flow occurs at each step of the ⟨Perform Transaction⟩ use case whenever the actor submits a request. The system gets the correct handler to service the request. The system generates an HTML output.
Alternate Flows
A1. Handle submission from different browsers.
A2. Handle long requests.

Listing 15–1 further shows an example of an alternate flow, which in this case is to handle the specifics of different browsers. There will likely be other alternate flows, such as handling requests with long service times by displaying a "please wait" message. You will likely find other alternative flows or special requirements of the ⟨Handle Presentation⟩ use case. However, we do not go into such details but proceed with the discussion on how to keep presentation specifics separate.

15.2.1   Minimal Use-Case Design without Presentation Specifics

In the minimal use-case design, user interaction is encapsulated within boundary classes. A ⟨Boundary⟩ instance handles requests from the ⟨Actor⟩ instance, as shown in Figure 15–4. Request handling is often delegated to a control class, which is not shown in Figure 15–4 for brevity. In addition, the ⟨Boundary⟩ instance holds in itself temporary data values. These temporary values can be accessed by the ⟨Actor⟩ instance for displaying. Thus, a ⟨Boundary⟩ class provides two kinds of operations to the ⟨Actor⟩, collectively represented as ⟨handleRequest⟩ and ⟨access-Data⟩ in Figure 15–4.

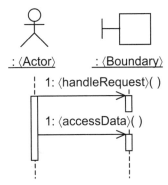

Figure 15-4 *Minimal use-case design for presentation.*

When designing and implementing the ⟨Boundary⟩ class, you create a simple test-case instance to invoke it. The test case plays the role of the actor. This follows the concept of test-first design, which we discuss in greater detail in Chapter 16, "Separating Tests with Use-Case Test Slices." Developing the ⟨Boundary⟩ class in this way helps you identify in detail the operations needed in the ⟨Boundary⟩ class as well as their parameters.

15.2.2   A Web Presentation Mechanism in J2EE

If you want to incorporate an actual user interface, you need user interface elements on top of the minimal use-case design. Additional classes are also needed by the user interface framework. For example, if you want the user interface to be Web-based, you need additional classes to execute the boundary class on a Web server. You also need classes to generate the actual Web display (i.e., HTML pages). In the J2EE core patterns, the Front Controller pattern provides the recommendations on how to design the Web-presentation mechanism. Specifically, it helps you to identify the classes needed and the interaction between their instances to realize the Web user interface. The typical interaction between the participating instances is shown in Figure 15–5.

As you can see, instead of having one boundary class in the minimal use-case design (see Figure 15–4), there are now four classes in the Web presentation mechanism (see Figure 15–5). Each class deals with a particular concern and has a distinct set of responsibilities.

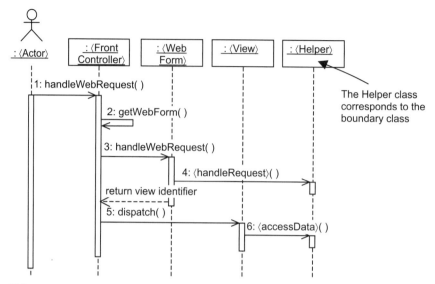

Figure 15-5   *Web presentation mechanism based on Front Controller pattern.*

Briefly, the interaction in Figure 15–5 is as follows. The user, through the browser, sends Web requests (specifically, HTTP requests) to the Web server. Upon receiving the request, the Web server invokes the ⟨Front-Controller⟩. Thus, the ⟨FrontController⟩ is the very first contact from the outside world to the system. It is responsible for finding an appropriate WebForm to handleWebRequest().

The ⟨FrontController⟩ is implemented as a servlet in this case. The Web server knows the existence of the ⟨FrontController⟩ class through an XML configuration file known as a deployment descriptor.

The ⟨WebForm⟩ is responsible for extracting the parameters from the HTTP request and converting them to data objects. The ⟨WebForm⟩ then delegates the actual handling of the request to the ⟨Helper⟩ instance. The ⟨Helper⟩ is a POJO. It corresponds to the ⟨Boundary⟩ class. It makes no references to HTTP requests but works on the data objects passed in by the ⟨WebForm⟩. All HTTP request-related processing is localized to the ⟨WebForm⟩ class.

After handling the request (e.g., reserving a room, querying the reservation status), the ⟨WebForm⟩ returns an identifier indicating which ⟨View⟩ must be displayed. The ⟨View⟩ instance accesses the data from the ⟨Helper⟩ instance and display them. This ⟨View⟩ instance is responsible for all the work in generating HTML content.

15.2.3 Designing the Presentation Mechanism

We now design the use-case slice for the Web presentation mechanism. In designing the presentation mechanism, you have to keep separate:

- that which is specific to the minimal use-case design.
- that which is specific to the presentation of that use case.
- that which is common across the presentation of any use cases.

Accordingly, there are three slices: the Minimal Use-Case Design slice, the Use-Case Presentation slice, and the Presentation slice. These slices are depicted in Figure 15–6. For generality, we model the use-case presentation slice as a parameterized use-case slice. The parameters must be substituted when you apply the slice on a specific use case.

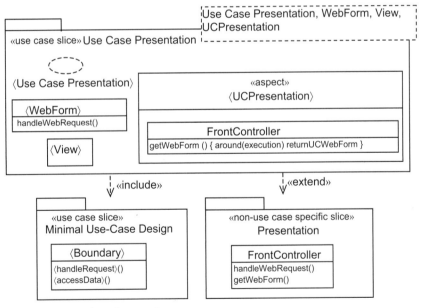

Figure 15-6 *Use-case presentation slice template.*

Minimal Use-Case Design Slice. The Minimal Use-Case Design slice is the result of refining the use-case analysis. It contains boundary, control, and entity classes and aspects that are specific to the use case. Since in this case we are only interested in user interaction, only the ⟨Boundary⟩ class is shown. The ⟨Boundary⟩ corresponds to the ⟨Helper⟩ class discussed earlier.

Presentation Slice. The presentation slice is non-use-case-specific and contains classes that are common across the presentation of any use case. Specifically, it contains the FrontController class, which is shared by many use cases. It is the first point of contact for the system when the system receives a Web request. The FrontController needs to find the correct ⟨WebForm⟩ to service the request through the getWebForm() operation. Consequently, the getWebForm() has many operation extensions containing if-statements to determine which ⟨WebForm⟩ will indeed handle the request. These operation extensions are use-case-specific and will be overlaid by the Use-Case presentation slice.

Use-Case Presentation Slice. The use-case presentation slice contains a ⟨WebForm⟩ and one or more ⟨View⟩s that are specific to the presentation of a use case. All ⟨WebForm⟩s should conform to the same interface. In this case, let's assume that they conform to the IWebForm interface. This interface is not shown in Figure 15–6 for brevity. We depict the IWebForm in Figure 15–7.

There is also a ⟨UCPresentation⟩ aspect to add the operation extension to the FrontController to forward the request to the ⟨WebForm⟩. The declaration for the operation extension is as follows:

```
getWebForm() { around (execution) returnUCWebForm }
```

It means that in the getWebForm(), you will have an operation extension returnUCWebForm. This operation extension determines which use case is being requested through the HTTP request parameters and returns the appropriate ⟨WebForm⟩.

Figure 15-7 *WebForm.*

The use-case presentation slice also contains a collaboration parameterized as ⟨Use Case Presentation⟩ to describe the interaction between user interface elements (e.g., views and Web handlers).

15.2.4   Applying the Presentation Mechanism

What we just achieved in the previous section is a template use-case slice for the presentation of a use case. To apply the template use-case slice, you need to substitute the parameters with actual classes and aspects. Figure 15–8 shows the result after applying the template use-case slice for the Reserve Room use case. The result is the Reserve Room Presentation use-case slice.

In Figure 15–8, the following substitutions are made:

- The ⟨Use Case Presentation⟩⟨Perform Transaction⟩ collaboration parameter is replaced by ReserveRoomPresentation collaboration. It describes the interaction between user interface elements that are involved in the Reserve Room use case.
- The ⟨WebForm⟩ class parameter is replaced by the ReserveRoomWebForm. This class is responsible for extracting HTTP request parameters.
- The ⟨UCPresentation⟩ aspect parameter is replaced by the ReserveRoomPresentation aspect. It contains an operation extension that will be overlaid onto the common FrontController so that requests from users can be forwarded to the ReserveRoomWebForm.
- You also need one or more views to display HTML results. You can create one view per Web request. Alternately, you can consolidate all requests into a single view, which is the case depicted in Figure 15–8.

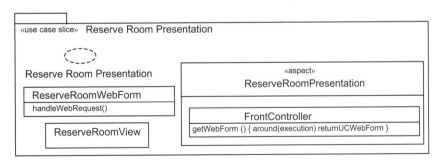

Figure 15-8   *Presentation slice for the Reserve Room use case.*

The strategy you choose is project-specific and is outside the scope of this book.

When you design user interfaces, you usually do *not* do so one use case at a time. Instead, you consider many use cases at once. Frequently, you must consider all the use cases associated with a specific actor. By taking the perspective of an actor, you have a better appreciation of the usability requirements—that is, what navigability is needed and what user interface elements are needed. Accordingly, you also design and implement user interfaces for many use cases at once. You will likely then incorporate use-case presentation slices for these different use cases together.

15.3   Overlaying Distribution

Distribution helps you improve the scalability and reliability of the system, but it does not add any functionality to the system. To the developer, incorporating distribution is one of the most repetitive tasks when developing an application. If there is a means to generate all the codes related to distribution, you can reduce such laborious work. You make this possible by keeping all distribution-related codes separate. If you ever need to modify the distribution mechanism, all you need do is regenerate the codes. Since use-case slices help you keep the codes separate, there is no worry about overwriting the work you have done.

Let us look at how you can incorporate distribution (i.e., EJB distribution in this case) onto the minimal use-case design slices. This is modeled in the use-case model through the ⟨Handle Distribution⟩ use case, as shown in Figure 15–9.

Listing 15–2 briefly describes the ⟨Handle Distribution⟩ use case. It is a pure extension use case as in the case of the ⟨Handle Presentation⟩ use case. The extension flow for the ⟨Handle Distribution⟩ use case essentially

Figure 15-9   ⟨Handle Distribution⟩ use case.

relays a local call to a remote machine. The alternate flows handle cases when the remote machine is not available.

Listing 15-2 Brief Description of ⟨Handle Distribution⟩ Use Case

Extension Flow: ⟨Handle Distribution⟩
This extension flow occurs at each step of the application use case. For each call to a remote machine, this use case intercepts the call from the caller and relays the call over the network. When the remote call completes, the base use case resumes.
Alternate Flows
A1. Handle remote machine unavailability.

You will expect to find alternate flows in the ⟨Handle Distribution⟩ use case. Listing 15–2 provides an example for handling remote machine unavailability. There can be more alternative flows.

15.3.1   Minimal Use-Case Design without Distribution

Let us now look at how you can incorporate distribution into use-case design. During analysis, you assume that instances reside in one process space and communication is via direct calls. During minimal use-case design, you have some idea which class you want to distribute. For example, you might decide to distribute the control class into a separate machine. Note that in general you can distribute any class, boundary, control, or entity. But for the purpose of discussion, we have chosen to distribute the control class. The same principle works for any class you want to distribute.

The usual interaction between the boundary class and the control class is depicted in Figure 15–10.

In general, there are two kinds of operations that the boundary instance might perform on the control instance:

1. Creating a control instance, such as through the **new** operation in Figure 15–10.
2. Invoking a normal operation, such as `makeReservation` on the `ReserveRoomHandler` instance in the case of the Reserve Room use case (see the discussion of the realization of the Reserve Room use case in Section 12.1).

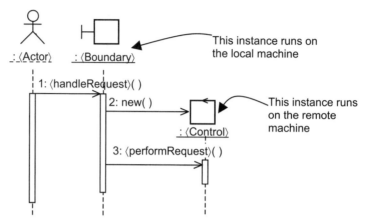

Figure 15-10 *Design realization of ⟨Perform Transaction⟩ use case.*

Since you are now distributing the control instance to a remote machine, you must intercept all these operation calls and replace them with remote calls.

Aspects do not provide any support for making remote calls and they do not create and manage remote instances for you. Aspects are just a general-purpose mechanism to provide the means to add behaviors to existing classes only. You must use some kind of middleware services to create and manage remote instances.

15.3.2   An EJB Distribution Mechanism

J2EE provides EJBs to help you create and manage remote instances. EJBs execute in what is called an EJB container. An EJB exposes two interfaces, a home interface and a remote interface:

1. Through the home interface, a client can create a remote EJB instance.
2. Through the remote interface, a client can invoke the remote EJB instance.

Recall that you want to distribute the control class (Figure 15–10) to a machine separate from that of the boundary class. You can wrap the control class within an EJB. To create an instance of the control class, you invoke the home interface on this wrapper EJB. You make a call to a control instance through the remote interface of this same EJB.

Next, you must intercept calls from the boundary class and replace it with calls to some proxy class. This proxy class uses the EJB services to call the control class through the wrapper EJB.

The J2EE core patterns provide a set of patterns to allow a ⟨BusinessClient⟩ instance on one machine to interact with a ⟨BusinessService⟩ instance on a remote machine. The ⟨BusinessClient⟩ and ⟨BusinessService⟩ correspond to ⟨Boundary⟩ and ⟨Control⟩ classes, respectively, in our minimal use-case design case above. Additional classes are involved to provide EJB distribution. They are based on the Business Delegate, Service Locator, and Session Facade patterns in the J2EE core patterns, as shown in Figure 15–11. We describe what each of these is responsible for. The vertical dashed lines in Figure 15–11 indicates which instances execute on the local machine and which instances execute on the remote machine.

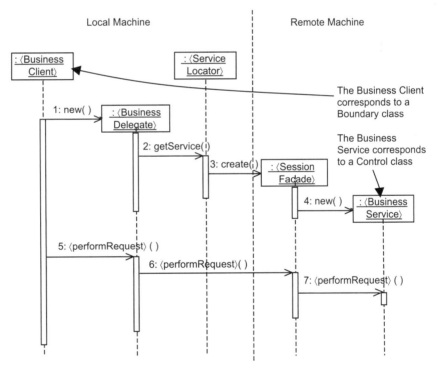

Figure 15-11 *EJB distribution mechanism.*

The purpose of the ⟨BusinessDelegate⟩ is to shield the fact that the ⟨BusinessService⟩ actually executes on a remote machine. It is the proxy class we mentioned earlier. The role of the ⟨ServiceLocator⟩ is to hide the details of the network structure (location and names of nodes, etc.) from the ⟨BusinessDelegate⟩. Both the ⟨BusinessDelegate⟩ and the ⟨ServiceLocator⟩ execute on the local machine. The ⟨SessionFacade⟩ executes on the remote machine and is the wrapper EJB we mentioned earlier.

Recall in the minimal use-case design, the ⟨Control⟩ class provides two kinds of operations: new() to create an instance of the ⟨Control⟩ class and ⟨performRequest⟩ to invoke some functionality on a ⟨Control⟩ instance. These two operations are refined by operations named the same way in the EJB distribution mechanism depicted in Figure 15–11.

Creating an Instance of ⟨BusinessService⟩. A ⟨BusinessClient⟩ creates a ⟨BusinessService⟩ instance by first creating a ⟨BusinessDelegate⟩ locally. The ⟨BusinessDelegate⟩ makes use of the ⟨ServiceLocator⟩ to locate the ⟨SessionFacade⟩ in the network. Basically, this means getting the IP address and name of the ⟨SessionFacade⟩. The EJB container (i.e., the underlying J2EE platform) creates an instance of the ⟨SessionFacade⟩, which then creates an instance of the ⟨BusinessService⟩. The reference to the ⟨SessionFacade⟩ is returned to the ⟨BusinessDelegate⟩.

Making a Call to a ⟨BusinessService⟩ Instance. A ⟨Business Client⟩ makes a call to a ⟨BusinessService⟩ instance through a series of calls all named ⟨performRequest⟩ in Figure 15–11. Even though the name is the same, each class deals with it differently. They collaborate together to hand over the call from the local machine to the remote machine where the ⟨BusinessService⟩ is located.

As mentioned, the ⟨BusinessDelegate⟩ shields the fact that the ⟨BusinessService⟩ is actually executing on a remote machine. So, if there are any network-related exceptions—for example, if the remote machine is not available or has restarted—it will handle them. The ⟨BusinessDelegate⟩ has a reference to the desired ⟨SessionFacade⟩ instance. The ⟨BusinessDelegate⟩ call the ⟨SessionFacade⟩, which then calls the ⟨BusinessService⟩ instance. The ⟨SessionFacade⟩ is implemented as an EJB and, therefore, can use the underlying EJB platform to manage its instances in memory. The ⟨SessionFacade⟩ in this case encapsulates all EJB specifics on the remote machine from the ⟨BusinessService⟩. Thus, the ⟨BusinessService⟩ (i.e., the ⟨Control⟩ class) only needs to be a POJO.

Since communications between instances are over the network, you need to serialize data into byte streams. These data elements being passed around as byte streams are known as Transfer Objects (TOs). In Java, serialization is achieved simply by making data classes implementing a Serializable interface. This Serializable interface is part of the Java platform. Basically, by implementing this interface, the Java compiler is able to convert each Transfer Object into a byte stream, and vice versa.

15.3.3   Designing the Distribution Mechanism

Let's consider how you can design the EJB distribution mechanism as a use-case distribution slice to keep distribution specifics separate from the Minimal Use-Case Design slice. To achieve this, the use-case distribution slice must do the following:

- Intercept calls from a ⟨Boundary⟩ instance to a ⟨Control⟩ instance and replace it with remote calls for both the creation of the ⟨Control⟩ instance and the invocation of any other operation on the ⟨Control⟩ instance.
- Hide all exceptions (such as remote machine not available, etc.) that are due to distributing the control class.

Figure 15–12 illustrates how we achieve this. At the top of Figure 15–12, we have the classes that are in the Minimal Use-Case Design slice. There is a ⟨Boundary⟩ class and a ⟨Control⟩ class. In addition, there is a data class ⟨TransferObject⟩ whose instances get passed as parameters in operation calls.

Figure 15–12 further separates the classes according to the containers they execute within. The ⟨Boundary⟩ class will be executing in the Web container. The ⟨Control⟩ class will be executing within the EJB container. The ⟨TransferObject⟩ is just something that gets passed around between the ⟨Boundary⟩ class and the ⟨Control⟩ class and between the Web container and the EJB container. Hence, it needs to realize the Serializable interface.

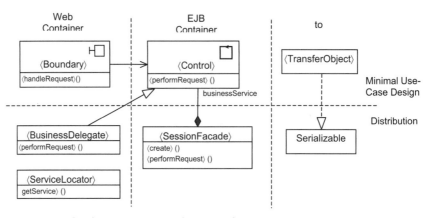

Figure 15-12 *Incorporating distribution into minimal use-case design.*

At the bottom, you see the classes that are needed to provide distribution. On the Web container, we have the ⟨BusinessDelegate⟩ and the ⟨ServiceLocator⟩. We have taken the approach to make ⟨BusinessDelegate⟩ a specialization of the ⟨Control⟩ class. Calls to create the ⟨Control⟩ instances are intercepted, which means you need to identify a pointcut for that. We return the ⟨BusinessDelegate⟩, which is a child of the ⟨Control⟩ class. In this way, we are substituting a ⟨Control⟩ instance with a ⟨BusinessDelegate⟩ instance.

The benefit of this approach is that you no longer need to intercept other calls from the ⟨Boundary⟩ to the ⟨Control⟩ using pointcuts and advices. Instead, you intercept calls through the inheritance mechanism. All you need to do is specialize each operation in the Control instance with a remote call to that operation. Thus, you are using the inheritance mechanisms to intercept calls rather than using the pointcut mechanism in AOP. Inheritance is much simpler than identifying pointcuts. Each operation in ⟨BusinessDelegate⟩ shields exceptions due to distribution from the ⟨Boundary⟩ class.

The ⟨SessionFacade⟩ holds a reference to the ⟨Control⟩, which plays the role of a business service. Each operation in ⟨SessionFacade⟩ invokes a corresponding operation in the ⟨Control⟩ class.

Because the developer of the ⟨Boundary⟩ class and the ⟨Control⟩ class— that is, the minimal use-case design—is aware that these classes run within separate processes (i.e., the Web and the EJB container), he or she will try to reduce the number of calls between the ⟨Boundary⟩ class and the ⟨Control⟩. Thus, the minimal use-case designs do take into account some distribution considerations. Nevertheless, this is just a guideline to the developer. Other than such guidelines, he or she will not have any EJB-related codes in the ⟨Boundary⟩ and ⟨Control⟩ classes. They are just POJOs.

All EJB-related code will be in the classes at the bottom of Figure 15–12. As per Figure 15–10, the ⟨Boundary⟩ class makes a direct call to the ⟨Control⟩ class. But this must be intercepted by a use-case distribution slice, as you shall see shortly. So, what you achieve is better modularity and separation of concerns. The minimal use-case design has no EJB-related code whatsoever. In addition, you design the use-case distribution slice as a template. This allows you to apply the use-case distribution repeatedly in a consistent manner.

Some parts of the distribution mechanism will be common across the distribution of any use case and separated into a distribution slice.

Accordingly, you will have three use cases, as shown in Figure 15–13: the Minimal Use-Case Design slice, the Use-Case Distribution slice, and the distribution slice.

Minimal Use-Case Design Slice. As mentioned, the Minimal Use-Case Design slice contains the specifics to realize use-case flow of events. It does not have any distribution design at all. The ⟨Boundary⟩ class and the ⟨Control⟩ class correspond to the ⟨BusinessClient⟩ and the ⟨BusinessService⟩, respectively.

Distribution Slice. The distribution slice is a non-use-case-specific slice. It contains the ServiceLocator for the system. In this example, we use one ServiceLocator for all use cases.

The distribution slice has also an EJB deployment descriptor, which is an XML file that identifies the EJBs (i.e., the SessionFacades) in the system. This allows the EJB container to locate and manage EJBs.

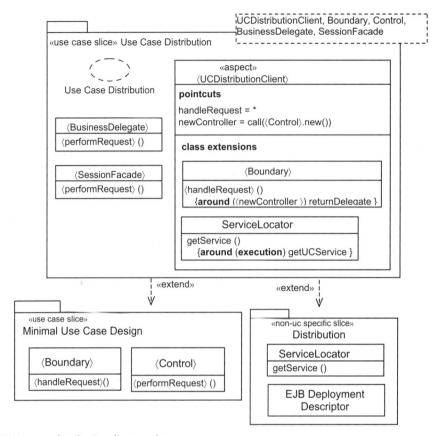

Figure 15-13 *Use-case distribution slice template.*

Use-Case Distribution Slice. You can categorize the contents of the use-case distribution slice into whether it will execute on the Web container (i.e., the client) or the EJB container (i.e., the server), or is shared by the two.

The ⟨BusinessDelegate⟩ executes on the Web container. The ⟨UCDistributionClient⟩ aspect intercepts calls made by the ⟨Boundary⟩ class to create a ⟨Control⟩ instance on the client and returns the ⟨BusinessDelegate⟩. The ⟨UCDistributionClient⟩ aspect also adds operation extensions into the ServiceLocator to return the ⟨SessionFacade⟩ for the use case. The ⟨SessionFacade⟩ executes on the EJB container. You need to have home and remote interfaces for the ⟨SessionFacade⟩. For brevity, we do not show them in Figure 15–13.

Each use-case distribution slice must add a small XML extension into the EJB deployment descriptor to indicate the existence of its EJBs (i.e., the `SessionFacades`) in the use-case distribution slice. Since AspectJ is only designed for Java, it is unable to add extensions to XML files. You need a different technology to do that. Today, a number of code-generation tools are available for you to achieve this. They range from open source utilities to commercial code generation tools.

Figure 15–14 shows how code-generation tools are used to generate EJB deployment descriptors. Basically, the code generator accepts a number of `SessionFacades` (which are implemented as EJBs) as inputs. This can be achieved either by parsing the source codes of the EJBs or through some other means of defining EJBs. The `SessionFacades` become parameters that are applied on the deployment descriptor template to generate the desired deployment descriptor. Thus, in effect, the code generator merges multiple EJB definitions into a single EJB deployment descriptor.

You can model what these code generators do as shown in Figure 15–15. We take the same approach of overlaying a use-case slice on a non-use-case-specific slice. After all, we are, in reality, overlaying an XML extension onto an XML file (the deployment descriptor). Figure 15–15 models the deployment descriptor as a classifier stereotyped as «deployment descriptor».

Each entry for an EJB description in the deployment descriptor is modeled as an attribute stereotyped as «ejb entry». In Figure 15–15, the name of the descriptor is ejb.xml. Through an additional ⟨UCDistributionServer⟩ aspect, the use-case distribution slice overlays the XML extension onto the deployment descriptor in the distribution slice. We model the XML extension as a class extension—special kind of class

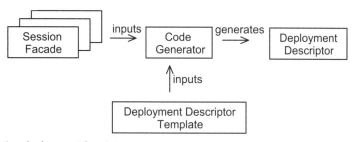

Figure 15-14 *Generating deployment descriptors.*

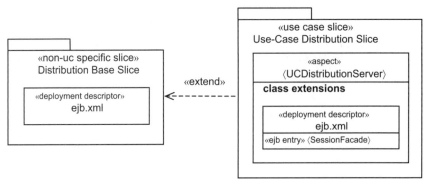

Figure 15-15 *Modeling overlaying deployment descriptor extensions.*

extension—which also resides in the class extensions compartment of the ⟨UCDistributionServer⟩ aspect.

So, indeed, you add two aspects: one ⟨UCDistributionClient⟩ aspect on the Web container and one ⟨UCDistributionServer⟩ aspect on the EJB container. But both aspects are part of the use-case distribution slice. As you can see, the use-case distribution slice cuts across the process structure.

Recall in Figure 15–12 that the ⟨TransferObject⟩ needs to realize the Serializable interface to support distribution. You can get the ⟨UCDistri-butionServer⟩ aspect to overlay this relationship on top of the ⟨TransferObject⟩, but this is not a good idea. It is just a trivial addition that will lead to scattering of such relationships that are an integral part of ⟨TransferObject⟩s. This will make the ⟨UCDistributionServer⟩ aspect look like patchwork and is poor modularity. Since the developer knows that the ⟨TransferObject⟩ needs to be serialized anyway, a better approach would be to let this relationship be part of minimal use-case design.

15.3.4   Applying the Distribution Mechanism

Let us now look at how you can apply the use-case distribution slice template discussed above. This is achieved by simply substituting the template parameters with actual classes and aspects into the template. As an example, Figure 15–16 shows the Reserve Room distribution slice.

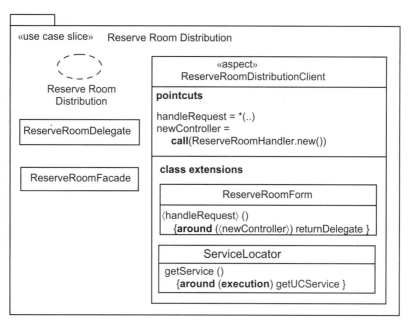

Figure 15-16 *Reserve Room distribution slice.*

The Reserve Room distribution slice contains the following:

- The `ReserveRoomDistributionClient` aspect, which substitutes the ⟨UCDistributionClient⟩ parameter.
- The `ReserveRoomForm`, which substitutes the ⟨Boundary⟩ parameter.
- The `ReserveRoomHandler`, which substitutes the ⟨Control⟩ parameter.
- The `ReserveRoomDelegate`, which substitutes the ⟨BusinessDelegate⟩ parameter.
- The `ReserveRoomFacade`, which substitutes the ⟨SessionFacade⟩ parameter.

The template parameters ⟨Boundary⟩ and ⟨TransferObject⟩ are used in the contents of `Distribution` aspects and are substituted, respectively, by `ReserveRoomForm` and `ReservationData`. This allows the `ReserveRoomDistributionClient` aspect to intercept calls by the `ReserveRoomForm` to create a control class, and the `ReserveRoomDistributionServer` aspect to make the `ReservationData` serializable.

To make the discussion more concrete, Listing 15–3 shows the AspectJ source code for the `ReserveRoomDistributionClient` aspect.

Listing 15-3 Source Code for ReserveRoomDistributionClient

```
1. public aspect ReserveRoomDistributionClient {
2.   pointcut newController() : within(ReserveRoomForm)
3.                   && call(ReserveRoomHandler.new(..)) ;
4.     ...
5.   ReserveRoomHandler around() : newController() {
6.     return new ReserveRoomDelegate() ;
7.   }
8.     ...
9. }
```

The `newController` pointcut in lines 2 and 3 refers to all operations in `ReserveRoomForm` that make calls to create a new `ReserveRoomHandler` instance. The advice in lines 5, 6, and 7 implements the operation extension:

```
handleRequest()  {around (⟨newController⟩) returnDelegate }
```

It intercepts calls to create a new `ReserveRoomHandler` and returns a `ReserveRoomDelegate` instead.

The use-case distribution slice template looks much more complicated than the use-case presentation template, however, looks can be deceiving. Many of the parameters in use-case distribution slice template can be generated automatically because their implementation is similar across use cases. All you need to do is work out a code sample for one use-case distribution. Other use-case distribution slices can follow this code template. In fact, you can generate the entire Reserve Room distribution slice once you have implemented the use-case distribution slice.

This is unlike use-case presentation, where you need to do user interface design and add the implementation details on generating HTML content and extracting request parameters from the submitted requests.

In Chapter 12, "Separating Functional Requirements with Peer Application Use Cases," we described the `ReserveRoomHandler` component from the minimal design perspective. The left-hand side of Figure 15–17 shows the `ReserveRoomHandler` component prior to the overlaying of the use-case distribution slice. After overlaying the distribution slice, the `ReserveRoomHandler` component is endowed with additional classes and interfaces. The interfaces are depicted in the right-hand side of Figure 15–17.

The contents of the `ReserveRoomHandler` component are depicted in Figure 15–18 using the notation in UML 2.0. The `ReserveRoomHandler` component has the three provided interfaces and two required interfaces.

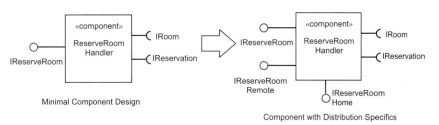

Figure 15-17 *Component with and without distribution specifics.*

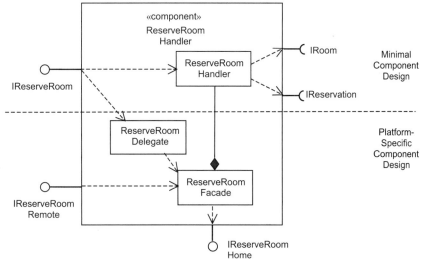

Figure 15-18 *ReserveRoomHandler component.*

The horizontal line across Figure 15–18 separates the minimal component design from the platform-specific component design parts. The latter is overlaid onto the `ReserveRoomHandler` component through the use-case distribution slice.

The classes overlaid onto the `ReserveRoomHandler` component are the `ReserveRoomDelegate` and the `ReserveRoomFacade`. The platform-specific interfaces added are the `IReserveRoomHome` and `IRemoteReserveRoom`. The `IReserveRoomHome` is an EJB home interface. It is used by the EJB container to manage the EJBs (creating, pooling, etc.). The `IRemoteReserveRoom` permits clients to make calls over the network. Thus, you have three interfaces through which you make calls to the `ReserveRoomHandler` component:

- **IRemoteReserveRoom**. The `IRemoteReserveRoom` interface is a platform-specific interface to the `ReserveRoomHandler` component. It is an EJB remote interface. To make a call to this interface, the caller must be aware of the platform specifics (i.e., EJB distribution). This means creating the `ReserveRoomHandler` component remotely and so on.
- **IReserveRoomHome**. The `IReserveRoomHome` interface is also a platform-specific interface to the `ReserveRoomHandler` component. It is an EJB home interface. It is used by the EJB distribution mechanism to create and manage instances of the `ReserveRoomHandler` component.
- **IReserveRoom**. The `IReserveRoom` interface is a minimal design interface provided by the `ReserveRoomHandler` component. EJB distribution is hidden from callers to this interface.

15.4   Overlaying Persistency

The purpose of many systems, especially business systems, is to manage a set of information about customers and/or similar concerns. The Hotel Management System is one such example. It manages information about the hotel, and it automates a set of business processes. The use cases for this system are largely about accessing information about some persistent datastore. Consequently, a large part in the development of the system is about accessing the datastore. A change in the implementation specifics of the datastore often has a huge impact on the project.

Figure 15-19 ⟨Handle Persistence⟩ use case.

Keeping the platform-specific persistence separate not only limits the impact of such changes, but also makes it possible to have early, useful testing in the beginning of a project. This is because you can now test the use case even when the persistent datastore has not been selected yet. Figure 15–19 shows the ⟨Handle Persistence⟩ use case as an extension of the ⟨Perform Transaction⟩ use case.

Listing 15–4 shows the ⟨Handle Persistence⟩ use-case specification. We kept it very simple and merely indicate that the system can access the datastore.

Listing 15-4 Brief Description of ⟨Handle Persistence⟩

Extension Flow: ⟨Handle Persistence⟩
This extension flow occurs at each step of the ⟨Perform Transaction⟩ use case whenever there is a need to access data from a datastore. The system accesses the datastore from the designated database.
Alternate Flows
A1. Handle datastore access concurrency.

Listing 15–4 also shows an example of an alternative flow, which is to handle access concurrency.

15.4.1   Minimal Use-Case Design without Persistence

Let's consider how you keep codes pertaining to persistence separate. Recall that the minimal use-case design assumes that data structures persist beyond the lifetime of entity instances; that is, the data structures remain in memory even when the entity instances are destroyed. This is illustrated in Figure 15–20, whereby the data structures labeled as ds are declared static (i.e., in memory). In UML, this is indicated with an underline. Thus, the underline beneath ds indicates that ds is a static attribute of the ⟨Entity⟩ class.

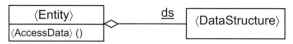

Figure 15-20 *Accessing the data structure through an* ⟨Entity⟩*class.*

The advantage in using the minimal design entity class is that you can quickly proceed to design the data structures, code them, and evaluate the way you structure them. Does a particular structure have too many fields? Can you generalize the structure? What are the relationships between the structures? These questions are important because the data structure will need to be mapped into the actual datastore (possibly a relational database). Thus, this approach helps you kick-start database design. In addition, since you are able to go down to code quickly, you can define the operation parameters of your entity classes.

Note that putting all data elements in memory might not be something you would like to do when the system goes live. However, it provides a convenient way to test the boundary and control classes. Usually, when conducting tests, you need to ensure that the system under test is in some known initial state. If you are using an actual database, you must initialize it to a known state every time you run a test. This can be quite tedious and may take considerable time. Using the minimal use-case design, however, testing the use case is significantly simpler. All you need to do is initialize the static data structure in memory. Thus, this minimal design of the ⟨Entity⟩ class serves as a test stub. We talk more about testing in Chapter 16.

15.4.2   A Relational Persistency Mechanism in J2EE

If you want to incorporate a persistency mechanism, you must substitute the ⟨Entity⟩ class with another one that is able to access data from a datastore (such as a relational database). Such a class is called a data access object (DAO) according to the J2EE core patterns. As the name implies, they are responsible for accessing data from a particular datastore using a particular data-access mechanism. DAOs hide all the specifics about that datastore or that mechanism from their callers, and if there are any changes to the way the datastore is structured, such changes will be encapsulated within the DAOs.

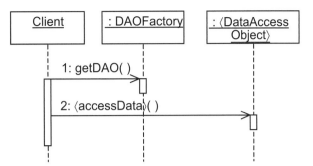

Figure 15-21 *DAO factory.*

Recall that in minimal use-case design, the ⟨Entity⟩ class uses a static data structure in memory. But the actual system uses a real datastore. Thus, you need a way to decide which data-access class you need. Do you want the minimal ⟨Entity⟩ class or the actual DAO, which perhaps might access the actual relational database? This selection is made through a DAO Factory class. The purpose of this class is to return an appropriate DAO class based on the datastore type (see Figure 15–21).

In J2EE, the usual practice is for the DAOFactory to determine the type of DataAccessObject to be returned based on some environment variables provided by the execution platform (i.e., J2EE). Thus, by changing the environment variable, you can configure which data-access class to use, whether it is minimal use-case design ⟨entity⟩ class, or a class that accesses a real data store, be it a SQL datastore, an XML datastore, or other type of datastore.

15.4.3 Designing Persistency Mechanism

Let's consider how you can apply the DAOFactory pattern on the minimal use-case design. Figure 15–22 shows the usual case of accessing data managed by ⟨Entity⟩ instances. The ⟨Control⟩ instance first creates an instance of the ⟨Entity⟩ and thereafter makes calls to ⟨AccessData⟩ in the ⟨Entity⟩ instance.

To introduce the DAOFactory pattern, you intercept the call to create instances of the ⟨Entity⟩ and call the DAOFactory instead. The DAOFactory determines whether to return the minimal use-case design ⟨Entity⟩ instance or a platform-specific DAO.

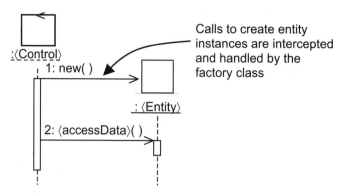

Calls to create entity instances are intercepted and handled by the factory class

Figure 15-22 *Accessing the ⟨Entity⟩ class.*

You can substitute an ⟨Entity⟩ instance with a ⟨DataAccessObject⟩ instance, but you still must design the ⟨DataAccessObject⟩. Today, relational databases are commonly used as a persistent datastore, and developers spend considerable time writing code to perform object-relational mappings. It is no wonder that many competing persistency frameworks are available. There are tools available even to generate code to perform data access from relational datastores. Although this is attractive, the problem is that they take a data-centric view and generate essential create, read, update, and delete operations for you. There are more sophisticated tools to generate even more of such code, but there will always be a need for some use-case-specific manipulation of records. Thus, you often need to supplement with additional codes to do just that. You can keep codes that perform use case specific manipulation within Use-Case Persistence slices.

You can put the use-case-generic part of persistency in an entity-persistent slice. You make this entity-persistent slice a template, since you want to take advantage of the available tools to generate the essential create, read, update, delete, and other operations.

You still have the usual Minimal Use-Case Design slice and a slice to hold what is common across the persistence of all entities (e.g., the DAOFactory). This results in four use-case slices: the Minimal Use-Case Design slice, the entity-persistence template slice, the persistence slice, and use-case persistence slice. The first three slices are shown in Figure 15–23.

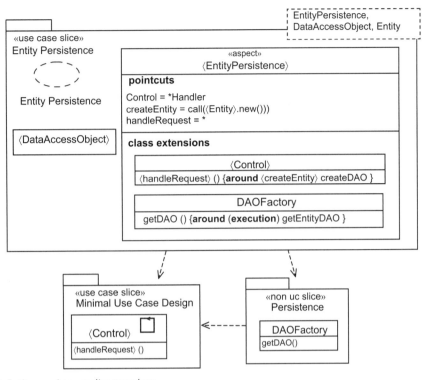

Figure 15-23 *Entity-persistence slice template.*

Minimal Use-Case Design Slice. As before, the minimal use-case design contains only the logic specific to the use case. It contains no platform-specific persistence contents. We show the ⟨Control⟩ class in Figure 15–23 to indicate that the behavior of the Control class will be modified by the use-case persistence slice.

Entity-Persistence Slice. The entity-persistence slice is different in nature from the use-case presentation and use-case distribution slices we discussed earlier. In the previous examples, these slices are applied on a per-use-case-design slice. However, you will have one entity-persistence slice per entity instead. This is because entity persistence is use-case-generic.

The entity-persistence slice contains an entity-persistence collaboration that describes the data-access mechanism used. The entity-persistence slice has three template parameters: the ⟨EntityPersistence⟩ aspect, the ⟨DataAccessObject⟩ class, and the name of the ⟨Entity⟩, which will be replaced by the ⟨DataAccessObject⟩. The name is used by the

DAOFactory to return the appropriate DAO. Potentially, the DAOFactory is responsible for creating many DAOs, one set for each entity class.

The ⟨EntityPersistence⟩ aspect contains two class extensions. The first is a class extension for the ⟨Control⟩ class. In essence, this class extension intercepts calls to create ⟨Entity⟩ instances and replaces them with calls to the DAOFactory to return an appropriate DAO.

The ⟨EntityPersistence⟩ aspect contains several parameters implemented using the parameterization (i.e., regular expression) capability provided by AOP pointcuts. All three parameters are used in the ⟨Control⟩ class extension. The ⟨Control⟩ parameter is bound to any class whose name ends with Handler (i.e., the regular expression *Handler). The ⟨handleRequest⟩ parameter is bound to *, which means all operations. The parameter ⟨createEntity⟩ is bound to call(⟨Entity⟩.new()), which means to all calls to create a new ⟨Entity⟩ instance. So, collectively, they are used to intercept all operations within *Handlers that attempt to create a new ⟨Entity⟩ instance.

The second is a class extension for the DAOFactory class. This extension indicates the existence of the ⟨DataAccessObject⟩ defined in the entity-persistence slice.

Persistence Slice. The persistence slice contains the DAOFactory class to control which DAO is returned. In this example, there is one DAOFactory for the system.

Use-Case Persistence Slice. As the name implies, the use-case persistence slice provides the means for you to overlay use-case-specific data access operations. It is shown in Figure 15–24. It simply adds these operations through the ⟨DataAccessObject⟩ class extension.

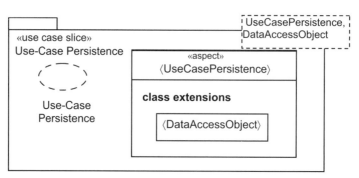

Figure 15-24 *Use-Case Persistence slice.*

15.4.4 Applying the Persistency Mechanism

You apply the entity-persistence template slice by substituting the template parameters. Figure 15–25 illustrates what happens when you apply the entity-persistence template slice on the `Reservation` entity class.

As mentioned, there is plenty of room for you to automatically generate the codes for the reservation-persistence slice, since it merely provides the usual create, read, update, and delete operations for the `Reservation-SQLDAO`.

The main idea is this: by separating what is use-case-specific and what is use-case-independent, you can automatically generate a lot of code that would otherwise take up much of your precious time. If you need more sophisticated data-access operations, you can then create a Use-Case Persistence slice.

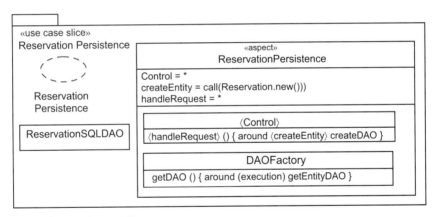

Figure 15-25 *Reservation-persistence slice.*

15.5   Preserving the Use-Case Structure

In the preceding sections, we described how you can design the various tiers for the system. These tiers involve platform specifics, which you want to keep separate. Let's compare how a use-case realization looks like before and after overlaying the platform specifics. Figure 15–26 depicts the realization of the Reserve Room use case from a minimal design perspective. Figure 15–27 depicts the same use-case realization after overlaying the presentation, distribution, and persistency slices.

As can be seen from Figure 15–26, the minimal use-case design realization of a use case looks very similar to the use-case realization in analysis. Even after the incorporation of the platform specifics (see Figure 15–27), the components and the relationships between them still conform to what you have created during analysis. This illustrates what is meant by preserving the structure of the analysis model in design. It makes the design of the system more understandable than a design that does not attempt to preserve the analysis structure.

Within each component in Figure 15–27, we depict the minimal design classes (i.e., POJOs) at the top and classes that link the POJOs to the infrastructure below. In addition, the bottom of Figure 15–27 shows interfaces that are used to plug the components into the selected platform—in this case, J2EE. Depicting components in this way has several benefits. It helps the reader clearly distinguish which parts are:

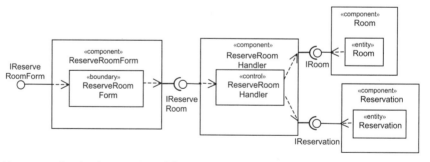

Figure 15-26 *Use-case realization from a minimal design perspective.*

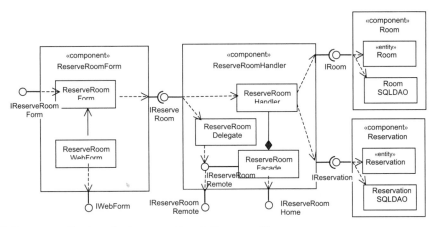

Figure 15-27 *Use-case realization after incorporating platform specifics.*

- use-case-specific
- use-case-specific and platform-specific
- platform-specific

This is precisely what a good architecture is about—keeping concerns separate. Frequently, the parts that are both use-case specific and platform specific can be automatically generated. This is yet another advantage for us to keep these different parts separate.

15.6   **Summary and Highlights**

A significant portion of the code used to implement a typical system has to do with platform specifics. This usually means that the system becomes tightly coupled with the selected platform. In this chapter, we show how you can keep platform specifics separate through use-case slices. The advantages of doing so are many. First, you can easily replace the platform specifics by replacing the slices. Second, by keeping the platform specifics separate, you can quickly build and test the non-platform-specific parts of the system. In this way, you can quickly and objectively evaluate the platform-independent structure you have established in analysis.

In this chapter, we use templates extensively. The platform-specific parts of a use case are designed as template use-case slices (use-case presentation slice, use-case distribution slice, etc.). This makes incorporation of platform specifics simpler and more consistent because developers have a template to follow. More importantly, templates provide opportunities for significant automation. Tools and utilities are already available to generate codes based on code templates. This improves your team productivity dramatically.

16

Separating Tests with Use-Case Test Slices

So far in this part of the book, we have discussed how to drive different kinds of use cases from requirements to code. Testing is an integral part of this work and should not be perceived as a separate activity done at the end. In fact, design is not complete until you know how to test your design elements. Likewise, implementation (coding) is not complete until the actual tests pass. When testing each element, you often need to somehow control the execution of the element being tested to follow the execution path stipulated by the test scenario. You also need to instrument (i.e., check and collect information about) the execution to determine that the behavior of the element is indeed correct. Use-case test slices help you localize such control and instrumentation extensions, which can be easily removed when you have completed executing tests. More importantly, when use cases of different kinds are kept separate, the system is much easier to test and defects are more readily isolated.

16.1 Test-First Approach

Testing should not be seen as the final border to cross before releasing the system to users. Testing should occur throughout the project life cycle, from requirements to code. In fact, whatever you do, you are not done until you have verified (and validated) that you did what you wanted to do. This applies not just to coding, but to design, requirements, and basically every task. You need to clarify the acceptance criteria for everything you do, and progress is measured with respect to meeting these acceptance criteria. Thus, test cases have to be identified *before* a single line of code is written, not after the code is written. This is because unless implementation passes the tests, implementation is not complete. Having tests identified and specified up front is crucial to an objective evaluation of the progress of the system. When a developer says she has completed 70 percent of the code, it has to be 70 percent working—that is, she passes 70 percent of the test identified. Anything else, such as saying, "Seventy percent of the code written," when testing has not yet been completed, is potentially misleading.

You must identify test cases early. But writing test cases that you know will definitely pass is not useful. You should always attempt to write test cases for parts of the system that may fail. Why write tests for parts you know will pass?

The test-first design principle emphasizes this even further—you write test cases for parts of the system that have yet to be implemented. Of course, they will fail—they have not been implemented yet! So, you start to implement parts of the system to pass this test case. You then write a test case for another part of the system that has yet to be implemented. This test case will fail too, so you code parts of the system to pass this test case. The cycle repeats and each time, you write test cases for parts of the system that have yet to be implemented and thereafter implement them according to the test case. In this way, testing is very much part of coding rather than a separate activity or an afterthought. Testing thus becomes more meaningful. In addition, since you are always thinking about test cases that will fail the system, your system will be robust to a wide variety of scenarios.

One of the critiques about test-first design is that you might write the wrong tests and then design to pass the wrong tests. So, you need to anchor the test cases to something useful, something important. This anchor is in the form of use cases. From use cases, you derive a good initial set of test cases through which you apply the test-first-driven design.

Use cases are also specified using the same test-first principle, but with a difference—you base your use cases on stakeholder concerns, specifically on what each actor needs to do with the system and the variations the stakeholder wants the system to handle. You begin with an empty use case and start to specify the basic flow. You explore with the stakeholder another scenario that the use case has yet to handle, and then you specify an alternate flow to handle that scenario. This repeats until you have adequately explored your stakeholders' concerns for each use case. Thus, you have an advantage with applying use cases, because use cases are written in a manner that facilitates testing. They should be written in that way—a use case that is not a good test case is not a good use case; more specifically, good test cases start with good use cases. This is because each use case systematically leads to many test cases. So, use cases provide a framework for you to organize and structure test cases. The use-case technique is quite helpful in getting stakeholders and end users, not just the developers and testers, to think in terms of test cases. This certainly promotes a better common understanding between team members on the acceptable behaviors of the system.

The fact that you have been able to keep use cases separate means that the system is much easier to test. Each use-case module is a unit of analysis, design, implementation, and *testing*. You test a use-case module separately from other use-case modules. Thus, you have test cases for: application use cases, infrastructure use cases, platform specifics, and so on. In this way, you can isolate defects quickly. Thus, use-case-driven development is indeed about testing first and testing early.

16.2   Identifying Test Cases from Use Cases

In Part II, we discussed in fairly good detail how you capture stakeholder concerns in use-case specifications. You have much to gain by getting use cases right at the beginning of the project. This is because test cases are derived from and organized around use cases.

However, you have to take note that use cases are not test cases. Use-case specifications are written for stakeholders to help explore and clarify their concerns. Test-case specifications are for testers and are significantly more detailed and much wider in coverage than use-case specifications. Test cases evaluate the behavior of a use-case implementation against its specification. Test cases can be identified to evaluate the behavior of a single use-case instance or multiple use-case instances, as we demonstrate in this section.

16.2.1   Identifying Test Cases from Use-Case Flows

Let's look at how you can identify test cases for each use case. A use case is specified in terms of flow of events—basic flows and alternative flows. Figure 16–1 depicts the different paths for the Reserve Room use case.

Figure 16–1 shows various execution paths from the instantiation of the Reserve Room use case until its termination. The basic flow is depicted by the dashed arrow, and the alternate flows are depicted with labels prefixed by Alt.

Each path through a use-case specification is a use-case scenario. It chains various flows together into a single sequence. It describes the desired behavior of one use-case instance. You evaluate the implementation of a use case against use-case scenarios. Since there are many different flows, you have many different use-case scenarios. You have at least one use-case scenario per flow of events. That is, each use-case flow of events must appear within at least one use-case scenario.

For each use-case scenario, you identify the actual test cases (with test data, test environment, etc.) for that use-case scenario.

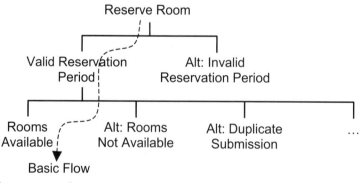

Figure 16-1   *Identifying test cases from use cases.*

16.2.2 Identifying Test Cases from Use-Case Variables

Earlier in the book, we discussed identifying variables that drive the variations in use-case flows of events. For example, the Reserve Room use case is subject to different customer types (individual, corporate, etc.), different reservation periods (reservation periods in weekdays, across weekends, during peak seasons, etc.), and so on, as shown in 16–2.

In Figure 16–2, each axis represents a variable, and each item on an axis represents a variation for that variable. During use-case modeling, you usually identify these variables, enumerate their values, and determine how the use case deals with each variation. However, when you identify test cases, you must explore their possible intersections of the variables and identify test cases for each intersection.

Use-case variables are useful for organizing alternate flows, as discussed in Part II. They are also useful for systematically exploring the test space—the total possible test cases for the use case. This test space will be large. Although it is important to test, you should not *overtest*. The meaning of overtest varies among systems—a life-critical system should be tested much more rigorously than a Hello-World application. Your tests should be driven by what is critical to the system.

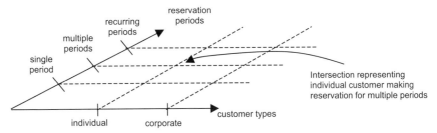

Figure 16-2 *Identifying test cases from use-case variables.*

16.2.3   Identifying Test Cases across Multiple Application Use Cases

You should also identify test cases that evaluate the behaviors of multiple use cases. For example, you might want to have a test case that executes a Reserve Room instance, followed by a Check In Customer use-case instance, and then a Check Out Customer use-case instance. This constitutes what is known as business-cycle testing, which is extremely important for validating how well the system supports business operations.

In real life, when using the system, use cases get instantiated concurrently, as the actor instance might be processing multiple customer requests at the same time. You can identify such test cases by first brainstorming business scenarios with the stakeholder, determining which use cases are involved, and then defining the test cases.

16.2.4   Identifying Test Cases for the Infrastructure and the Platform Specifics

You definitely need to test the infrastructure and platform specifics. One way to do so is to combine them with application use cases, as shown in Table 16–1.

Table 16-1   *Test Cases That Facilitate Defect Isolation*

Test Case	Reserve Room	Handle Authorization	Use-Case Distribution	Outcome
Test Case 1	Yes	No	No	Pass
Test Case 2	Yes	Yes	No	Fail
Test Case 3	Yes	No	Yes	Pass

Table 16–1 depicts three test cases, each using a combination of an application use case (i.e., the Reserve Room use case) and some infrastructure use cases. As you can see, the test cases are identified to deliberately help locate the possible existence of defects. For example, Test Case 2 fails, indicating that there is a defect in the Handle Authorization use case. If every test case for an application use case involves every single infrastructure use case, then it will not be easy to isolate the defect—you will need to resort to low-level tracing and debugging. However, by carefully designing

your test cases, you can indeed reduce such efforts. This is the benefit of keeping use cases separate.

16.2.5   Identifying Performance Test Cases

You should also have test cases that evaluate the performance of the system. For such test cases, you must combine the application use cases with the infrastructure use cases. For these tests, the use cases should already have been working. The focus of these tests is on timing issues and system configuration issues such as the number of threads you are using and the size of the memory pools.

You analyze different usage loads, such as the number of users making reservations, checking reservations, checking in, and checking out. From these usage models, you formulate performance test cases. These cases can be designed to evaluate such questions as the following:

- What is the response time, and what is the time to service a request when the system is subject to a certain workload (i.e., number of requests per second)?
- What is the maximum workload when the response time exceeds acceptable values? For example, what is the number of concurrent users the system can accept before the response time for each user exceeds 2 seconds?

You can run these tests with or without infrastructure or platform specifics composed. This facilitates the isolation of bottlenecks. Again, this is the benefit of keeping concerns separate—it is so much easier to isolate problems and fix them.

If you are still in the architectural iterations, the measurements you have at this moment are only for a very early stage of the system—not the final system. Still, these measurements are useful. You can use them to project the actual ones in the final system. In this way, you can evaluate whether your chosen architecture is feasible to build the rest of the system.

If, for example, the performance characteristics of the architecture might already be approaching the acceptable limits, you can predict that after incorporating the remainder of the system, the performance characteristics will not be acceptable. It is much better that you know such issues at the beginning of the project than later. This gives you ample time to find a better solution.

16.3   Identifying Elements to Be Tested

Use cases are also useful for identifying unit tests—tests for each element in the design model. Although you like to have a good test coverage, it is not practical to achieve complete coverage. You could not possibly test every single class. Instead, you choose a subset of classes to be tested more thoroughly than others. So, how do you determine which classes should be subject to unit testing, and also which operations should you focus more on? To find these classes, go back to the use-case realization. Figure 16–3 depicts the realization for the Reserve Room use case during design. These are Plain Old Java Objects (POJOs).

You should at least test the control class (i.e., The `ReserveRoomHandler` in this case) because it coordinates the other classes to realize the use case. You might also wish to test the boundary class (i.e., the `Reserve-RoomForm`) as well, because it is the facade through which the Web presentation must access the POJO elements. Since the `ReserveRoomForm` does not involve any Web presentation elements, it is possible to conduct unit testing without worrying about changes in the user interface.

The entity classes here need not be tested because they are just dummy classes—they do not access the actual datastore. The classes that do access the datastore are data access objects (DAOs), which we discussed in

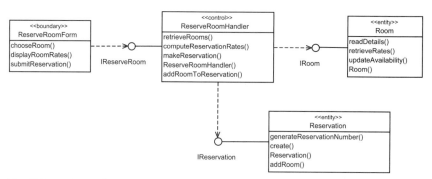

Figure 16-3   *Identifying unit tests from use-case analysis and design.*

Chapter 15, "Separating Platform Specifics with Platform-Specific Use-Case Slices." The entity classes, however, are excellent mock objects when it comes to testing. Even for the DAOs, they can be tested as part of testing the control classes.

Boundary classes to external systems are also good candidates for mock objects since the boundary classes contain now platform specifics. We discuss mock objects in a moment, but the truth of the matter is that the use case driven approach together with the separation of platform specifics from minimum design provides a systematic approach to finding mock objects.

The test cases you implement for the POJOs are also applicable even after you incorporate the platform specifics. Let's consider the control class for the ReserveRoomHandler. When you incorporate EJB distribution (see Chapter 15), you introduce a business delegate, ReserveRoomDelegate, which makes a call over the network and eventually to the ReserveRoom-Handler. Both the ReserveRoomHandler and ReserveRoomDelegate conform to the same interface. This means that you can use the same test case for both classes, illustrated in Figure 16–4.

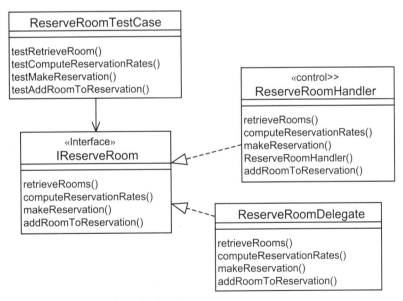

Figure 16-4 *Testing classes with or without distribution.*

In Figure 16–4, we have a test case class named `ReserveRoomTestCase`. This class contains operations to test the realization of the `IReserveRoom` interface, which can be either the `ReserveRoomHandler` or the `ReserveRoomDelegate`. This is advantageous because you have a single test implementation to verify behaviors with or without distribution.

16.4   Designing and Implementing Tests

Now that you have a set of test cases, you can start to design and implement them. When designing tests, you must be very clear on what the element under test (EUT) is. The EUT can be as simple as just an operation in a class, a set of operations in a set of classes, or a set of classes that realize a use case. The EUT defines the subset of the system being tested. All other parts of the system are part of the EUT's execution environment.

For instance, if you want to test the Reserve Room use case, specifically the operation `makeReservation()`, in the `ReserveRoomHandler` class, then the `makeReservation()` operation would be the EUT. A partial description of this operation is shown as a state chart in Figure 16–5. Suppose you want to develop the test case for a successful reservation. The dashed line in 16–5 depicts the execution path that you are interested in.

Test design and implementation is about forcing the behavior of the EUT to follow the desired execution path so that we can verify that the EUT

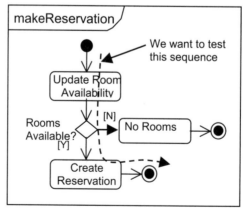

Figure 16-5   *Testing the makeReservation operation.*

does indeed behave as desired. There are two major considerations when designing and implementing tests: control and instrumentation.

Control. Control means forcing the EUT to follow the desired execution path defined in the test case. In addition, the EUT must reproduce the same behavior every time you execute the test case. If, on the other hand, you cannot control the execution or are unable to reproduce the same execution conditions, then you might get different outcomes. In this case, it would be impossible to verify the behavior of the EUT. The consequence is that you will not really be sure if the EUT works.

You can control the execution of the EUT in several ways. You can use parameters passed into the operations being tested, or you can set the global variables accessed by the EUT. This is relatively simple, since you are testing the EUT from its interfaces.

However, in many cases, the EUT requires the support of other elements. These elements might be developed by a different team or might be nondeterministic and extremely difficult to control. In this case, you might want to replace the supporting elements with mock elements. Mock elements substitute the actual supporting elements during testing. This is useful under the following conditions:

1. The actual supporting elements have not been developed. For example, you have yet to decide how to integrate with an external system. In this case, to test the realization of the use case without the external system, you need a mock element in place of the external system.
2. Setting up the actual supporting elements for testing takes a long time. It might not be easy to set up the relational database for each test case you need to execute and reset the database after each test. In this case, you might create a mock element to replace the DAOs. If you follow our approach, the entity classes become natural candidates for such mock elements.
3. The behavior of the actual supporting element is nondeterministic. The supporting element involves sending messages over the network, and the network response is not deterministic. In this case, you can replace it with a mock element that simply provides a delay and returns a fixed result.

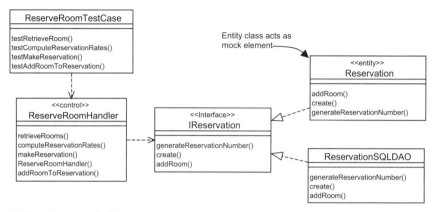

Figure 16-6 *POJO entity as mock element.*

Figure 16–6 shows the classes needed to test the `ReserveRoomHandler` class. The `ReserveRoomTestCase` is the class that tests the `Reserve-RoomHandler` class. The `ReserveRoomHandler` needs the `ReservationSQLDAO` to function. However, we do not use the `ReservationSQLDAO` for testing because the database setup might take up time. Instead, we use the `Reservation` entity class as a mock element.

Instrumentation. In addition to controlling the execution of the EUT, you must be able to extract (instrument) information about the execution state and outputs of the EUT. This can be achieved through checking return values and values set on global variables.

If the EUT makes calls to the other elements, you might want to check the actual parameters being passed to these elements. You can use the mock objects to perform these checks as well.

16.4.1   Designing a Test Infrastructure

If you add control and instrumentation code into the EUT directly, you experience tangling—you have both EUT code and testing (control and instrumentation) code all mixed up together. Application and testing are two different concerns, and hence you must keep them separate. To keep the control and instrumentation code separate from the EUT, you can define a separate slice that overlays on the EUT. In addition, you need a test infrastructure mechanism to manage tests and store test results for further analysis.

Let's design the test infrastructure. This is done in much the same way as analyzing and designing use cases, discussed in preceding chapters. You begin by identifying needed classes and determining how their instances interact. Thereafter, you allocate the behaviors to use-case slices.

To model the test infrastructure as a pattern, we identify the participating classes as parameters, which we denote using brackets: ⟨ ⟩. A ⟨TestManager⟩ executes one or more ⟨TestCase⟩ instances. Each ⟨TestCase⟩ invokes operations on some ⟨EUT⟩. The ⟨EUT⟩ itself may depend on other classes that are not within the scope of testing. We refer to these classes as *supporting classes*. If the supporting classes have not been developed yet, or you want to keep them separate, you replace them with mock elements: you substitute the supporting classes with a mock element. The mock element is parameterized as ⟨MockElement⟩.

Now that the classes (more specifically, template parameters) have been identified, you describe the interaction between their instances. A typical interaction sequence (i.e., basic low) between their instances is depicted in Figure 16–7.

In Figure 16-7, we want to test operation ⟨operationUnderTest⟩ on the ⟨EUT⟩ instance. The ⟨TestCase⟩ invokes this operation via ⟨testOpera-

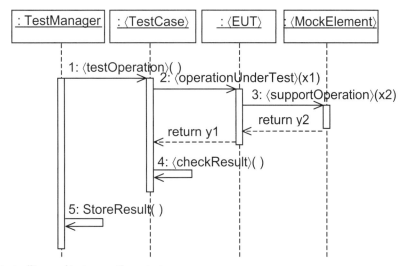

Figure 16-7   *Controlling and instrumenting a test sequence.*

tion). The ⟨TestManager⟩ is responsible for managing test cases, executing them, and storing the results. As part of the executing ⟨operationUnderTest⟩, the ⟨EUT⟩ might need support from other instances. This is provided by the ⟨MockElement⟩. For example, an operation might be invoked to perform some computation needed by ⟨operationUnderTest⟩.

Merely checking the return value of ⟨operationUnderTest⟩ is not sufficient. You must also check that the operation ⟨supportOperation⟩ in the ⟨MockElement⟩ instance is indeed invoked and that the parameter passed in (i.e., x2) is of the correct value. In addition, you must control the return value (i.e., y2) from the ⟨MockElement⟩ instance. The use of the variables x1, x2, y1, and y2 are summarized in Table 16–2.

Table 16-2   *Test Data and Verification*

Variable	Type	Purpose in testing
x1	Operation parameter	Test data
x2	Operation parameter	Test verification
y2	Operation return value	Test data
y1	Operation return value	Test verification

The test data for the test case in Figure 16–7 are x1 and y2, and test verification is performed by checking the values of x2 and y1. ⟨TestCase⟩ and ⟨MockElement⟩ need to output the test data and perform the test verification accordingly.

Now that we have described the interaction between the participating parameters, we proceed to keep the test infrastructure separate from the test case and the test case separate from the use-case slice being tested. This yields the following three slices, shown in Figure 16–8:

- The use-case design slice, which contains the elements being tested.
- The test-case slice, which contains the specifics of a test case.
- The test infrastructure slice, which contains elements that are common across test cases.

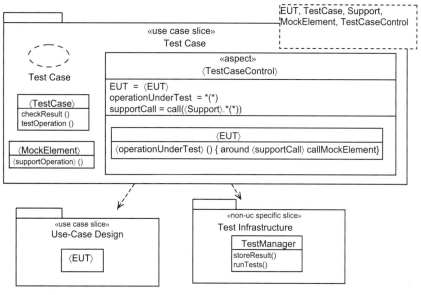

Figure 16-8 *Test-case slice template.*

Use-Case Design Slice. The use-case design slice contains the elements being tested. Collectively, these elements are represented by ⟨EUT⟩. They can be boundary, control, or entity classes.

Test Infrastructure Slice. The test infrastructure is a non-use-case-specific slice. It contains the `TestManager`, which manages and runs various test cases. It is responsible for storing test results. If the test infrastructure provides the ability to do performance tests, then the `TestManager` must be responsible for generating threads to run test cases in parallel. This requires further design and refinement of the `TestManager` class.

Test-Case Slice. The test-case slice contains the specifics of a test case. It contains the ⟨TestCase⟩ and one or more ⟨MockElement⟩s, depending on how many supporting elements are needed. There is also a ⟨TestCaseControl⟩ aspect to control the behavior of the ⟨EUT⟩. Figure 16-7 shows the use of an operation extension to introduce the ⟨MockElement⟩. The operation extension declaration is as follows:

```
⟨operationUnderTest⟩ () { around ⟨supportCall⟩ callMockElement}
```

In essence, when the operationUnderTest() makes a call to an operation in ⟨Support⟩, it is replaced by a corresponding call to the ⟨MockElement⟩. Both ⟨TestCase⟩ and ⟨MockElement⟩ are responsible for conducting test verification where appropriate.

16.4.2   Designing a Test Case

Now that you have established a test infrastructure and a template for designing test cases, you can apply it to test a specific use case. To do so, you must substitute the parameters in the test-case slice template. You also must work out the test data and test values needed during the execution of the test case.

Figure 16–9 illustrates the application of the test-case slice template to test the Reserve Room use-case slice. In this case, the ⟨EUT⟩ is the Reserve-RoomHandler, and the ⟨Support⟩ class is the RoomSQLDAO class. Hence, the RoomSQLDAO class is replaced with a Room entity class.

The mock element in this case is a Room class. Recall that in Chapter 15, we use a DAOFactory class to determine if an entity instance should be used or a DAO should be used. Thus, instead of using an operation extension as shown in Figure 16–9, you can also use the DAOFactory to introduce a mock element. Both approaches—using operation extensions and factory classes—are possible. The benefit of aspects is that since you are able to intercept calls to each operation, you have the option to substitute an operation instead of an entire object.

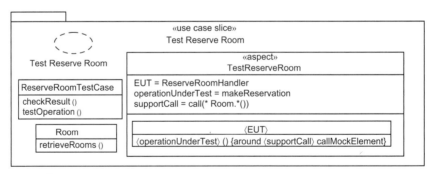

Figure 16-9   *Testing the Reserve Room use case.*

What we have shown in Figure 16–9 is only one test case and one operation being tested. In general, for each use case, there are many operations being tested and accordingly many test cases. You must apply the test case template many times.

For each operation or sequence of operations being tested, you must also identify the test data values and the test verification values. These values are usually stored in a data file, and you can easily execute more tests by providing more test data.

16.5   Summary and Highlights

To recap, testing should not be seen as a final stage of development. In fact, it should be one of the first things to do in every project. Test cases are an effective means of defining the completion criteria for development—a developer's job is not complete until the test cases pass.

You must systematically identify test cases for the system. Use cases help you identify and organize test cases systematically. You identify a set of test cases for each use case separately. This is important, since you can easily localize the presence of defects and bottlenecks. Furthermore, with test-case slices, you can keep test control and implementation separate from the use-case slice being tested. This is quite powerful because you can remove test codes from the production system after you are done with testing and leave the production system intact. With all these benefits, your approach to testing the system is streamlined significantly. You can test first, test early.

17

Evaluating the Architecture

It is important that you get the architecture correct. If you follow the approach described in earlier chapters, you will approach a resilient architecture quickly. But you must continually evaluate and improve the architecture. This necessitates viewing the architecture from various perspectives, which allows you to evaluate if the use cases are indeed kept separate and whether systemwide concerns such as maintainability, extensibility, portability, reusability, performance, and reliability are met. If necessary, you make some improvements. The techniques we describe in this chapter constitute what is commonly known as refactoring. Martin Fowler and his colleagues list a number of such techniques [Fowler et al. 1999]. The refactoring we discuss has an essential difference. Since use-case slices cut across the element structure, refactoring is conducted along two dimensions—along the element structure and along the use-case structure.

17.1 Putting It Together

Before we conduct the evaluation, let us summarize what you have learned so far. From the discussion in the preceding chapters, you probably notice there is a general approach to analyzing and designing use cases and through them different kinds of crosscutting concerns.

- **Identify Classes or Parameters.** You identify classes that are involved in the use case. If you are analyzing use cases generically, then instead of identifying classes, you identify parameterized classes. These parameterized classes subsequently are substituted with actual classes.
- **Identify Pointcuts.** If the use case is an extension use case—whether an application-extension use case, infrastructure use case, or just platform specifics—you must identify pointcuts and operation-extension declarations. The pointcuts and operation-extension declarations define where the extension will be executed. They can be derived from the use-case specifications.
- **Allocate Use-Case Behavior to Classes.** You consider how the classes or parameterized classes interact to realize the use case. At this point, you do not worry which parts of the interaction are specific to the use-case realization and which are not. The focus is on understanding the interaction and finding responsibilities of classes or parameters.
- **Separate the Use-Case Specifics.** With a good understanding of the interaction, you determine which classes or features of classes are specific to the use case and which are not. You collate the use-case specific parts into use-case slices and the common parts into non-use-case-specific slices.
- **Bind Parameters.** If you have been analyzing and designing the use cases generically (i.e., you are using class parameters instead of actual classes), you must define these class parameters. This can be achieved through pointcut expressions or by binding template parameters. Once you understand this general approach, understanding each special case is much simpler.

In the remainder of this section, we compare and contrast ways to analyze and design the different kinds of use cases you have encountered in preceding chapters.

Application Peer Use Cases (Chapter 12, "Separating Functional Requirements with Application Peer Use Cases"). Application peer use cases provide end-user functionality on top of the element structure that defines the problem domain. The emphasis when analyzing peers is on distinguishing what is common and what is specific to a use case. The Reserve

Room use case is an example of an application peer use case. Its use-case slice is depicted in Figure 17–1. The aspects within application peer use-case slices contain primarily intertype declarations (additional and complete operations) to be added to existing elements.

Peer use cases do not extend other use cases and do not have extension flows and pointcuts. Thus, you do not identify pointcuts during analysis. However, aspects in peer use-case slices have operation extensions to list services they offer and to allow actors to initiate the appropriate ones.

Application-Extension Use Cases (Chapter 13, "Separating Functional Requirements with Application-Extension Use Cases"). Application-extension use cases add additional behaviors on top of the use cases they extend. They may have basic flows through which actors can initiate them directly. They also have extension flows that are executed in the context of an extended use case. The Handle Waiting List is an example of an application-extension use case. It has an extension flow that puts the customer into a waiting list when there are no rooms available during a reservation. It typically also has basic flows to view who are in the waiting list and their waiting status. Thus, application-extension use cases are a special case of application use cases.

The use-case slice for the Handle Waiting List is shown in Figure 17–2. Application-extension use cases contain pointcuts from which you identify corresponding pointcuts in extension use-case slices. Since you normally analyze the extension use case with reference to the use case it extends, the pointcuts refer to the classes in the base slice directly. This differs from infrastructure use cases (discussed below) that are analyzed with reference to a generic application use case.

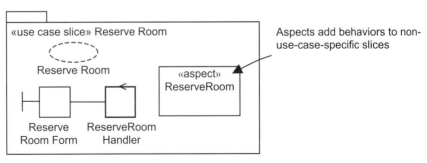

Figure 17-1 *Reserve Room use-case slice.*

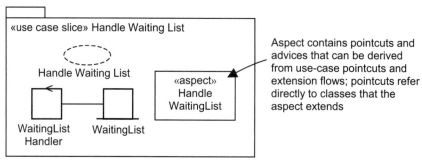

Figure 17-2   *Handle Waiting List use-case slice.*

Infrastructure Use Cases (Chapter 14, "Separating Nonfunctional Requirements with Infrastructure Use Cases"). The infrastructure use cases keep nonfunctional requirements separate from the application. The analysis and design of infrastructure use cases follows a two-step approach. In the first step, you attempt to extend a generic Perform Transaction use case to yield an abstract use-case slice. This use-case slice is abstract because the pointcuts are identified with reference to a generic application use case. Therefore, you cannot have a precise pointcut expression defined, so the aspects are usually abstract. In the second step, you specialize the abstract aspect by defining pointcut expressions for the specific application use case you want to extend. This two-step approach is exemplified by the Handle Authorization use case, whose use-case slice is depicted in 17–3.

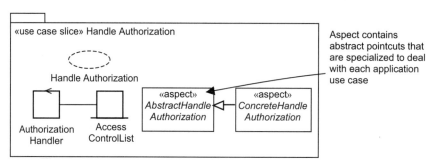

Figure 17-3   *Infrastructure use-case slices.*

Platform-Specific Extension Use Case (Chapter 15, "Separating Platform Specifics with Platform-Specific Use-Case Slices"). Platform-specific extension use cases are special infrastructure use cases that require additional classes on a per-use-case basis. You still use the same two-step approach as in the case of normal infrastructure use cases. This is exemplified by the Handle Distribution use case, which requires a `BusinessDelegate` and a `Session  Facade` be added to each application use case (e.g., Reserve Room).

The design of the platform-specific use-case slice is conducted in two steps. You first define the additional behavior and pointcuts on top of a generic base behavior. This results in a parameterized use-case slice, illustrated in Figure 17–4, which shows the parameterized use-case slice for Handle Distribution.

In the second step, you bind the parameters with the actual classes and aspects for a particular application use-case slice. It is common practice to explore the possibilities of automatically generating parameters. For example, `BusinessDelegate` and `SessionFacade` can usually be generated based on some code templates.

Test Cases (Chapter 16, "Separating Tests with Use-Case Test Slices"). Test-case slices are very much like extension use-case slices, but instead of adding more functionality, they provide additional code to support test-case execution. Figure 17–5 depicts the test slice for the Reserve Room test case.

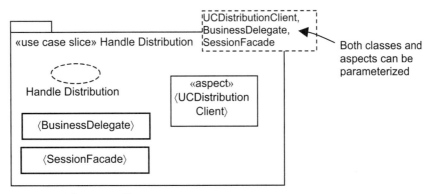

Figure 17-4 *Parameterized use-case slices.*

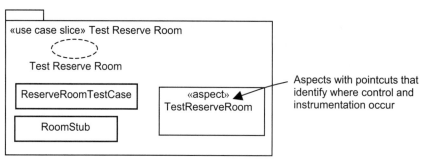

Figure 17-5   *Test slices.*

In the test slice, you need test case, a class that drives the test, and possibly some test stubs. The aspects in the test slice provide control and instrumentation capability to force the use case under test to adhere to the desired execution path and to check if the execution path is indeed correct.

We have highlighted the use of abstract and concrete aspects, parameterized use-case slices, and so on. Although these concepts are discussed with reference to specific examples dealing with particular concerns, the techniques themselves are general. You can apply any of these techniques to any kind of use-case slice. For example, you might want to parameterize an application use-case slice.

17.2   Evaluating Separation of Concerns

Evaluating the separation of concerns across elements and slices occurs all throughout the project. It is not a separate activity from use-case modeling, use-case analysis, and use-case design. You do them as an integral part of these activities.

Recall that the analysis model and the design model each have an element structure and use-case structure. Consequently, you must evaluate along both structures. In this section, we discuss how to evaluate the element structure. Whether it is the analysis element structure or the design element structure, the same principle of separation applies. In this section, we assume that you are evaluating the design element structure.

17.2.1 Evaluating Design Elements

When you evaluate a design element, you must consider it in a composed manner: a design class (e.g., the Room class) may have several features (attributes, operations, and relationships) from one use-case slice (e.g., the Reserve Room use-case slice) and several features from another use-case slice (e.g., the Check In Customer use-case slice). The total composed number of features for this class (i.e., the Room class) is the total number of features from all use-case slices.

To evaluate the goodness of a design class, you compose the class and consider the following:

- Does the design class represent a meaningful abstraction with respect to the system?
- Does the class obey the responsibilities hinted at by its name or stereotype?
- Does the class own a cohesive set of responsibilities?
- Can the responsibilities of the design class be delegated to another class, perhaps a child class, or parent class, or even some helper classes?

17.2.2 Evaluating Design Packages

Considering each design class individually is not enough. You need to consider the design class as part of a design package in some design layers. We take this opportunity to depict the design element structure after composing the minimal design package with the platform-specific design elements based on the principles discussed in Chapter 15.

Figure 17–6 depicts the design elements that participate in the Reserve Room use case. It shows the classes separated into packages, which are in turn separated into other packages or layers.

Details of the classes in Figure 17–6 are described in Chapter 15. Basically, Figure 17–6 shows the three design element layers: application layer, domain layer, and infrastructure layer. Within them are packages such as customer, room, and so on. Each of these may have nested packages named app, web, ejb, and db.

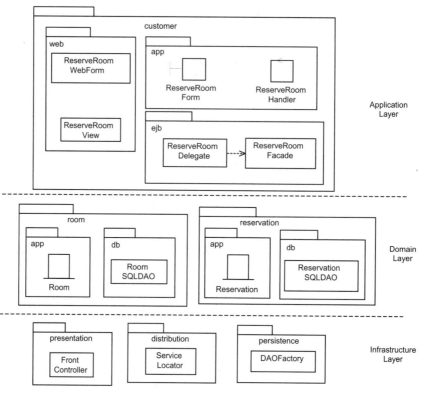

Figure 17-6 *Design element structure.*

The app package contains boundary, control, and entity classes that are derived from the analysis model. The Web package contains design classes that are needed to provide a Web user interface. The ejb package contains design classes needed to provide EJB-based distribution. Finally, the db package contains classes that provide relational persistency. We have discussed them earlier in Chapter 15.

The following questions help you evaluate the goodness of the design element structure:

- Is there a clear separation of responsibilities across the packages in the respective layers?
- Does each package contain classes that are functionally related to each other? Is there loose coupling across packages and tight cohesion between classes within the package?

- What if the user interfaces change? What if the object structure changes? What if the deployment structure of the system changes? Would the impact of such changes be limited to only a few slices in the use-case structure and only a few packages in the element structure?

There are several rules you can use to enforce the separation defined in the design element structure:

- Design classes in the app package should contain no platform-specific operations. They are minimal design packages. Their operations may have extensions that are platform-specific (these are added by platform-specific use-case slices), but the operations themselves must be platform-independent.
- Design classes in the app package cannot make calls to classes in the infrastructure services layer.

The above checkpoints help you to evaluate the architecture you have established so far. Additional checkpoints can be added to the list as you continue with your project.

After evaluation, what kinds of improvements do you make? Generally, you relocate responsibilities from one class to another, or relocate classes from one package to another, or even repackage the classes. As you relocate responsibilities across classes, remember that you have to preserve the semantics of the analysis stereotypes. For example, you should never relocate a responsibility to retrieve some data elements to a boundary class or relocate a responsibility to display some data to an entity class.

17.2.3   Evaluating Use-Case Structures

The use-case structure represents another dimension of the model. It is used to preserve separation of use cases from requirements to code. As you may recall, use-case slices are used to keep crosscutting concerns of various kinds separate—separating functional requirements, nonfunctional requirements, platform specifics, and so forth.

To make our discussion concrete, let's consider the slices involved in the Reserve Room use-case design. Figure 17–7 depicts the slices that are relevant to the Reserve Room use case. We do not show the features (attributes, operations and relationships) within the class extensions—if we did, Figure 17–7 will be very large indeed. The intent of Figure 17–7 is to provide an overview of the contents in the various use-case slices.

In essence, when you evaluate whether you have a good use-case structure, you are asking if you have good use-case slices, good aspects, and good operation extensions (i.e., advices). So, you ask questions like these:

- Is the separation between what is use-case-specific and what is use-case-generic appropriate? We draw dashed lines in Figure 17–7 to help you consider if there is appropriate separation between what is Reserve Room–specific and Reserve Room–generic, what is platform-specific and what is platform-independent. If it is not appropriate, you may need to relocate extensions across slices.
- If a use-case slice extends more than one other slice, is it sufficient to use only one aspect, or should you split the aspect to make individual aspects more resilient to changes?
- Is the behavioral and structural context of each operation extension clearly defined? Otherwise, you may add behaviors to places where they are not needed and thereby cause unwanted side effects.

Again, what we have above is a small checklist. As aspect-oriented software development matures, this list will be more comprehensive.

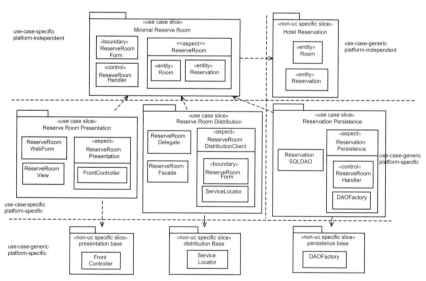

Figure 17-7   *Slices within the use-case structure.*

17.2.4 Automating the Evaluation

The system grows as you start to add more use cases into it. This makes it increasingly more difficult for you to conduct the evaluation because you have more use cases to consider, more classes to consider, and so on. Finding errors is more difficult if you must find them manually. You want to spend more time improving the architecture than hunting for errors. Naturally, you look for ways to automatically hunt possible errors. We explore two ways for automation: through metrics and access rules.

You can formulate some measurements on the various system attributes, such as size, complexity, and dependency of each element within the system, to determine which areas need more attention. These measurements should preferably be automated so that you can quickly scan through the architecture.

- Size refers to the number of classes in a package, the number of features in a class, and so on.
- Complexity refers to the number of paths through a class. So, if a responsibility of a class has many conditions, then it is considered complex.
- Dependency refers to the number of classes a class depends on, the number of packages a package depends on, and so on.

In addition, you must consider the three attributes from several perspectives:

- From the perspective of one use case—that is, from one use-case realization.
- From the perspective of the system—that is, after the composition of multiple use-case realizations.

A class that is simple in the eyes of one use-case realization may in reality be quite complex after adding all the responsibilities from various use-case realizations.

In general any element that is big in terms of size, complexity, and dependency is difficult to understand, and you will have to retry to make it smaller. If the system is comprised of only a few classes, then each of these classes will be complex. Since there are few classes, the dependencies between them will be few.. The degenerate case occurs when the entire system has only one class. In this case, the dependency is zero, but the complexity of each class is huge. If you have many small classes, each individual class may be simple, but there will be a large number of classes in a package. So, refinement is a tradeoff between size, complexity, and dependencies.

However, numbers are just numbers. They serve only to highlight potential problems in the system. You must do some structuring work (discussed above) to determine where best to locate classes and their features.

17.2.5   Enforcing the Separation of Concerns

During analysis and design, you define the permitted relationships between classes belonging to different packages. For example, classes in package A cannot access classes in package B. In a team with many people, there are bound to be developers who break such rules for some reason—lack of training, lack of understanding, convenience, and so on. This is illustrated in Figure 17–8.

Figure 17–8 contains no modeled dependencies between the app package and the db package. This is because the architect does not want any classes within the two accessing each other (i.e., making calls to each other) or any kind of dependencies between them. First, the app package is supposed to be free from any platform specifics that are in the db package. Second, the db package should not make calls to classes in the app package, since there should be no calls from the domain layer to the application layer.

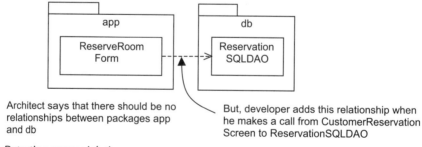

Figure 17-8   *Detecting access violations.*

However, during implementation, a developer for some reason makes a call from the `ReserveRoomForm` class to the `ReservationSQLDAO`. This is a violation of the access policies defined by the architect. Although such errors are obvious, finding them is laborious work.

AspectJ provides facilities to detect such access errors, illustrated in Listing 17–1.

Listing 17-1 Dependency Checks with AspectJ

```
1.  public aspect DependencyCheck {
2.    declare error : within(app.*) && call(* db.*.*(..))
3.          : "app class should not access db classes directly";
4.  }
```

Lines 2 and 3 declare an error. The error occurs when any class within the app package makes a call to any operation in any class in the db package. If such a call is made, the AspectJ compiler displays an error message defined in Line 3: "app class should not access db classes directly."

The advantage of doing such checks as part of compilation is that the developer is notified of the error and must fix it immediately. This is much better than a separate code review, which usually occurs many days and even months after implementation, if it is ever done at all. Errors are usually detected too late in the project. The result is schedule slippage. This follows the principle of the test-first approach—you want quality from the beginning, not as an afterthought.

We do not model errors, so we do not have a UML notation for Listing 17–1. You model what is allowed and thus define permitted dependencies between packages. If no such dependency exists in the model and such calls are in the code, there is an access error, and you have to declare an error check in AspectJ for every unmodeled dependency between packages. Usually, quite a large number of error declarations are needed. Therefore, you might create a utility to generate all these AspectJ error declarations. In addition, you should always strive to detect such errors even earlier, for instance, during analysis.

17.3   Evaluating and Achieving Systemwide Concerns

It is important to keep use cases and concerns separate. However, there are a number of system qualities that are not restricted to a single use case but span the entire system. Such qualities include maintainability, extensibility, portability, configurability, reusability, reliability, and performance. We discuss each of these qualities and how to evaluate whether your system has such qualities. More importantly, we demonstrate how to achieve these qualities. As you read this section, you will notice a key theme: By keeping concerns separate, you naturally achieve these architectural qualities.

17.3.1   Evaluating and Achieving Maintainability

Maintainability is about whether a system is easy to understand and modify. When a requirement changes, you want to be able to quickly identify which parts of the system are affected, and as far as possible, the parts affected should be few.

Separation of concerns is key to maintainability. In this part of the book, we discuss how to keep concerns of different kinds separate. By following the approach discussed throughout the book, you should have systematically arrived at a system that is easy to understand and maintain.

To evaluate if your system is indeed maintainable, you must evaluate the element structure and the use-case structure. We discussed this in the preceding sections (see Section 17.2).

17.3.2   Evaluating and Achieving Extensibility

Extensibility is about whether you can easily incorporate enhancements to the system. To evaluate extensibility, you must first think about what kind of enhancements you want and what kinds of changes you might have. These are called *change cases*. Change cases attempt to predict possible changes that you will encounter in the near future. For example, you might foresee that the Hotel Management System will need to handle new kinds of reservation schemes or manage hotel chains rather than individual hotels.

In Chapter 7, "Capturing Concerns with Use Cases," we highlighted the identifications of variables during use-case modeling. These variables give a systematic basis for considering potential variations (changes). You will evaluate extensibility with respect to each variation or change case for your system.

In this book, we go a step further. We show how you can achieve extensibility. In essence, we treat each change case as an extension use case. So, you identify these extension use cases at the beginning of the project and analyze and design the system to realize them. A large part of Chapter 13 deals with the design of such extension use cases.

Configurability is about changing the behavior of the system by changing some settings instead of changing its design or implementation. This system quality is closely related to extensibility. In essence, your system must be able to read some configuration parameters and use them during execution. These configuration files and related elements can be easily incorporated as part of your extensibility mechanism.

17.3.3   Evaluating and Achieving Portability

Portability is being able to run a system on different execution platforms. To evaluate portability, you need to identify change cases for porting scenarios as well. You consider the potential parts of the system that you will port and evaluate the system accordingly.

Portability is largely about changing the infrastructure and platform specifics, discussed extensively in Chapters 14 and 15. You model portability change cases as extension use cases. Thus, you can have extension use cases for authorization, distribution, presentation, persistence, and so on. So, if you want to change from a browser client to a thick client, you just need to consider the Handle Presentation extension use case (see Chapter 15) and determine how you can perform the port.

This book goes further by showing how you can design the infrastructure and platform as an extension use case. You can have different realizations for each of these extension use cases. Thus, porting would simply mean replacing an existing extension use-case slice with a new extension use-case slice.

17.3.4   Evaluating and Achieving Reusability

Reusability is about using the same design element under different contexts. In a system, some parts are reusable, and some are project-specific and not so reusable. To evaluate reusability of a system, you evaluate how well the reusable parts are modularized and kept separate from the parts that are project-specific—how the design elements are organized in separate layers. Thus, you look for reusable elements in lower layers or lower packages in each layer. For example, in the application layer, you find lower packages that are application-generic. These packages are utilized by application-specific packages. Likewise, you find domain-generic packages that are used by domain-specific packages. Use-case slices and extension use-case slices are potentially reusable elements as well. Each of these realizes a specific stakeholder concern. You can pick the appropriate ones to compose the desired system.

In this book, we discussed such layering, packaging, and modularizing concepts and guidelines extensively. Following the approach discussed in this book will help you achieve reusability.

17.3.5   Evaluating and Achieving Performance and Reliability

To evaluate the performance and reliability characteristics of a system, you have to execute it. A system executes in a composed manner that involves several use-case slices, including the platform-specifics, at once.

We use the Reserve Room use case as an example. Figure 17–9 shows the participating elements within the Reserve Room use-case realization. These elements execute within two processes: the Web container and the EJB container.

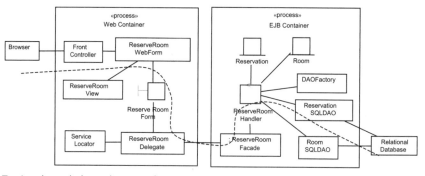

Figure 17-9   *Tracing through the realization of Reserve Room use case.*

The Web container is responsible for serving HTML pages to the browser. It contains the `ReserveRoomForm`, which is a boundary class, and also a number of elements to provide Web-presentation support. Since the control class (`ReserveRoomHandler`) is distributed over the EJB container, the Web container must have elements to support making remote calls.

The EJB container includes elements that perform the actual processing. It comprises control classes (e.g., `ReserveRoomHandler`) and entity classes (e.g., `Room` and `Reservation`). It also has elements to provide distribution and elements to provide access to the relational database.

You can determine the response time to handle an actor request by tracing how the request is processed and passed between the elements. As you trace the request, you sum up how long each element takes. The total time will be the response time. To be really sure about the performance characteristics of the system, tracing request flows is not sufficient. You need to conduct performance tests in which you measure turnaround time, throughput, and other performance attributes of the requests.

There are many different kinds of application use cases. Some involve short user requests, while others involve batch computations and similar tasks. You must evaluate each different type.

If there are more requests coming into the system than can be processed, you probably need to consider buffers to queue up the requests, or you may consider load balancing or other request-handling methods. It should be easy to add these additional capabilities. For example, you might extend the Service Locator with the ability to schedule between different processing nodes, and so on. Because you have been keeping infrastructure and platform specifics separate, you can make such changes easily.

It is important to emphasize that the architectural qualities (e.g., extensibility, performance, reliability) cannot be evaluated and achieved in total isolation. There are tradeoffs. Frequently, these architectural qualities conflict with one another. For example, extensibility implies that you add new elements to the system. As can be seen in Figure 17–9, new elements introduce additional delay, increasing the total response time of the entire system and degrading performance quality. You must also bear in mind that not all systems require all architectural qualities. For example, a system might not need to have a rich extensibility mechanism. There is also a question of time and resources, neither of which is unlimited. The goal when building the whole system, then, is to find the correct balance. The architect must be able to distinguish between what is important and what is not.

Sidebar 17–1 How Do Use Cases Help to Evaluate Architecture?

Some of you may be familiar with the Architecture Tradeoff Analysis Method (ATAM) to evaluate the goodness of architectural decisions [Clements et al. 2002]. In essence, the ATAM involves identifying architectural scenarios and conducting the evaluation based on these scenarios.

Architectural scenarios can be effectively modeled as use cases or extension use cases. You can consider the pros and cons of different realizations for each use case. Thus, by applying the use-case-driven approach, you are employing a method similar to ATAM. In fact, you are conducting analysis, design, and evaluation in parallel.

The use-case-driven approach helps you further. Use cases help you explore the different variations for each use case and each architectural scenario. The use-case-driven approach further helps you visualize and communicate the different realizations with your team members. From this basis, you can weigh the relative merits of different realizations and make correct choices. In the event that a wrong choice is made, the impact is not severe because by following the approach of keeping concerns (use cases) separate, you can re-implement the defective parts without significant impact to other parts of the system. This is why we dare say that by following the approach in this book, you will naturally achieve an effective architecture.

17.4   Summary and Highlights

In this chapter, we discussed how to evaluate and achieve system qualities such as maintainability, extensibility, performance, and reliability. Key to achieving these qualities is the concept of separation of concerns. By following the approach outlined in Part IV, you can achieve effective separation of concerns and these qualities.

You probably noticed as you read preceding chapters in this part of the book that there is a general approach for dealing with concerns of different kinds—you model them with use cases; you analyze them and start separating use-case specific from use-case-generic; and you proceed in this manner all the way to code. Once you understand this general approach, aspect-oriented software development with use cases us easy.

It is important that you have an architecture that is of some minimum quality to start with. If you follow our approach, you will have a good candidate architecture to begin with, and you can commence evaluations and refinements iteratively. If you have a poor architecture to start with, the refinements you do will not give you the desired benefits. Your work will be time consuming. If your system is poorly organized in the first place, we strongly suggest that you take a step back and begin from analysis to establish a good candidate architecture of sufficient quality. Then consider how you can migrate the elements from the disorganized structure into this new candidate structure. Remember, it is architecture first.

Remember, too, that architectural evaluation is not a task that you do at the end of certain milestones. No—you evaluate the architecture continually in a project. If there are necessary improvements to be made, you make them immediately. Thus, achieving that an effective architecture and evaluation occur in parallel.

18

Describing the Architecture

Architecture is about everything, yet it is not everything. It is about the architecturally significant things in everything that stakeholders and developers must understand in order to comprehend the whole system. The architecture description is an important artifact because it describes the architecture as manifested in the architecture baseline—a skinny system that will become the final system. Recall that the architecture baseline is an early version of the system. Since a system is described by a set of models, the architecture baseline is also described by an early version of these models. The architecture description has views of these models—we call them architectural views—which it collates and presents in an understandable way to both stakeholders and developers. Through the architecture description, you can evaluate whether the goals and constraints of the system are met and whether there is effective separation of concerns. The architecture description serves as the roadmap by which the rest of the system is developed.

18.1 Architecture Description Comprises Architectural Views

The architecture encompasses the important decisions that make the project successful—decisions about the structure of the system, about how functionality, performance, reliability, and other requirements are met, and so on. The architecture is manifested in an early version of the system, which we call the skinny system or the architecture baseline. It demonstrates that the decisions you have made are valid in the sense that they have correctly and feasibly addressed stakeholder concerns.

Since the system is described by a set of models, the skinny system (architecture baseline) is also described by a version of these models (see Figure 18–1).

The skinny system also has an accompanying architecture description. The architecture description is, at the end of elaboration phase, an extract (i.e., a set of views) of the models in the architecture baseline. The architecture description thus manifests what the architecture is—major decisions made about the system.

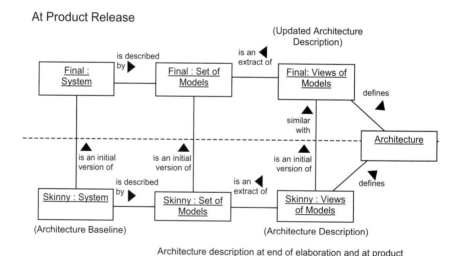

Figure 18-1 *System models, views, and architecture.*

You may need to rewrite the views and remove the non-architecturally significant elements to make them more readable. The views include the architecturally significant elements. Thus, the architecture description includes descriptions of architecturally significant use cases, architecturally significant analysis elements, architecturally significant design elements, and so on. Many model elements that are part of the architecture baseline also show up in the architecture description. However, not all of them do, because to get an operational system, you may need to develop some model elements that are not architecturally interesting but are needed just to produce executable code. When it comes to the use-case model, you may need to specify much more than the architecturally significant use cases because you need to know about more use cases to be able to pinpoint the use cases that are indeed architecturally significant. The same goes for the analysis model, but to a lesser extent. When it comes to the design model, at the time that you establish the architecture baseline, the version of the contents within the design model is largely architecturally significant.

Actually, the architecture description is developed concurrently, often even ahead of the activities that result in the version of the models that are parts of the architecture baseline. The architecture description is the standard for the development team to build the rest of the system. Since the architecture should be stable, the standard (i.e., the architecture description) should be stable after the elaboration phase.

The architecture description must be updated throughout the system's lifetime to reflect the changes and additions that are architecturally relevant. The architecture description itself may need to be modified, but it need not grow in size. It is just updated to stay relevant.

Recall that the architecture description is just a proper extract of the models of the system (i.e., it does not add anything new). Given that we don't try to make a more readable rewrite of these extracts, the architecture description looks very much like ordinary models of the system. This appearance means that the architectural view of the use-case model looks like an ordinary use-case model. The only difference is that this architectural view contains only architecturally significant use cases and more specifically only the scenarios that are architecturally significant, whereas the final use-case model contains all the use cases. The same goes for the architecture view of the design model. It looks like a design model, but it realizes only the use cases that are architecturally interesting.

The truth is this: *Even though architecture is extremely important, it is not that special when it comes to content and modeling.* In a book like this, it is practically impossible to show how to develop both the architecture and the models. We can only give you a feeling for how it proceeds.

In the following sections, we describe the architectural views of the use-case model, the analysis model, and the design model. Since the implementation model is a straightforward mapping, there is usually no need to describe its view.

Our intent is to provide an extract of the important pieces in the respective models; we do not describe the contents in detail, since they are explained in preceding chapters. Our discussion in this chapter focuses how you choose architecturally significant elements.

18.2   Architectural View of the Use-Case Model

The architectural view of the use-case model presents the most important actors and use cases (or scenarios of these use cases). Many architecturally significant use cases come from risks of different kinds. Risks can be associated with functional requirements, nonfunctional requirements, or platform specifics. Thus, architecturally significant use cases encompass both application and infrastructure use cases.

Groups of use cases in a system follow similar behavioral patterns. You naturally choose one representative use case per group to be part of the architecturally significant use cases, because once you solve that particular use case, you can solve the other use cases in the group. After all, they use the same design principles. This is also why, in the preceding chapters, we explored use cases that belong to different categories— application use cases, application extension use cases, infrastructure use cases, and so forth.

The architecturally significant use cases for the Hotel Management System are depicted in Figure 18–2. It shows both application and infrastruc-

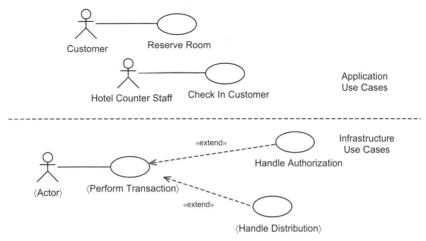

Figure 18-2   *Architecturally significant use cases.*

ture use cases, albeit only the important ones. Note that the architectural view of the use-case model is not just a diagram. The use-case diagram itself does not say much. You need to describe the critical scenarios or at least a brief description of the use cases to help the reader understand what the architecturally significant use cases are about.

The Reserve Room use case is the most important use case, as the fundamental goal of the system is to provide online reservations to customers. Whereas the room reservations by customers are conducted over the Internet, customer check in is performed by counter staff at the hotel itself, and it involves an entirely different set of user interfaces (a thick client as opposed to a Web-based client). The Check In Customer use case is chosen as a representative of functionality provided to hotel staff. Together, the realizations of these three use cases exercise a large portion of the application and domain layers in the design model.

In this case, Handle Authorization is deemed critical, since stakeholders are concerned with security. ⟨Handle Distribution⟩ is also critical, since stakeholders are concerned with scalability of the system.

The ⟨Perform Transaction⟩ use case is not considered architecturally significant in this case. Nevertheless it is still depicted in Figure 18–2. This is because Handle Authorization and ⟨Handle Distribution⟩ are extension use cases and it is necessary to show the use case which they extend. In this case, it is the ⟨Perform Transaction⟩ use case.

To simplify our discussion, we choose only one use case, Reserve Room, to drive the architectural views of the analysis model and design model. In an actual project, you will probably need to describe all the identified architecturally significant use cases.

18.3   Architectural View of the Analysis Model

The architectural view of the analysis model presents the architecturally most important classifiers of the analysis model. Recall that the analysis model comprises an analysis element structure (a containment hierarchy of layers, packages, and analysis classes: i.e., boundary, control, and entity) and a use-case analysis structure (comprising use-case slices, aspects, class extensions). The architectural view of the analysis model also presents how the most important use cases are realized in terms of these elements (i.e., use-case realizations). It is natural to find architecturally significant classifiers present in these realizations. You extract several diagrams to describe these architecturally significant elements and realizations.

18.3.1   Architecturally Significant Analysis Elements

Figure 18–3 identifies the architecturally significant analysis elements from among others in the analysis element structure. The shaded packages indicate these important elements.

The choice of architecturally significant analysis elements is motivated by the same criteria that motivates the choice of architecturally significant use cases. Reservation is central to the Hotel Management System, and so are security and distribution. In addition, the rich-client interface used at the staff counters is critical and must be responsive.

You do not need to describe every subsystem or package in detail, but only the architecturally significant ones, and you often find them participating in the realization of architecturally significant use cases.

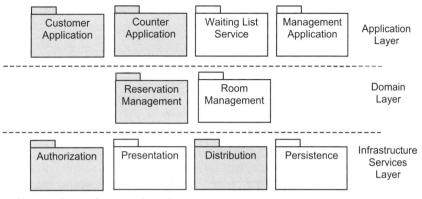

Figure 18-3   *Architecturally significant analysis elements.*

You depict the realization of architecturally significant use cases in a diagram. Figure 18–4 depicts the realization of an architecturally significant use case—the Reserve Room use case—as an example.

You can depict the Reserve Room use-case realization with authorization added, or you can depict the realization of Handle Authorization in a separate diagram.

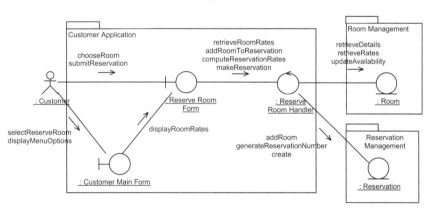

Figure 18-4   *Communication diagram: Reserve Room use-case realization.*

18.3.2   Architecturally Significant Use-Case Analysis Slices

The analysis model also contains a use-case structure. The use-case structure attempts to keep the specifics of use cases separate in the analysis model. Figure 18–5 depicts some of the slices, and highlights (shaded) those that are of architectural significance. As you might expect, the choice of the architecturally significant use-case slices follows naturally the architecturally significant use cases. That is why the Reserve Room and Check In Customer use-case slices are shaded.

In the architecture description, you depict the contents of architecturally significant use-case slices. Figure 18–6 shows the contents of the Reserve Room use-case slice as an example.

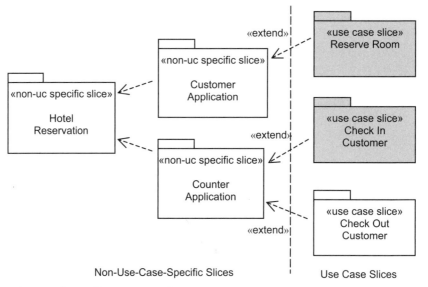

Figure 18-5   *Architecturally significant use-case slices.*

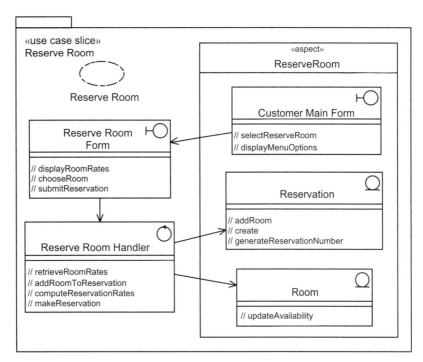

Figure 18-6   *Architecturally significant use-case slice: Reserve Room use case.*

18.4   Architectural View of the Design Model

The architectural view of the design model presents the most architecturally significant elements in the design model. Recall that the design model comprises a deployment structure, a process structure, a design element structure, and a use-case design structure. The architectural view of the design model is an extract of these structures. Frequently, you find that a sizeable portion of the deployment and process structures are architecturally significant.

The purpose of the design model is to deal with platform specifics. These platform specifics are driven not by functionality, but by the deployment environment and the technologies available in that environment. So, you present the extract of the deployment structure first. You then zoom down to an extract of the process structure and show how they map to the chosen elements in the deployment structure. Thereafter, you zoom down to an extract of the design element structure and the use-case design structure.

18.4.1 Architecturally Significant Deployment Elements

Figure 18–7 depicts the architectural view of the deployment structure. It comprises the deployment elements (i.e., nodes) that participate in the realization of the Reserve Room and Check In Customer use cases. Both of these, as you recall, are architecturally significant use cases. Figure 18–7 is also annotated with the architect's choice of communication mechanisms, implementation languages, and technologies. The shaded elements are architecturally significant.

18.4.2 Architecturally Significant Process Elements

Figure 18–8 depicts the architectural view of the process structure. It refines Figure 18–7 to show how these processes map to the deployment elements. The Web container and EJB container are both architecturally significant process elements in this case. So is the thick client, because a very responsive user interface is needed.

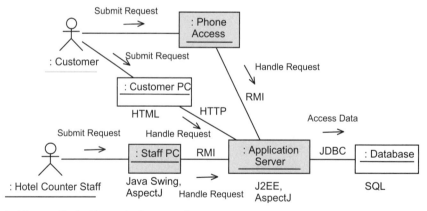

Figure 18-7 *Architecturally significant deployment elements.*

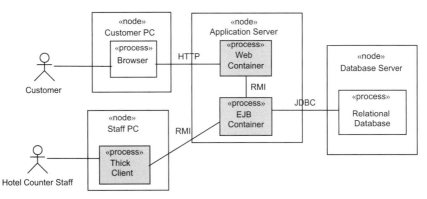

Figure 18-8   *Architecturally significant process elements.*

18.4.3   Architecturally Significant Design Elements

The architectural view of the design element structure comprises several diagrams depicting the architecturally significant design elements individually and their relationship with elements in other structures.

- **Minimal Design**. You can have diagrams to describe design elements before the incorporation of platform specifics (see Figure 18–9).
- **Platform Specifics**. You can have diagrams to describe design elements after the incorporation of platform specifics (see Figure 18–10).
- **Process Mapping**. You can have diagrams to describe how design elements map to the process structure (see Figure 18–11).

The design realization of the Reserve Room use case demonstrates how you describe architecturally significant design elements.

Figure 18–9 depicts the components realizing the Reserve Room use case. It illustrates how the components interact with one another and what primary classes are needed to realize the architecturally significant use case.

Figure 18–10 depicts the components realizing the Reserve Room use case, but unlike Figure 18–9, it shows the platform-specific parts. This is useful in understanding which classes are needed to adapt the minimal design classes, or POJOs, onto the runtime platform.

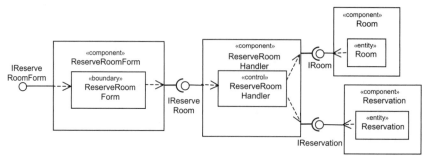

Figure 18-9   *Use-case realization from a minimal design perspective.*

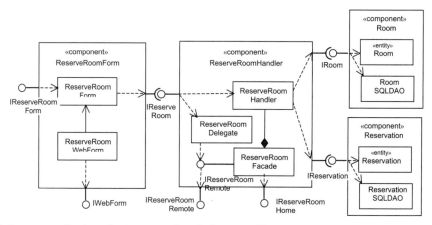

Figure 18-10   *Use-case realization after incorporating platform specifics.*

Figure 18–11 shows the design elements participating in the Reserve Room use-case realization. These design elements are mapped to the process structure, specifically to the Web container and the EJB container within the application server. This diagram clarifies where the design classes execute and is useful for determining which artifacts (binaries, etc.) run on which node. These artifacts are subsequently deployed onto the respective containing nodes.

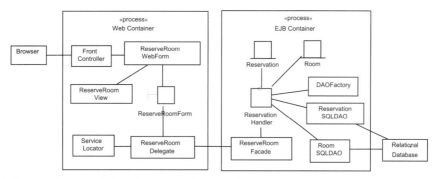

Figure 18-11 *Mapping between design elements and process elements.*

18.4.4   Architecturally Significant Use-Case Design Slices

The architectural view of the use-case design structure comprises a number of diagrams depicting the architecturally significant use-case design slices. Since distribution is a critical part of the Hotel Management System, and the Reserve Room use case is an important use case, the Reserve Room distribution use-case slice is architecturally significant. This is depicted in Figure 18–12.

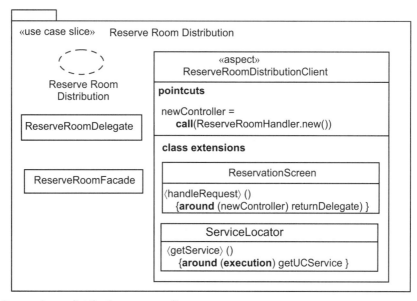

Figure 18-12 *Reserve Room distribution use-case slice.*

Sidebar 18–1   What Are the Typical Contents of an Architecture Description?

An architecture description describes the architecturally significant elements in the system. It usually contains the following sections:

- Architectural goals and constraints.

- Architectural representation.

- Architectural view of the use-case model.

- Architectural view of the analysis model.

- Architectural view of the design model.

The architectural goals and constraints section lists the important decisions you need to make. These goals can be expressed as change cases (see Chapter 17, "Evaluating the Architecture") and are the basis by which a reviewer evaluates the key decisions.

The architectural representation section describes the models used to describe the system. If project-specific tailoring of the UML notation is necessary, it is described in this section.

The remainder of the architecture description presents the architectural views of the various models, as discussed in this chapter. We explained but one way to present architectural views; you will need to apply project-specific tailoring. Nevertheless, we believe our method is a good starting point that is applicable to most software projects.

18.5   Summary and Highlights

The architecture description is the most important artifact. It is used to clearly communicate the architecture to stakeholders and project members. It contains detailed descriptions of the architecturally important views of the models that represent the system. Thus, in the architecture description, you find architectural views of the use-case model, the analysis model, the design model, and so on. To show how the various views relate to each other, it is useful to describe them from the perspective of the realization of some critical use case. In this way, you can systematically guide the reader from a very high-level description in the use case and analysis model to the smallest details in the design model. From this understanding, the reader can better evaluate all kinds of structures in the system—element structure, use-case structure, and so on—and, if necessary, improve these structures.

It is important to note that what we have discussed in this chapter is but one way to describe the architecture. You must choose diagrams according to the needs of your project. Drafting the architecture description takes some effort. However, this investment is well worth the effort, as it ensures that you can gracefully grow the system during the rest of the project lifetime, and even more importantly, throughout the system's lifetime.

PART V

Applying Use Cases and Aspects in a Project

In Part V of the book, we show how you can apply aspect orientation in your project. We demonstrate how to estimate, plan, and track the progress of your project, and we explain the productivity improvements you gain from applying better separation of concerns. Whether you are just starting a new project, in the middle of one, or in the final stages of one, you can apply the practices advocated in this book. We demonstrate how to tailor our software development approach to different project scenarios so that you can reap immediate success.

Part V includes the following chapters:

Chapter 19, "Running a Project"

Chapter 20, "Tailoring the Approach"

Chapter 21, "Aspects and Beyond"

19

Running a Project

Developing a system is an iterative process. In each iteration, you deliver useful capabilities in terms of use cases or use-case scenarios that are tested and working. At the beginning of the project, you estimate the size of the system in terms of use cases—both application and infrastructure use cases—and in each iteration, you assess project progress according to the progress on these use cases, i.e., the degree to which they have been specified and analyzed, the degree they have been design and implemented, etc. Planning and tracking development in this way provides you with an objective assessment of the project's status. Moreover, keeping concerns separate not only makes the system more understandable and extensible, it also provides significant savings in terms of development effort.

19.1   Iterative Development

Managing and controlling a project with aspect orientation is quite similar to managing and controlling any other project—it is iterative. Each iteration defines a time period for the development team to achieve some demonstrable results of value. The time period can be as short as one or two weeks for small projects or as long as three months for large projects. Normally, long iteration duration is a sign that either the system is extremely complex or, more likely, the team cannot define smaller

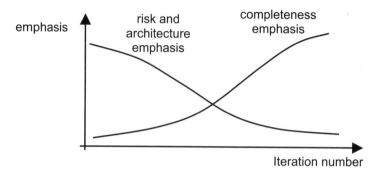

Figure 19-1   *Shifting emphasis in iterative development.*

increments or get its act together to collaborate properly—it has development-process problems.

The earlier iterations in a project are driven by risks of all kinds, technical and architectural risks, business risks, process risks, and others. The later iterations are driven be completeness as the team seeks to make the system sufficiently mature for the end-user community. The gradual shift from a risk and architecture emphasis to a completeness emphasis occurs through the project life cycle and is depicted in Figure 19–1.

19.1.1   Phases in a Project

The Unified Process breaks down the project life cycle into four phases: inception, elaboration, construction, and transition.

- In the inception phase, the primary goals are to set the scope of the project, reduce the business risks, and prepare an initial business case to indicate if the project is worth pursuing from a business standpoint.
- In the elaboration phase, the goal is to capture most of the requirements, reduce risks further, and establish the architecture baseline—the skinny system. By the end of the elaboration phase, you can estimate the costs and schedule, and plan the construction phase in detail.
- In the construction phase, the primary goal is to develop the full-fledged system.
- In the transition phase, the primary goal is to ensure that the system is mature enough to be released to the end-user community.

19.1.2   Activities in an Iteration

Please remember that inception is not requirements, elaboration is not design, construction is not code, and transition is not test. In each phase, there is one or more iterations. Within each iteration, many things happen, often in parallel. You do requirements, analysis, design, implementation, test, and many other activities, and you move back and forth between them. It is useful to allocate development to a team member in terms of use-case modules because she must have freedom to move between the activities surrounding the use case.

Although some project managers like to plan an iteration in terms of activities in some form of a schedule, it is more fruitful to plan iterations in terms of results you want to achieve in that iteration and let the team coordinate itself to achieve those results. After all, achieving results is more important than meeting a schedule of activities. Certain activities, such as meetings with stakeholders, must of course be planned. However, when it comes to what the development team must do, management by results is more appropriate. This means that it is important to clarify the acceptance criteria for each target—for example, the number of use cases specified to a defined level of detail, the number of use cases designed and implemented (with test cases defined), the number of test case passed, and so on.

At the end of each iteration, some new capability will have been added to the system to demonstrate that some risks and some concerns have been resolved. This new capability is often described in terms of use cases or use-case scenarios—that is, you build a system use case by use case across iterations.

19.2   Estimating Development Effort

At the beginning of the project, you must systematically estimate the size and complexity of your system and determine how long the development will take. There are many software estimation techniques available, ranging from the simple to the complex. An effort estimation technique is usually in the form of:

$$\text{Effort Required} = \text{Size}/\text{Team Productivity}$$

You can compare this formula to that of driving a car:

$$\text{Time Required} = \text{Distance}/\text{Speed}$$

A good estimation technique has the following characteristics:

1. The size estimates must be verifiable.
2. The productivity estimate must be tunable.

To be verifiable, the unit by which you measure the size of the project and the progress of development must correspond to what you deliver. This means that units are in terms of use cases or their derivatives, such use-case scenarios, use-case flows, use-case steps, and test cases.

To be tunable, your team productivity must be in a form that you can easily calibrate to your project. Many estimation techniques such as COCOMO [Boehm et.al. 2000], Use-Case Points [Karner 1993], and so on. use a list of parameters with values for high, low, and nominal. But a finite number of parameters is never able to capture characteristics of each project.

Another alternative to estimate team productivity is to totally ignore the use of parameters. Instead, measure what the team is actually capable of producing in each iteration. Simply get the team to work on a number of use-case scenarios for an iteration and track how much is accomplished in that iteration. This gives you a data point to estimate your team's productivity. The data point encompasses the time that team members spend talking to each other about work, responding to emails, performing secondary duties, taking coffee breaks, dreaming about their next job, planning their vacation, and last but not least, working on delivering the use-case scenarios. It does not matter whether the developers are truthful about the use of their time because you only check the results at the end of the iteration. After observing several iterations, you have a set of historical data that is collected from your project (and not other projects) to support your productivity estimation.

19.2.1   Estimation at the Beginning of a Project

At the beginning of the project, you may not have any historical basis for the team's productivity estimates. An alternate way to estimate productivity is as follows: Choose several use cases and conduct a quick use-case analysis and design. Once you understand the complexity of the use case, you can get your team members to estimate how long each use case or its derivative might take.

As an example, you can consider a typical use-case step. The realization of a use-case step involves the submission of a request until the result is displayed to the actor. This is captured in the design realization of the Perform Transaction use case, shown in Figure 19–2.

You can get a consensus from your team members on the amount of time needed for development of a use-case step, together with the use-case presentation, use-case distribution, and use-case persistence, as discussed in Chapter 15, "Separating Tests with Use-Case Test Slices." From our experience and interaction with various project teams, this may take between one to five man days depending on the skills of the team and the complexity of the use-case step. Let's take two and a half man days as the average. You can then count the number of use-case steps in the system for both application and infrastructure use cases. Suppose you have 10 application use cases, each with five steps in the basic flow and maybe another five steps in the alternate flow. In this case, you have about 100 use-case steps in the system. So, the development effort for the application use case alone will be 250 man days.

Suppose you have five infrastructure use cases, and each has three steps as well as three steps in the alternate flows. That's about 30 use-case steps for the infrastructure use cases. However, your team might indicate that infrastructure use cases are technically more complex and will take twice as much effort, say, five man days. The effort required for the infrastructure use cases, therefore, will be 30 × 5 = 150 man days.

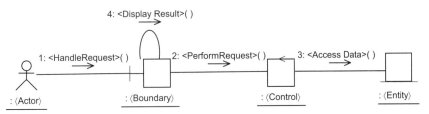

Figure 19-2 *Developing a use-case step.*

So, the total effort will be 250 + 150 = 400 man days, and if we take each man month to be 20 man days, then the effort will be approximately 20 man months. If you want the system to be delivered in five months, you need four people on the development team and one more person to play the role of a project leader, analyst, and architect. Of course, if this is a more complex project, you need more than one person to play these roles. There is a limit to how many people you can put on a project, however. You cannot put 20 people on this project and expect the project to be delivered in a month. Time must be invested to get the architecture right, and that occurs in the elaboration phase. In this five-month project, elaboration might possibly take one or two months. It is only when you have completed elaboration that it is possible to have more people on the team. Otherwise, you have some people waiting for the architecture to be stabilized and much of the work they do in the meantime will likely have to be redone.

You probably notice that we keep the estimation of application and infrastructure use cases separate. This is only possible because, if they follow the approach described in this book, they are indeed separate.

19.2.2   Refining the Estimates

The estimation above makes two additional yet important assumptions:

- You have a good idea of the system scope.
- You have a good idea of the architecture you will be using.

If these assumptions are true, then your estimates will be quite credible. If not, what most project managers do is add some buffers, perhaps an additional resource, and probably more time.

In the early architectural iterations of the project, you must ensure that the assumptions are true and the estimates to develop each use-case step (application or infrastructure) are accurate. This involves observing how much the team can deliver at the end of each iteration over several iterations. At the end of the architectural iterations, you have not only an established architecture, but also a credible basis to estimate the time required to complete the remaining parts of the system.

19.3   Planning and Controlling the Project

The progress of a project usually follows an S-curve, as shown in Figure 19–3. This curve represents the accumulative number of use-case steps you complete over time. It takes an S shape because your project team normally takes time to ramp up productivity and also because of time spent on resolving critical risks early in the project. During the later part of the project, you tend to exercise more rigor, make more checks, and so on, as you attempt to get the system ready for end users. The added efforts take a toll on the team productivity and results in the S-curve.

The middle part of the project is the generally the most productive. So, for example, if the project needs to be delivered in six months, you probably have, in reality, about four to five months for the bulk of the development.

19.3.1   Estimating Project Delays

Continuing with our example, there are 100 application use-case steps and 45 infrastructure use-case steps: 145 use-case steps in total. These have to be developed in about five months, and if you take each iteration to be two weeks, you have about 10 iterations for development. In each iteration, you must complete about 15 use-case steps—implemented and tested just to be on track. If you cannot keep this productivity value, your project will be delayed.

Suppose you are in the fifth iteration and you have completed 45 use-case steps. That means that you have another 100 use-case steps to go in the remaining five iterations. If you continue development at the same pace

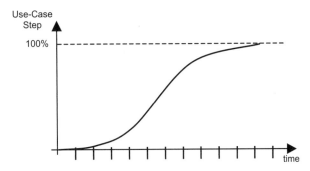

Figure 19-3   *Planning iterative development.*

(i.e., 45/5 = 9 use-case steps per iteration), then you need 100/9 = 11 iterations more. However, you only have five left. This means that you are six iterations late! Such computation is simple and even obvious, but it does give a numerical basis about the project's health.

Sidebar 19–1 Number of Iterations and Duration of Iteration

In the example above, the project plan has 10 iterations of two weeks each. Are there too many iterations? Iteration is not dependent on the length of a project. A project with six iterations is not good if the project runs for six years—that's one iteration per year! Instead, iteration length should be dependent on the time needed for some useful increment. In this case, the team can complete 15 use-case steps (i.e., a couple of scenarios), and this is a reasonable increment.

In many cases, a long iteration duration usually signifies that the team has difficulty breaking down development into smaller chunks of work. This is not good: it is normally impractical to track progress within an iteration because so many things happen in parallel. So, in a way, what occurs within an iteration is a management black hole. Each iteration gives the team a sense of closure and a chance to re-evaluate the project status based on what it has completed. Iterations, therefore, should not be too long. In fact, the riskier the project, the shorter should be the iteration to provide better visibility.

19.3.2 Keeping the Project on Track

Keeping track of the remaining time required is an important part of a project manager's job. It helps you ascertain ahead of time whether you can meet the deadline and take remedial action if necessary to improve team productivity.

You have several options to improve productivity. One method, of course, is to streamline the development process and reduce unnecessary documentation effort. Another method is to add additional development resources. But this is useful only if you have an established architecture. Otherwise, you simply have more resources *waiting* for the architecture to be established, as previously mentioned. Another technique is to use more powerful tools to automatically generate the repetitive parts of the system. However, if such tools are not tailored or configured during elaboration, you must invest additional time just to keep them working. As a project manager, you need to decide if the expected productivity improvements outweigh the investment.

Sidebar 19–2   How Does Aspect Orientation Impact Iterative Development?

You might find that what we have just described about managing a project iteratively for aspect-oriented software development is very much the same as you would do for any project. That is true. Iterative development is applicable to software development projects of any kind. In fact, the more difficult a project is, the more you need to iterate.

Aspect orientation does facilitate iterative development. Since crosscutting concerns (modeled as use cases) are kept separate, you have greater freedom to plan your iterations.

19.4   Productivity Gains by Keeping Concerns Separate

You achieve significant productivity gains with an architecture that keeps concerns separate. To justify this claim, let's consider a system with N requirements. Let's assume that these N requirements are independent, and the effort to develop each requirement is X. The effort required to develop the N requirements, then, is NX.

Let's suppose the N requirements are not well separated (i.e., there has been no attempt to keep concerns separate). This means that the realization of each requirement will overlap the realization of other requirements. Let's assume the worst case that occurs when the realization of each requirement touches the realization of $N-1$ requirements (i.e., every other requirement), and the effort to integrate the overlapping parts is Y. Now the effort required to develop each requirement is $X + (N-1)Y$, and the effort for the entire system of N unseparated requirements is $NX + N(N-1)Y$.

Figure 19–4 compares systems that are well separated (best case demanding NX effort) and unseparated (worst case demanding $NX + N(N-1)Y$ effort). In Figure 19–4, we have set $X = 20$ and $Y = 1$; that is, the effort to realize each requirement takes 20 times more effort per integration.

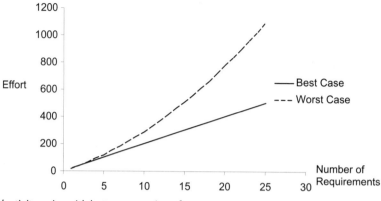

Figure 19-4 *Productivity gains with better separation of concerns.*

From Figure 19–4, you can see the need for better separation in a large system with a large number of requirements (i.e., N is large).

You do not need to achieve the ideal case to reap the benefits of better separation. Even by separating different kinds of concerns, such as application from infrastructure, you gain an advantage. Suppose you have 20 application and 20 infrastructure requirements: a total of 40 requirements. According to the worst-case formula $NX + N(N - 1)Y$, the effort is:

$$40(20) + 40(39)1 = 32,760$$

Suppose you have kept the application and infrastructure requirements separate so that each application requirement is separate from the other. However, the realization of each application requirement still needs to invoke each of the 20 infrastructure requirements. There is still some savings, because now the effort required per application requirements is $X + 20Y$, and the total effort for the whole system is $20(X + 20Y) + 20X$. The last term, $20X$, is the effort to realize each infrastructure requirement. After substituting $X = 20$ and $Y = 1$, the effort required for the whole system is 16,400, which is about half that of the worst case.

With the use-case slice and aspect approach, since infrastructure services are composed into the application by the aspect weaver, you no longer need to code each call to the infrastructure services; thus, the integration effort Y is reduced tremendously. Let's assume that Y is now 0.5; the effort $20(X + 20Y) + 20X$ now becomes 12,400.

From these simple calculations, you can see that there is much productivity to be gained by keeping concerns separate and leaving the development environment to compose the realization of concerns. Surely this is an incentive to apply the approach demonstrated in this book to your projects.

19.5   Summary and Highlights

Software development is iterative. In each iteration, you add some useful capability. The early iterations focus on resolving risks, and the later iterations focus on completeness. You need to systematically track the progress of the project and determine if there are any delays. If there are, you must improve team productivity. By keeping concerns separate as use cases, the effort to realize each concern is reduced dramatically, and team productivity is increased.

20

Tailoring the Approach

In the preceding parts of this book, we demonstrated how you can systematically capture and model concerns with use cases and, with aspect orientation techniques, preserve the separation of use cases all the way to code and test. How far you apply our approach in a project depends on a number of factors. Every project is different, and you must tailor your approach. Frequently, you will apply aspect orientation in conjunction with several other techniques. The key idea is to find the right balance and steer the project to success. In this chapter, we enumerate different project scenarios and prescribe a roadmap for you to find that balance for these scenarios.

20.1   Achieving the Right Balance

In the preceding parts of this book, we went into great detail on the theoretical basis for aspects. We provided a systematic approach for applying use cases and aspects to achieve better separation of concerns. We demonstrated how to apply the approach from requirements to code and how to establish a resilient architecture based on the approach.

It is time for you to apply the approach to *your* project. We recognize that every project is different—different complexity, different technologies, different levels of formality, and so on. Every project team is different as well, with various backgrounds and skill sets. You definitely need to tailor the approach to suit the specific needs of your project.

In this chapter, we discuss how you can adopt aspect orientation, specifically, the approach described in this book. This chapter is *not* about adopting a new approach in an organization. Adopting a new technology in an organization means organizational change, and it involves getting a champion, identifying pilot projects, and more—that is an entirely separate topic.

Rather, the premise is this: given that you want to apply use cases and aspects on an already chosen project, what should you do in that project? Which areas of our approach should you apply? How do you balance your existing approach with the new approach?

The remainder of this chapter is a guide to adopting the approach to a project discussed in this book. In particular, we look at the following considerations:

- Selecting the areas (or disciplines) within the methodology you want to adopt—requirements, design, implementation, testing, and so on.
- Balancing current and proposed approaches for software development at different phases of a project.

For each consideration, we discuss some of the adoption challenges you are likely to face and show you how to resolve them.

20.2   Selecting Disciplines to Apply

In the earlier parts of this book, we described how you capture and model concerns with use cases. We demonstrated how you specify use cases and analyze them, and how you can keep the realization of use cases separate during analysis as distinct use-case slices. These use-case slices are then designed, implemented, and tested with the available aspect technologies. Do you want to apply our approach during requirements and analysis? Do you want to apply it during design and implementation? During testing? How far you apply our approach depends on the aspect technologies available on your target platform.

Use-Case Modeling and Analysis. It is important that you capture stakeholder concerns correctly and accurately. The use-case specification technique attempts to do just that. Use cases capture stakeholder concerns, and the final deliverable is in the form of working use cases. Use-case analysis is part of the requirements and should be applied together with use-case modeling to better understand the requirements for the system. It is through this understanding that you shape and structure the system and keep the different concerns about the system separate.

You can most definitely apply use-case modeling and analysis to any project, since they are applicable to any software development in general—aspect-oriented, object-oriented, or otherwise. They are not limited to a specific aspect technology like AOP or AspectJ. Nevertheless, how far and how detailed you want to apply use-case modeling and analysis depends on the technology available in your development and target environment. If, for instance, you do not have any AOP technology available, you can still identify use-case slices, but you would probably not describe pointcuts in detail during use-case modeling and analysis. If AOP is available, you will probably specify pointcuts in greater detail.

We encourage you to write use cases for infrastructure services and explore the different scenarios in which they are applied. Frequently, only the basic flows of infrastructure services are described. When actual design and implementation occurs, there are many open and unresolved issues simply because they have not been sufficiently analyzed. Again, how far you want to go in writing use cases for the infrastructure services depends on the project. If you need to develop the infrastructure service, then you want to specify it in detail. If it is already existing, perhaps reused from a previous project, and your project team is familiar with it, you will need less detail. In this case, identifying the key scenarios the infrastructure services need to handle is quite sufficient.

While use-cases modeling and analysis are simple concepts, their application requires some practice. Writing use cases at an appropriate level of detail that meet your project's needs take some experience. Writing effective use cases that are easily understood by customers and by the development team also takes some experience. Fortunately, the use-case technique has gained widespread acceptance, and most practitioners have some understanding of use cases.

Design and Implementation. The introduction of use-case slices and the use-case structure represent the key differences between our approach and those applying just object orientation. The use-case slice concept is probably new to members of your project team. AOP and AspectJ (if your project team is using it) also are probably new to the project team. This represents a barrier for your team members. Your team must learn how to model aspects and use-case slices, and how to specify pointcuts. They also have to learn how this maps to an aspect technology such as AOP. A large part of this book is about doing just that.

To overcome the barrier, choose a particular concern that you want to solve through our approach. Express the concern as a use-case, and drive it all the way to code and test. You should not emphasize too much analysis and design at this point. Just dive in and quickly get out a working executable, much like a prototype solution. By developing this little prototype, you gain the experience of applying our approach and how use cases lead to use-case slices and how they are implemented in code. With a better understanding, you can proceed to apply the approach on the architecturally significant use cases.

A team attempting to implement infrastructure services is faced with two options: use either an aspect technology or an architecture framework such as J2EE. For example, most architecture frameworks have some support for security. Frequently, a combination is used, as implementation aspects provide the glue from the application layer to invoke such services. Early in the project, as you develop the architecture, you establish guidelines to achieve that balance. In Part IV, we provided several examples.

What if you do not apply use cases to capture stakeholder concerns? Would our approach work for design and implementation? The answer is a resounding yes. If you capture concerns as features, then you have feature-specific slices and non-feature-specific slices in place of use-case slices and non-use-case-specific slices. The approach during design and implementation would be similar. But still, we recommend that you do use cases, since they capture stakeholder concerns, and they capture what the system is supposed to do for each user in a manner that facilitates the identification of test cases.

Testing. If you are a risk-adverse person, then testing represents the most profitable area for you to apply our approach. Testing often requires the introduction of control and instrumentation code. With use-case slices, you can, in a blink, remove all such code from the final delivered system. Thus, it is a small wonder that the logging example is one of the most frequently used examples to introduce aspect orientation. You want to remove such instrumentation code in the final system and, hence, aspect orientation is a welcome solution to many project teams. In addition, our approach through use-cases helps you to systematically identify and organize test cases.

20.3   Adopting at Different Phases of a Project

You might not have the luxury of adopting aspect orientation on a completely new project. Your project might be an enhancement to an existing system. In general, when you adopt aspect orientation, you might be in any of the project phases enumerated in Figure 20–1.

1. **Planning Stage.** If you are developing a new system, you have a clean slate. You can easily apply the entire approach in this book—from requirements to code as well as in the development of the architecture and the rest of the system.
2. **Early Elaboration.** If you have already completed some initial iterations, you likely have a number of use cases working and several infrastructure services in place. You can definitely apply use-case slices on those areas that you have yet to develop. For those infrastructure services that you have already developed, consider whether it is worthwhile to redesign them as use-case slices.

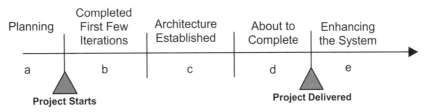

Figure 20-1   *Phases of software development.*

3. **Late Elaboration.** If you have a firm architecture in place, you are unlikely to make any revisions or changes unless there are significant productivity gains. Consider the possibility of using code templates and pointcut parameterization to help you incorporate infrastructure services and platform specifics into the system. AspectJ, as a programming technique, also provides the means for you to determine whether dependencies between layers and packages are violated.

4. **Construction.** If you are nearing the completion of your project, you are unlikely to make significant changes. But during this time, there is heavy emphasis on testing, tracing, and debugging. You can apply our methods to testing—identifying test cases from use cases, designing and implementing test slices, and so on.

5. **Enhancements.** If you have already delivered the system, your users might have some enhancement requests, or you might want to customize the system for another group of users, possibly at a different site. Such revisions can be mapped into either new use cases or extension use cases. Implementing them using aspect technology makes such revisions composable, and you can easily select the ones needed for a particular end-user group.

20.4   Summary and Highlights

Every project has its own individual characteristics. No two projects are the same. Although the same general principles of sound software engineering apply, they need to be tailored to the specific needs of a project. Our approach, to keep concerns separate as use cases and maintain that separation all the way to code and test, is not exempt. When you attempt to apply our approach to your project, you need to do some tailoring. But how can you tailor the approach when the team is unfamiliar with it?

This chapter enumerated various project scenarios and prescribed some tailoring considerations. Nevertheless, the rest is up to you. It is useful to choose a specific concern in your project and solve it with use-case slices and aspects. Produce a prototype solution and from it gain some experience. Thereafter, you can tackle larger problems.

21

Aspects and Beyond

Keeping concerns separate not only makes the system more understandable and extensible, it also gives rise to significant savings in terms of development effort. Aspect orientation—a powerful technique indeed—can help you achieve this. Nevertheless, aspects and even use cases are not silver bullets. They are but just two best practices in software development. In addition to use cases and aspects, you must build the system from the basis of a solid architecture, and you must progress iteratively, tailoring the approach to meet your project's needs. Once you master and balance these best practices, you can ensure success in your project.

21.1 Building a System in Extensions

As you know, successful software development is about being able to build and evolve a system incrementally to meet the evolving needs of the stakeholders. You give the development team some new or changed requirements, and the development team produces the changed system, as depicted in Figure 21–1.

Thus, software development is about changing from "something" to "something else." Even the first development step is a change from "nothing" to "something." In each development step, you add a new extension to the existing system to address some stakeholder concern, and as far as

Figure 21-1   *Software development is about changing.*

possible, you want to have minimal impact on that which already exists and already works. Thus, new extensions must be clearly separated from preceding extensions. This is achieved through use-case slices. Here, *extension* refers to a new concern or capability that you will add to the system at each point in time. Thus, you can have extensions comprising application use-case slices, application-extension use-case slices, infrastructure use-case slices, platform-specific use-case slices, and so on. Extensions occur during the whole life cycle of the system—over all releases, iterations, and builds. Organizing the system development as successive extensions makes the system easier to understand, grow, shrink, and maintain; the cost, quality, and time measures dramatically improve.

21.2   Balancing Best Practices

Obviously, we view aspect orientation as an extremely important contribution to the software world. Being able to separate use cases or extensions of various kinds and keep them separate all the way down, and later being able to compose them, gives us a tremendous boost in all measures: costs, quality, and time.

Keep in mind, though, that software development is much more than aspects and use-case-driven approaches. Several key practices discussed in this book can help you become successful in software development:

Use-Case-Driven. Every software development approach must start with capturing stakeholder concerns and must provide guidelines for analyzing, designing, implementing, and testing the system with respect to those concerns. Use-case-driven development precisely deals with stakeholder concerns. By walking through usages of the system, you have a better understanding of stakeholder concerns and their acceptance criteria. In

Part II, we discussed how to model concerns with use cases. In Part III, we showed how to drive the development of each use case with use-case slices and use-case modules.

Architecture-Centric. Every software system must be built on top of a sound and resilient architecture. A resilient architecture keeps concerns of various kinds separate, which localizes changes and prevents changes from propagating to other parts of the system. In Part IV, we explained how to keep variations from the core, nonfunctional requirements from functional requirements, platform-specific from the platform-independent elements, and tests from the subject being tested. We also showed you how to establish such an architecture with an accompanying architecture description.

Tailoring the Approach. Every project and team has its own specific characteristics. In Part V, we recommended ways to tailor our approach to apply to different project conditions.

Develop Iteratively. Every system has to be built iteratively, and in each iteration, you introduce some useful capability into the system. In Part V, we have described how to estimate, plan, and track iterative development projects and explained the productivity gains you can achieve by keeping concerns separate.

21.3   The Road Ahead

Once you have started to adopt aspect orientation, you will find even greater advantages in using it. In this book, we dealt largely with the more technical aspects of software development, but there are other dimensions, each with its own set of best practices.

- The technical dimension has best practices for modeling, programming, reuse, architecture, platforms, and so on.
- The project management dimension has best practices for planning, tracking, project metrics, configuration management, contract specifications, and so on.
- The human dimension has best practices on requirements elicitation, brainstorming, reviews, and so on.

- The organization dimension has best practices for organization structures (project versus product organization structures), outsourcing, process improvement, and so on.

A major project management woe is how to adapt and compose all these different best practices to formulate an effective project plan. Moreover, the emphasis on each dimension changes as a project evolves. A best practice may be extremely important in the beginning of a project but less so later on. Another may be more important at the end of a project. An effective project manager is one who can successfully balance these best practices.

The concepts of aspect orientation and extensibility provide the foundation for experts to define best practices separately, in a composable manner. We foresee a "best-practice weaver" who will compose project-relevant parts of the best practices together, eliminating static process descriptions that must be deciphered by the project teams. We also foresee automation to guide project managers in composing best practices to form a detailed plan for his or her team. Such possibilities represent a significant change to software development, but that is the subject of another book. For now, it is time to apply aspects in your project.

Modeling Aspects and Use-Case Slices in UML

This appendix provides a quick guide to notation for modeling aspects as used in this book. Let's recount the principles we use to model aspects. We treat aspect as part of an overlay (i.e., use-case slice) that is placed on top of an existing class or a set of classes. The names of the classes and operations must match those in the element structure before proper overlaying can take place. The use-case slice is a larger concept of an overlay than aspects. Whereas aspects can only add to existing classes, use-case slices can add entire new classes as well. Moreover, whereas parameterization of pointcuts is for binding existing locations (i.e., join points), use-case-slice template parameters allow you to define completely new elements. The key to understanding the notation is to know how overlaying is achieved.

A.1   Modeling Intertype Declarations with Class Extensions

A class extension is a modular extension to an existing class. It defines the features (attributes, operations, and relationships) to be overlaid onto an existing class. The name of the class and the class extension must correspond. See Figure A–1.

Overlay Semantics.   The logging aspect adds:

* an operation named `extractData()`
* to the `Room` class.

AspectJ Mapping.   This corresponds to an intertype declaration as listed below:

```
1.  public aspect Logging {
2.      public void Room.extractData() {
3.      // code
4.      }
5.  }
```

Notation

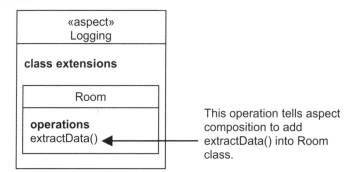

Figure A-1

A.2   Modeling Advices with Operation Extensions

An operation is the behavioral response when an element is invoked. An operation extension is a modular extension to an operation. Since operations are defined within classes, operation extensions are also defined within class extensions. See Figure A–2.

Overlay Semantics. The logging aspect adds:

- an operation extension `logData`
- to the `ReserveRoomHandler` class `makeReservation()` operation, that is, to the structural context,
- before the execution point when a call is made to `Room.retrieve()`, that is, behavioral context.

AspectJ Mapping. This corresponds to an advice as follows:

```
1.  public aspect Logging {
2.      before () :
3.          withincode(void ReserveRoomHandler.makeReservation())
4.          && call(void Room.retrieve())  {
5.          // code
6.      }
7.  }
```

Notation

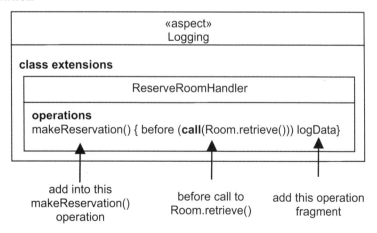

Figure A-2

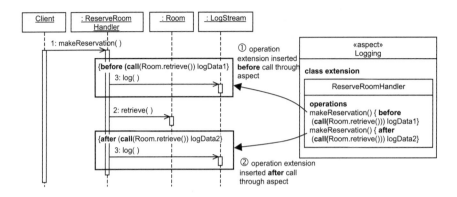

Figure A-3

A.2.1   Semantics of Before and After

`Before` and `after` operation extensions execute before or after existing execution points. Figure A–3 shows the use of `before` and `after` operation extensions.

The figure contains two frames:

- Frame ① shows the execution of operation extension `logData1` before call to `Room.retrieve()`.
- Frame ② shows the execution of operation extension `logData2` after call to `Room.retrieve()`.

A.2.2   Semantics of Around

`Around` operation extensions wrap up existing codes and determine if existing code can proceed. Figure A–4 shows how operation extensions execute around existing execution points.

The figure contains two frames:

- Frame ① shows the execution of operation extension `checkAuthorization` around call ⟨Control⟩.`performRequest()`.
- Frame ② shows the continuation of call to ⟨Control⟩.`performRequest()` when `checkAuthorization` initiates `proceed`.

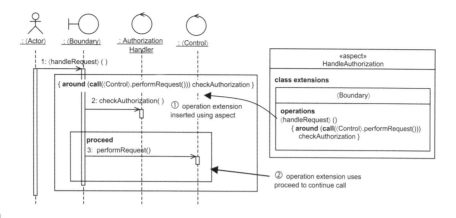

Figure A-4

A.3   Modeling Pointcuts

A pointcut gives the context in which an operation extension executes a name. This context can comprise structural context, behavioral context, or both. See Figure A–5.

Notation

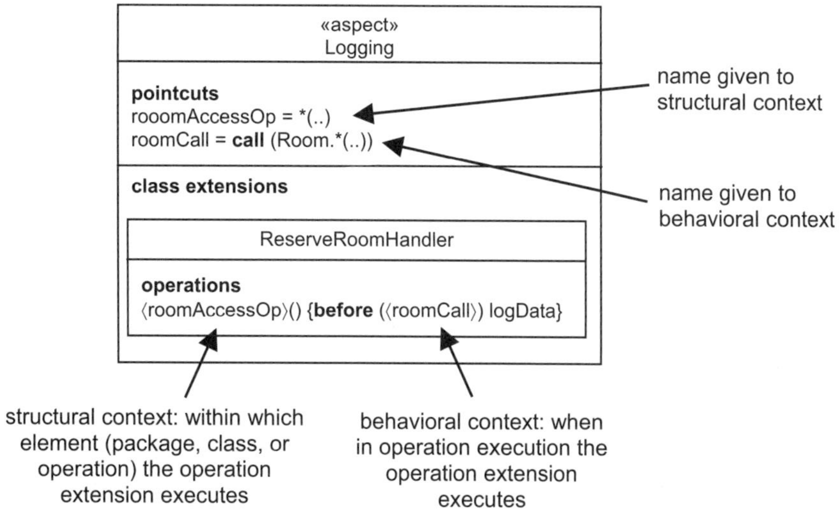

«aspect» Logging
pointcuts   rooomAccessOp = *(..)   roomCall = **call** (Room.*(..))
class extensions
ReserveRoomHandler
operations   ⟨roomAccessOp⟩() {**before** (⟨roomCall⟩) logData}

name given to structural context

name given to behavioral context

structural context: within which element (package, class, or operation) the operation extension executes

behavioral context: when in operation execution the operation extension executes

Figure A-5

Overlay Semantics.   The logging aspect adds:

- an operation extension `logData`
- to an existing operation within the `ReserveRoomHandler` class (This is parameterized as ⟨roomAccessOp⟩, and it establishes the structural context of the operation extension.)
- before a call to a Room operation (This is parameterized as ⟨room-Call⟩ and it establishes the behavioral context of the operation extension.)

AspectJ Mapping.   This corresponds to pointcuts as follows:

```
1.  public aspect Logging {
2.     pointcut roomAccessOp()
3.              : withincode(void ReserveRoomHandler.*(..)) ;
4.     pointcut roomCall()
5.              : call (void Room.*(..)) ;
6.
7.     before () : roomAccessOp() && roomCall() {
8.       // code
9.       }
10. }
```

A.4   Modeling Use-Case Slices

A use-case slice contains one collaboration, zero or more classes, and one or more aspects. The diagram in Figure A–6 depicts the various parts of a use-case slice.

A use-case slice is a
stereotyped package.

A use-case slice contains
one or more aspects.

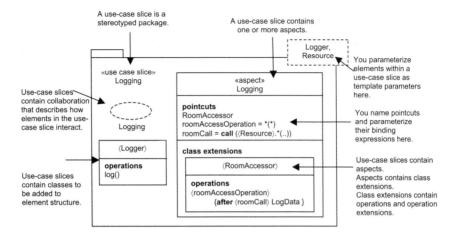

Use-case slices
contain collaboration
that describes how
elements in the use-
case slice interact.

Use-case slices
contain classes to
be added to
element structure.

You parameterize
elements within a
use-case slice as
template parameters
here.

You name pointcuts
and parameterize
their binding
expressions here.

Use-case slices contain
aspects.
Aspects contains class
extensions.
Class extensions contain
operations and operation
extensions.

Figure A-6

Notation Guide

In Appendix A, we gave an overview of the notation used to model aspects. In this appendix, we give a quick guide to the UML representation of other elements used in this book. The purpose is to highlight how these elements are used. For a more detailed discussion on the notation, please refer to the UML specification itself.

B.1   Package

A package is an element that is used to group other elements.

Notation

A package is denoted as a tab folder.

Usage

You normally assign work to developers in terms of packages rather than individual classes. We use different kinds of packages in the book.

Layers. Layers are used as the first-level partitioning in a model. Layers group software elements that are on the same level of abstraction. See Chapter 11, Section 11.4.1.

Tier Packages. A tier package is a package representing a subset of a logical tier in the design package. See Chapter 15, Section 15.1.2.

Model. A model contains a (hierarchical) set of elements that together describe the system being modeled. A model may contain more than one structure. In this book, the discussion is largely on the use-case model, the analysis model, and the design model. See Chapter 10.

Relationships Between Packages

A dependency can occur between two packages. This means that one package contains elements that need elements in another package.

B.2   Actors and Use Cases

An actor models a type of role played by an entity that interacts with the system. Actors may represent roles played by human users, external hardware, or other external systems.

A use case is the sequence of actions performed by a system, which yields an observable result that is typically of value for one or more actors or other stakeholders of the system. A use case models the behavior of the system, including possible variants when the actor uses the system.

Notation

An actor is denoted using a stick figure; a use case is denoted using an ellipse.

Customer   Reserve Room

The rectangular classifier notation provides another means to represent a use case, but it now shows the details of the use case. See Chapter 5.

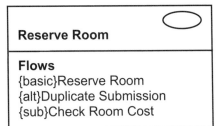

Using the rectangular classifier notation for use cases, you can highlight the different flow of events within a use case: basic flows, alternate flows, and subflows.

Usage

In this book, we apply use cases to model both application and infrastructure. Broadly speaking, application use cases capture concerns arising from functional requirements, whereas infrastructure use cases capture concerns arising from nonfunctional requirements. See Chapter 7.

Relationships Between Use Cases

There are three relationships between use cases: include, extend, and generalization.

B.3   Classes and Instances

A class models a set of objects that share the same specifications of features (attributes, operations, and relationships), constraints, and semantics. An instance is one such object.

In essence, a class represents a type, and an instance is a concrete manifestation of the type.

Notation

A class is represented as a rectangle with three compartments. The top compartment shows the name, the second compartment shows its attributes, and the third shows its operations. In this book, we frequently hide the second compartment and thus show only class names and operations.

RoomTO
- roomName - roomDescription - availableQty
+ getRoomName() + getRoomDescription() + getRoomAvailableQty() + setRoomName() + setRoomDescription() + setRoomAvailableQty()

An instance is also denoted as a rectangle, and the name of the instance is underlined. We use instances in interaction and communication diagrams.

: ReserveRoom Handler

The name of an instance is of the form X:Y, where X is the name of the instance and Y is the name of the class. In this book, we frequently leave the instance anonymous—that is, X is not defined.

Usage

There are many different kinds of classes used in this book. In the analysis model, are three stereotyped classes: boundary, control, and entity. See Chapter 10, Section 10.3.1.

boundary   control   entity

In the design model, the analysis classes are mapped to their design counterparts. To distinguish them, the boundary, control, and entity classes in design are depicted with rectangles; those in analysis are circles. See Chapter 10, Section 10.4.1.

boundary   control   entity

The design boundary, control, and entity classes are also known as POJOs (Plain Old Java Objects) in this book. They represent minimum design classes that make little use of platform specifics.

There are a number of class stereotypes in design, such as transfer objects, data access objects, and business delegates. These are discussed extensively in Chapter 15.

Relationships Between Classes

Between a class and an interface is a realization relationship. This relationship indicates that a class conforms to the behaviors specified in the interface.

Classes in different models can be related with a trace relationship, which indicates that one element in a model is mapped from one element in another model.

B.4   Components and Interfaces

A component is a modular part of a system that encapsulates its contents and the manifestation of which is replaceable within its environment. A component defines its behavior in terms of provided and required interfaces. As such, a component serves as a type, and its conformance is defined by these provided and required interfaces.

An interface is a named set of operations that characterize the behavior of an element (e.g., class, component).

Notation

A component is represented using a rectangle with a component stereo-type. Provided interfaces are denoted as balls, and required interfaces are denoted as sockets.

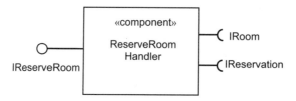

Usage

Components appear only during design. They do not appear in analysis. In other words, components are design elements.

In this book, we often discuss components in the context of incorporating extensibility into the system. Use-case slices are used to extend existing components with required interfaces through which other components can be plugged into the system. See Chapter 13, Section 13.3.

B.5   Processes and Nodes

A process is a unit of concurrency and execution in an operating system.

A node represents a runtime computational resource, which generally has at least memory and often processing capability.

Notation

A node is represented in this book by a rectangular stereotyped «node». A process is represented as a rectangular stereotyped «process».

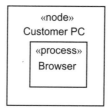

Usage

In this book, nodes and processes are used to model the deployment and process structures in the design model and to describe how the system is distributed.

References

[Alur et al. 2003] Deepak Alur, Dan Malks, and John Crupi. *Core J2EE Patterns: Best Practices and Design Strategies* (2nd ed.), Prentice Hall, Upper Saddle River, NJ, 2003.

[Aksit et A. 1998] M. Aksit and B. Tekinerdogan. "Aspect-Oriented Programming Using Composition Filters, in Object-Oriented Technology." In S. Demeyer and J. Bosch (Eds.), *ECOOP '98 Workshop Reader*, Springer Verlag, pp. 435, July 1998.

[Bergmans et al. 2001] L. Bergmans and M. Aksit. "Composing Crosscutting Concerns Using Composition Filters," *Communications of the ACM*, Vol. 44, No. 10, pp. 51–57, October 2001.

[Bittner et al. 2002] Kurt Bittner and Ian Spence. *Use Case Modeling*, Addison-Wesley, Boston, 2002.

[Boehm et.al. 2000] Barry W.Boehm, Ellis Horowitz, Ray Madachy, Donald Reifer, Bradford K. Clark, Bert Steece, A. Winsor Brown, Sunita Chulani, Chris Abts, *Software Cost Estimation with Cocomo II*, Prentice Hall, USA, 2000.

[Clements et al. 2002] Paul Clements, Rick Kazman, and Mark Klein. *Evaluating Software Architectures: Methods and Case Studies*, Addison-Wesley, Boston, 2002.

[Dijkstra 1976] E. W. Dijkstra. *A Discipline of Programming*, Prentice Hall, Englewood Cliffs, NJ, 1976.

[Eeles et al. 2002] Peter Eeles, Kelli Houston, and Wojtek Kozaczynski.

Building J2EE Applications with the Rational Unified Process, Addison-Wesley, Boston, 2002.

[Fowler et al. 1999] Martin Fowler, Kent Beck, John Brant, William Opdyke, and Don Roberts. *Refactoring: Improving the Design of Existing Code*, Addison-Wesley, Boston, 1999.

[Gabriel 1996] Richard Gabriel. *Patterns of Software*, Oxford University Press, New York, 1996.

[Gamma et al. 1995] Erich Gamma, Richard Helm, Ralph Johnson, and John Vlissides. *Design Patterns: Elements of Reusable Object-Oriented Software*, Addison-Wesley, Boston, 1995.

[Harrison et al. 1993] William Harrison and Harold Ossher. "Subject-Oriented Programming (A Critique of Pure Objects)." Proceedings of the 8th Annual Conference on Object-Oriented Programming Systems, Languages, and Applications, Washington D.C., 1993.

[Jacobson 1981] Ivar Jacobson (inventor) and Ericsson (applicant). Address Sequence Variator, 1981-09-21.

[Jacobson 1986] Ivar Jacobson. "Language Support for Changeable Large Real-Time Systems." Proceedings of OOPSLA '86, pp. 377–384, September 1986.

[Jacobson 1987] Ivar Jacobson. "Object-Oriented Development in an Industrial Environment." Proceedings of OOPSLA '87, pp 183–191, October 1987.

[Jacobson et al. 1992] Ivar Jacobson, Magnus Christerson, Patrik Jonsson, and Gunnar Övergaard. *Object-Oriented Software Engineering: A Use Case Driven Approach*, Addison-Wesley, Boston, 1992.

[Jacobson et al. 1994] Ivar Jacobson, Maria Ericson, and Agneta Jacobson. *The Object Advantage: Business Process Reengineering with Object Technology*, Addison-Wesley, Boston, 1994.

[Jacobson et al. 1997] Ivar Jacobson, Martin Griss, and Patrik Jonsson. *Software Reuse: Architecture, Process, and Organization for Business Success*, Addison-Wesley, Boston, 1997.

[Jacobson et al. 1999] Ivar Jacobson, Grady Booch, and James Rumbaugh. *The Unified Software Development Process*, Addison-Wesley, Boston, 1999.

[Jacobson 2003a] Ivar Jacobson. "Use Cases and Aspects—Working Seamlessly Together," *Journal of Object Technology* (http://www.jot.fm), July/August 2003.

[Jacobson 2003b] Ivar Jacobson. "Case for Aspects—Part I," *Software Development Magazine*, pp. 32–37, October 2003.

[Jacobson 2003c] Ivar Jacobson. "Case for Aspects—Part II," *Software Development Magazine*, pp. 42–48, November 2003.

[Karner 1993]Gustav Karner, Metrics for Objectory. Diploma thesis, University of Linköping, Sweden. No. LiTHIDA- Ex-9344:21. December 1993.

[Kiczales et al. 1997] G. Kiczales, J. Lamping, A. Mendhekar, C. Maeda, C. Lopes, J. M. Loingtier, and J. Irwin. "Aspect-Oriented Programming." In ECOOP '97—Object-Oriented Programming, 11th European Conference. LNCS 1241, pp. 220–242, 1997.

[Kiczales et al. 2000] Gregor Kiczales, Erik Hilsdale, Jim Hugunin, Mik Kersten, Jeffrey Palm, and William G. Griswold. "An Overview of AspectJ." Proceedings of the European Conference on Object-Oriented Programming, Budapest, Hungary, June 2001.

[Kiczales 2004] Gregor Kiczales. "A Little Goes a Long Way," *Software Development Magazine*, May 2004.

[Kleppe et al. 2003] Anneke Kleppe, Jos Warmer, and Wim Bast. *MDA Explained: The Model Driven Architecture—Practice and Promise*, Addison-Wesley, Boston, 2003.

[Kroll et al. 2003] Per Kroll and Philippe Kruchten. *The Rational Unified Process Made Easy: A Practitioner's Guide to Rational Unified Process*, Addison-Wesley, Boston, 2003.

[Kruchten 2000] Philippe Kruchten. *The Rational Unified Process: An Introduction* (2nd ed.), Addison-Wesley, Boston, 2000.

[Laddad 2003] Ramnivas Laddad. *AspectJ in Action Practical Aspect-Oriented Programming*, Manning, Greenwich, CT, 2003.

[Lieberherr et al. 1994] Karl J. Lieberherr, Ignacio Silva-Lepe, and Cun Xiao. "Adaptive Object-Oriented Programming Using Graph-Based Customisation," *Communications of the ACM*, pp. 94–101, May 1994.

[Martin 1994] Robert Martin. "OO Design Quality Metrics: An Analysis of Dependencies." (Abstract.) October 28, 1994. Available: http://www.oma.com/resources/articles/oodmetrc.pdf.

[Mellor et al. 2002] Stephen J. Mellor and Marc J. Balcer, *Executable UML: A Foundation for Model Driven Architecture*, Addison-Wesley, Boston, 2002.

[Ossher et al. 2000] H. Ossher and P. Tarr. "Multi-Dimensional Separation of Concerns and the Hyperspace Approach." Proceedings of the Symposium on Software Architectures and Component Technology: The State of the Art in Software Development, Kluwer, 2000.

[Overgaard et al 2004] Gunnar Övergaard and Karin Palmkvist, *Use Cases: Patterns and Blue Prints*. Addison-Wesley, Boston, 2004.

Reusable Asset Specification, Available: http://www.rational.com/ras/index.jsp.

[Racko 2004] Roland Racko "A Cool *Tool* Tool," *Software Development Magazine*, May 2004.

[Rashid et al. 2002] A. Rashid, P. Sawyer, A. Moreira, and J. Araujo. *Early Aspects: A Model for Aspect-Oriented Requirements Engineering.* IEEE Joint International Conference on Requirements Engineering. IEEE Computer Society Press, pp. 199–202, 2002.

[Rosenberg et al. 1999] Doug Rosenberg and Kendall Scott. *Use Case Driven Object Modeling with UML: A Practical Approach*, Addison-Wesley, Boston, 1999.

[Rosenberg et al. 2001] Doug Rosenberg and Kendall Scott. *Applying Use Case Driven Object Modeling with UML: An Annotated e-Commerce Example*, Addison-Wesley, Boston, 2001.

[Tarr et al. 1999] Peri Tarr, Harold Ossher, William Harrison, and Stanley Sutton. "N Degrees of Separation: Multi-Dimensional Separation of Concerns." ICSE 1999 Conference Proceedings, 1999.

[Walls et al. 2003] Craig Walls and Norman Richards. *XDoclet in Action*, Manning, Greenwich, CT, 2003.

Glossary

abstract.   An element that cannot be instantiated.

actor.   An element in the use-case model that represents something external to a system. It can represent the role a user plays with respect to the system. It can also represent an external system or an external device.

advice (AOP).   An extension to an existing method.

analysis.   The refinement of use cases to promote a better understanding of requirements and at the same time establish a platform-independent structure for the system. Analysis packages contain analysis classes, which can be boundary, control, or entity classes. Analysis use-case slices contain aspects as well.

analysis model.   An abstraction of the system from a platform-independent perspective. It contains the results of analysis.

architectural view.   An architectural view of a model highlights the important elements of a model and presents them through a set of diagrams and other accompanying description.

architecturally significant element.   A model element that is part of some key functionality/capability of the system that is affected by some critical risks and decisions about the system.

architecture.   The architecture of a system encompasses the major decisions about the system.

architecture baseline.   An early version of the system that exercises the important parts of the system. It is also known as the skinny system.

architecture description.   An architecture description describes the architecture baseline.

aspect (AOP).   A programming construct in AOP that gives the ability to add class extensions into existing classes. An aspect in AOP contains pointcuts, advices, and intertype declarations.

aspect (English).   A facet of the system.

aspect (stereotyped classifier).   A classifier that contains class extensions and instructions on how these class extensions will be overlaid to their respective classes.

aspect orientation.   A set of techniques to separate crosscutting concerns about a system in terms of aspects (or modularity units that can be composed into classes).

aspect-oriented programming (AOP).   A set of techniques that provides the means to add additional behavior into existing classes and operations during compilation or execution in an unintrusive manner.

AspectJ.   A Java language extension that implements AOP.

attribute-oriented programming.   A code-generation technique that uses tags on classes, operations and attributes as parameters to code templates. An example of attribute-oriented programming is XDoclet.

base use case.   When discussing the «include» and «extend» relationships between use cases, the base use case refers respectively to the use case that includes another use case and the use case that is extended by another use case.

basic flow.   The description of the normal, expected path through the use case. This is the path taken by most of the users most of the time.

class.   A class is a categorization of objects that share the same attributes, operations, relationships, and semantics.

class extension.   A modular extension to an existing class, the purpose of which is to realize a use case. It contains the features of the extended class that are specific to the use-case realization.

classifier.   From UML, a collection of instances that have something in common. A classifier can have features that characterize its instances. Classifiers include interfaces, classes, datatypes, and components.

code fragment.   A small sequence of a few statements (in some programming language) that achieves some task.

collaboration.   The description (or view) of a set of interacting elements required to fulfill a particular task, usually a use-case realization or a mechanism.

composition. The process of combining one or more slices (use case or non-use-case-specific) into the element structure.

concern. Anything that is of interest to some stakeholder, whether an end user, a project sponsor, or even a developer.

concrete. An element that can be instantiated.

crosscutting concern. A concern that affects more than one class. Since use cases are realized by multiple classes, use cases are considered cross-cutting concerns.

design. The translation of a system's requirement specification into a platform-specific implementation of the system.

design model. An abstraction of the implementation (i.e., code in any form—source files, scripts, configuration files).

element under test (EUT). The class or set of classes or a use-case slice that will be tested against some test cases.

exision. An existing software unit (class, component, system, etc.) on top of which you add additional capabilities.

extend relationship. A relationship between two use cases in which one use case adds to the behavior of another. The extend relationship is similarly defined between use-case slices and use-case modules.

extension. An extension represents additional behavior that executes in the context of an existing element. You can have extensions for operations, classes, and so on.

extension flow. A special case of an alternate flow, which executes in the context of a separate use-case instance (other than the one in which it is specified).

extension point. A named point in the execution path of a use-case instance.

feature. A high-level requirement normally used to justify the needs and benefits of a system.

feature (UML). A property, such as an operation or attribute, that characterizes the instances of a classifier.

flow. A full or partial path through a use-case description. There is always at least a basic flow, and there maybe alternate flows and subflows.

functional requirement. A requirement that involves user interactions.

identification. Giving something a name and possibly its location in some namespace.

implementation.   The implementation refers to code. An implementation model contains the code and other artifacts needed by the runtime environment.

include.   A relationship between two use cases—an including and included use case. The including use case specifies a location within itself in which the included use case is inserted.

infrastructure mechanism.   The technique of using infrastructure service.

infrastructure service.   A software unit within a system that provides nonfunctional capabilities of the system.

infrastructure use case.   The specification of the sequence of events that emerges when an infrastructure service is being used.

instance.   An instance of a class refers to a specific example of that class.

interface.   A named set of operations that characterize the behavior of an element.

iteration.   A time period in a project that normally has an executable release at the end to demonstrate that some functionality or some stakeholder concerns have been met.

join point.   A point in the execution of a system.

layer.   A high level of partitioning of the system through different levels of abstraction. The application-specific layer is at the highest level. The system-specific layer is at the lowest level.

mechanism.   A pattern that solves recurring computer science problems in a system, such as persistency and distribution. It can be specified with a use case and realized as a collaboration. In this book, a mechanism is modeled as an infrastructure use case.

merge.   When two elements are merged, their contents are superimposed on one another, and the result is their mathematical union. *See* **package merge**.

method.   A realization of an operation.

minimal use-case design slice.   Part of a use-case design slice that has minimal platform specifics.

mock element.   During testing, an element under test (EUT) may depend on some supporting elements. A mock element is a substitution for a supporting element to simplify the testing.

model.   A complete description of a system from a particular perspective. It contains one or more hierarchical structures of model elements.

model structure. *See* structure.

modularity. The localization of all artifacts, including specification, realization, and implementation of a concern or a set of concern(s).

module. A software unit that can be developed independently from other software units.

nonfunctional requirements. Requirements such as performance, reliability, usability, and supportability. They normally affect multiple use cases.

non-use-case-specific slice. A use-case slice that adds only classes into the element structure of the system. A non-use-case-specific slice does not contain any aspects.

object. An instance of a class.

object model. A model that contains classes. The analysis model and the design model are examples of object models.

object orientation. A set of techniques to separate concerns about a system in terms of classes.

operation. A service that can be requested from an object to effect behavior. An operation has a declaration, which may restrict the actual parameters that are possible.

operation extension. The additional behavior that executes in the context of an existing operation.

package. A UML element that contains other UML elements.

package merge. A package merge defines how one package extends another package by merging their contents.

pattern. A solution to a recurring problem.

Peer use-cases. Use-cases that have no explicit relationship between them and neither one depend on the other. They can, however, depend on something else.

phase. The time between two major project milestones during which a well-defined set of objectives is met, artifacts are completed, and decisions are made to move or not move into the next phase. A phase comprises one or more iterations.

pointcut. An expression that identifies a specific point or a set of points in the execution of a system.

provided interface. A provided interface of a component is one that is implemented directly by the component.

required interface.   A required interface of a component is one that the component needs to use.

requirement.   A description of what the system must do or a condition that the system must conform to.

responsibility.   The responsibility of a class is the description of what the class must do. Responsibilities are found during analysis and are refined into operations during design.

role.   Each instance in a collaboration plays a particular role, and from the role, the instance's responsibilities and operations are identified.

scattering.   The effect of having design of a concern spread across multiple design elements.

separation of concerns.   The technique of breaking down a complex problem into smaller problems so that the smaller problems can be solved individually and separately. The separation criteria are in terms of stakeholder concerns.

structure.   A containment hierarchy of elements of some kind. An analysis element structure is a containment hierarchy of analysis elements (boundary, control, entity classes). A model can have more than one structure.

subflow.   A self-contained, labeled section of a flow. Subflows can be reused in many places within the flow of events where they are defined.

tangling.   The effect whereby a particular design element or an operation needs to do more than its allocated requirements.

template.   A parameterized element. In UML, it is denoted by a dashed box on the top right-hand corner that lists the parameters in the template.

test case.   A set of test inputs, execution conditions, and expected results developed for a particular objective, such as to exercise a particular program path or to verify compliance with a specific requirement (use case).

test driver.   A program or tool that allows a tester to exercise/examine in a controlled manner the unit of software being tested.

test stub.   A program unit that stands in for another (more complex) program unit that is directly referenced by the unit being tested.

testing.   The evaluation of the behavior of a software element against its desired behavior.

trace.   A stereotyped dependency that relates how a model element from one model is derived from a model element in another model.

use case.   A use case models the behavior of a system. A use case is a sequence of actions performed by a system, which yields an observable result that is typically of value for one or more actors or other stakeholders of the system.

use-case model.   A model that describes the use of the system in terms of actors and use cases.

use-case module.   The localization of everything about a use case within a single package. It contains many use-case slices.

use-case slice.   A use-case slice contains the specifics of a model in a single package. A use-case slice of the analysis or design model contains classes and aspects of classes specific to a use case. It also contains the collaboration that describes the realization of the use case in terms of interaction, communication, class diagrams, and so on.

use-case specification.   A use-case specification is associated with a use case. It describes the behavior of a use case by walking through the interactions between actors and the system—what information is manipulated, presented, and persisted.

use-case structure.   The use-case structure of a model (analysis, design, and implementation models) describes the relationships between use-case slices and non-use-case-specific slices in that model.

user experience model.   The user experience model captures the interaction between the user and the user experience (i.e., user interface) elements.

utility-extension use case.   A use case that contains only extension flows and is meant only to extend other use cases.

utility use case.   A case that contains only subflows and is meant to be included by other use cases.

view.   A view presents parts of a model as seen from a given perspective or vantage point and omits elements that are not relevant to this perspective. It is normally depicted as a diagram.

Index